LOOSE HEAD

LOOSE HEAD

JOE MARLER

WITH RACHEL MURPHY

Confessions of an (un)professional rugby player

4

Ebury Press, an imprint of Ebury Publishing
20 Vauxhall Bridge Road
London SW1V 2SA

Ebury Press is part of the Penguin Random House group of companies
whose addresses can be found at global.penguinrandomhouse.com

First published by Ebury Press in 2020
This paperback edition published in 2021

www.penguin.co.uk

A CIP catalogue record for this book is available from the British Library

ISBN 9781529107531

Printed and bound in Great Britain by Clays Ltd, Elcograf S.p.A.

The authorised representative in the EEA is Penguin Random House
Ireland, Morrison Chambers, 32 Nassau Street, Dublin D02 YH68.

Penguin Random House is committed to a sustainable future for
our business, our readers and our planet. This book is made from
Forest Stewardship Council® certified paper.

For Daisy, Jasper, Maggie & Felix

When the ball is up in the air and it's a perfect kick, it doesn't matter how great it looks, cos there's no telling which way it's going to bounce when it hits the floor. That's a bit like life, isn't it? You think it's going great one minute and all looks wonderful, but you never know which way it's going to take you.

CONTENTS

PROLOGUE

If I were a horse, you could take me to water and ask me, 'Hey, horsey, do you want to have a drink or do you want to swim?'

I'm not sure if I'd be a slightly Irish horse or whether I'd just whinny in my own East Sussex accent, but I know I'd reply as quick as a wink, 'I want to go out on Saturday. I want to clippity-clop all the way to the Stoop and I want to say hello to the fans.'

I signed for Harlequins when I was a lardy, wayward 17-year-old, and for 13 years I've lived every rugby boy's dream, winning 71 caps for England, touring with the British and Irish Lions, being called up by the Barbarians and playing in the World Cup final in Japan.

It hasn't all been plain clippity-clopping, though. For a start, I never set out to be a professional rugby player. My body decided rugby was what I should do long before my head caught up with the idea. My attitude was even later to the party – much, much later. To tell you the truth, I think it only properly showed up in the last year or so.

I haven't taken the most conventional route to the top of my sport and I'm not the most professional player in the game. Not by a long chalk. I've retired and unretired twice from the England squad and my charge sheet is eclectic, to say the least. But it takes all sorts, as they say. And how boring life would be if we all trotted along in an orderly fashion, keeping our noses down and never refusing to drink the water.

This book is not about putting an egg-shaped ball over the whitewash. It's a rugby tour with a difference, an eye-opening journey through the professional rugby bubble, in and out of my topsy-turvy career and inside my (occasionally loose) head.

We'll visit my red-mohawk and red-mist moments. We'll stop off for beers with some of the world's top players and find out why they have names like Sloshbucket, Snorlax and Spidey. And we'll have a peek behind the curtains of the England team hotels and training camps.

Along the way we'll pass through some gates – Fondlegate and Gypsygate, to name a couple of them. We'll drop in for a chat with Eddie Jones and say hello to royalty, celebrities and the wonderful cast of fans that cross our path. We'll also look back at the hard men and amateur-era players who blazed the trail for today's modern game, soaking up some history and tradition as we go.

If you want to know what goes on when the ref can't see, step this way. We'll unveil the dark arts (and smells) of the scrum and uncover the naked truths and psychological secrets of playing your best game.

There'll be excursions into rugby's inner sanctum: the dope tests, the gym, the dressing room and the team meetings. If you dare, have a look beneath the surgical gowns to find out what happens when a player's body goes through the equivalent of 30 car crashes in every game.

As for onboard entertainment, I'll tell you what's tickled me, as well as the occasions when I've been the butt of the joke (quite a few times, it turns out). There's a catastrophic game of credit card roulette; naked wrestling in the England camp; barber-shop disasters in Japan; the curious incident of the tramp on Wellington harbour; the player who bought a car he couldn't fit his 20-stone arse into (that'll be me).

I don't mind a laugh at my expense. But be prepared. We might hit the occasional pothole in the road, moments when I have a meltdown and press the emergency stop button. We'll deal with those when we've got a few miles under our belt.

Up and down like a rugby ball, never knowing which way I'll bounce. That's how it goes. I've learned to take the rough with the smooth and I count my blessings every day.

I'm very lucky to be a professional rugby player. It's taken me to places I could never have imagined and I've learned so much. Not just about how to be a rugby player, but also about how the whole big rugby bubble bounces along, and how to look after yourself when you're in it.

It's a privilege to have the chance to share it all. Are you ready to go? Please sit back and enjoy the tour.

1

HAIR WE GO

'Got your kit sorted?'

I looked up and saw the bent nose and the huge squashed brow. It was Martin Johnson, England's best ever captain, booming down at me from his great height.

Intimidating doesn't even begin to cover it. I'd watched him lifting the 2003 World Cup on telly when I was a fat 13-year-old. He was one of the most phenomenal players the country had ever seen. Now here he was, not just standing in front of me, but eye-balling me at the start of my first England training camp in February 2010.

'Yes,' I squeaked. 'The kit man sorted me out.'

'So you're good to go? Good to train, are you?'

I detected an edge to his voice. 'Yeah, I'm good to go ...' I was shifting my weight from one foot to the other and mumbling my words. It wasn't the impression I wanted to give to one of rugby's hardest men.

'Well,' he barked, 'you're gonna have to get rid of that fucking stupid haircut before you do!'

I blushed. Did Martin Johnson really just say that? Was he serious? I was confused as well as shocked, because what did my haircut have to do with him, with rugby? He stalked off and I glanced around awkwardly, wondering what to do next.

The call-up to the England squad had come from another rugby legend, Graham Rowntree, aka Wig, then the England scrum-maging coach. I'd met him at Harlequins, but I thought it was a mate pissing about when he phoned me out of the blue.

'Hi, Joe, it's Wig here. Next week, what you up to?'

After an embarrassing altercation, during which I declared, 'I'm not falling for this – this is a fucking wind-up!' I realised it was no joke. Wig told me they had a couple of injured players and he wanted me to train with the squad at Pennyhill Park in Surrey.

I'd been playing for Harlequins for a couple of years, but I was still only 19 and not in the best of shape. My imposter syndrome kicked in, massively. *How can they want a lardy, lazy teenager like me? What if I balls it up and never get asked again?*

One thing I hadn't thought about was my haircut. Why would I? OK, you might get given a nickname like Wig if you had a dodgy flat-top like Graham Rowntree, but aside from that, who cared what hairstyle you had? And what did it have to do with Martin Johnson? I was here to play rugby, not be judged on my looks.

I could only assume he was showing me who was boss, stamping his authority on a new pup. Besides, how was I supposed to get rid of my haircut here?

I nipped to the toilet before the training session started and caught a glimpse of myself in the mirror. *It'll be fine*, I thought. *I'll just have to crack on and hope he doesn't mention it again.*

My mohican was dyed the brightest red you could imagine. During the week I'd had it trimmed into a very tight, neat stripe, so it looked like I had a giant scarlet-coloured caterpillar sleeping down the middle of my scalp. For a bit of extra pizzazz I had stars and stripes shaved around the sides of my head. It was an absolutely brilliant haircut, the best I'd ever had. There was no way in the world I was getting rid of it, not even for Martin Johnson.

I ran out onto the field. *Fuck you, Martin Johnson*, I thought. *You can't make me shave my head. My hair's got nothing to do with rugby!*

Despite my brave thoughts, I still felt like a little kid among so many legends. Jonny Wilkinson, Mike Tindall and Tom Palmer were helping with training. It was surreal.

Graham Rowntree spotted me on the sidelines, freezing my nuts off. 'Have you not got a gig?' he asked.

'Er, yeah,' I said, not wanting to admit that I was too scared to go up to Andrew Sheridan, the player I was meant to be swapping in and out with, and say, 'Do you mind if I come on now, mate?'

*

Over the years I've learned that hair has a lot to do with rugby, one way or another. If I had a time machine I would go back and say to Martin Johnson, 'Look, mate, I know that if I shave my head things won't go totally doolally, like they did when Samson had a crop. I won't be captured or have my eyes put out and I won't end up tied to a treadmill for the amusement of the Philistines. Apart from anything else, the gym manager at Pennyhill Park wouldn't have it. But I'm telling you, a rugby player's hair is very, very important to him.'

Martin Johnson would have laughed in my face. 'Son, has that ludicrous caterpillar on your head scrambled your brain?' he'd have replied. I'm guessing.

When Martin Johnson started out, rugby was still in the amateur era and nobody ever talked about their hair. All the players looked like farmers, solicitors or lorry drivers, because that's what they were. Typically, they had the no-nonsense short back and sides, classic army corporal crops or skinheads for anyone thinning on top. Practical, macho haircuts befitting of gentlemen who were as tough as old boots and played a brutal game.

One or two players bucked that trend. Legendary Welsh full-back J.P.R. Williams had flowing hair and magnificent sideburns, but it wasn't a fashion statement. He simply liked long hair and still has long hair today, plus silvery sideburns.

Mutton chops of all shapes and sizes weren't unusual back then, and the Welsh boys especially loved a moustache. Paul Ringer had a magnificent Mexican-style 'tache, and Mervyn Davies, aka Merv the Swerve, was known for pairing his luxuriant black moustache with a white headband.

Even so, there was no pre-match preening, not even for the backs, who even then were always better-looking than the ugly mugs who stuck their noggins in a scrum. Nobody cared if you hadn't shaved or had a haircut for weeks, or if you could grow mushrooms in your ears. You were there to play rugby and win. End of. There were no sponsors and advertisers to please or impress, and after the game it was Vosene and soap on a rope, a scrape through with a comb and straight out on the piss. Sounds wonderful.

The player who changed all this was Gavin Henson. Playing for Wales, he was the ultimate metrosexual icon. Shaved legs, a spray tan and silver boots, he pulled them all off perfectly. But it was his meticulously gelled, expertly spiked hair that was his pièce de résistance, on and off the pitch.

He had the match of his life in the 2005 Six Nations, putting in his famous monster tackle on the young England player Mathew Tait. I was 14, eating peanut butter and jam on toast on the sofa and thinking, *What a phenomenal tackle! And how good does he look?*

Henson's immaculate hair could have been a gladiator's crown that day. Smashing into Tait and carrying him forward with the momentum of his tackle, he was no longer in the Millennium Stadium. He was in Rome, carrying a body from the arena.

Henson was man of the match and Wales went on to win the Grand Slam. 'I like to look good,' he said. 'If I look the part it helps me to perform.'

I loved hearing that. I'd grown up thinking only footballers could be style icons because, try as I might, I couldn't find a rugby idol I wanted to look like. As a kid I had David Beckham-inspired curtains and I'd wash and condition my luscious blond locks three times a week, hoping that looking more like him would make me more popular. My two big sisters regularly enhanced my Beckham look. They never needed one of those Girl's World dummy heads to play with because throughout my childhood I was their real-life doll.

'Sit down and stay still,' they'd say, while forcing what looked like a gigantic condom with holes in it over my head. Then they would slowly pull strands of my hair through the holes and add highlights.

'It hurts!' I'd protest.

'Stop moaning!' they'd say.

I put up with it because my hair was my crowning glory. Well, it was my only glory, really, because not only was I a big fat kid, but I had a huge nose too. Life was so unfair.

I wished one of my childhood rugby heroes would inspire me like Beckham, but old amateur-era habits were dying hard in the nineties and very few players stood out because of their striking lids.

Will Carling had clearly smashed it in the sex-appeal stakes, but he was much older than me and his wavy black hair would have made me look like a melted strawberry ice-cream with chocolate sauce on top. Jonah Lomu stood out. I idolised him as a player and loved the fact that he dared to be different, but there was no way I could go into my local barbers and say, 'Do me a Jonah Lomu, mate.'

The random tuft that stuck out of the front of his bald head looked like a black chick breaking out of an egg. It was never going to be flattering on anyone, but who was going to tell a six-foot-five, eighteen-stone All Black his hairdo looked ridiculous? He could have had a penis tattooed on his head and nobody would have said a word.

Jerry Collins was another of my boyhood heroes. For most of his career he had the biggest biceps in the All Blacks squad and was renowned for melting people mercilessly in tackles. I was totally in awe of him as a player, and then he came out with the best haircut I'd ever seen in rugby.

Fucking great! I love it! I want to be like you!

Jerry Collins had the bottle to rock his famous Guinness haircut, turning it white on top and leaving the sides jet-black. What a sensational move! I looked at him and thought, *That's bold, and it's clever too. It's going to wind people up. It'll distract the opposition. It's absolutely genius.*

That was a turning point. I was learning that rugby is not just about beating your opposite number physically. You need to out-psych him, irritate him, make him lose the plot. Every rugby player knew that, but I don't think anyone had thought to use their hair as a weapon before. Jerry was having fun with it too. I rated that so much. The guy was a total inspiration to me.

I had my first mohawk when I was in the Quins academy. I was bald when I arrived because the girls at my old sixth-form college had used me as a prize to raise money for Children in Need: 'Pay up and Marler has his luscious blond locks shaved off!' I was left looking like a prisoner of war, and when my hair grew back I started to look like Scarecrow in *The Wizard of Oz*. I had to accept that the blond curtains were never coming back, because every time I tried to grow my hair Scarecrow reappeared.

I got my Quins teammate Chris Brooker to sort me out. He did his own hair with shears, shaving the sides and leaving a bit of a mullet at the back. I asked him to do the same to me, and each time I had more and more taken off the sides and let the top grow longer. The resulting mohawk wasn't a Jerry Collins showstopper, but it did make a statement.

When I unveiled it at the Stoop I could see some of the boys I'd come through the academy with giving me disapproving looks. The same happened when I started to dye it bright colours, like purple and pink and orange.

'Nice hair,' they mocked. 'What have you come as? Is the circus in town again?'

It was the private-school lads who took the piss, the ones who had the classic posh-rugby-boy look of the day: short back and sides and big floppy fringe falling slightly over one eye. By contrast, the working-class boys had shaved heads and eyebrow slits. The stereotypes were very real and very obvious.

The private-school boys not only looked prettier, they always occupied the most glamorous positions, at the back. The backs are the gazelles and the peacocks, sprinting around and showing off their skills and physical prowess, while we forwards are the slugs and the baby rhinos, the White Orcs. We thrive in muddy waters, dark corners, under rocks. We wallow and plod and thrust our heads into dangerous, shadowy caves – places where even a full tub of Dax isn't going to hold your fringe up.

You only had to look in the Quins changing room to understand where a prop stood in the glamour stakes. There was one full-length mirror next to the bench, where all the wingers and centres and some of the backs kept their stuff, and a second identical mirror opposite the spots occupied by the nines and tens. What did we have for the numbers one to eight? Nothing. Not even a shaving mirror.

I embrace my position now and I'm very proud to occupy it, but back then the combination of being a working-class kid and a prop forward made me feel bottom of the heap, with everything to prove.

I had a huge chip on my shoulder about the fact that I'd arrived at Quins via a comprehensive school rather than Epsom College or Cranleigh like so many of the academy boys. Some of it was my own fault. I let it get to me because I lacked confidence and self-esteem. That happens when you've grown up as the fat kid. The lad the girls don't fancy. The oik with the bad temper.

I felt judged when the other boys clocked my Asda Smart Price shampoo next to their Molton Brown in the shower. Stuff like that bothered me massively. What right did they have to sneer and mock and act all superior, just because their parents had more money? Fuck them!

When they started to take the piss out of my mohawk something changed. It was like a red rag to a bull. It was time for me to stand up for myself and be proud of who I was. *Bring it on,* I thought. *I'll show you lot.*

The mohawk became a great motivator. How much *more* of a prat would I look if I was crap on the pitch while sporting a brightly coloured mohawk? I wasn't going to let that happen. I had to win. I had to melt my opponents. I had to teach the posh boys not to underestimate me.

It started to work. My rugby was improving all the time. I was committed and ambitious and working my nuts off in the gym and in training. It's no exaggeration to say that my desire to show the snobs what I was made of vastly improved my game.

I'd shave my head from time to time to get rid of the latest dye. On one such occasion, when Quins were playing Leicester Tigers in 2012, I felt my ears were too exposed going into the game, so I decided to wrap tape round my head to protect my ears. I've no idea why I felt the need to do that. The mohawk didn't exactly cover my ears, did it?

Still, I did a proper good job of it, layering on the white physio tape and then the thick black tape on top. I was up against Leicester prop Boris Stankovich, a player who owned the 'headband of tape' look. Boris was so hard that he didn't bother with the white layer of tape. He went straight for what looked like black electrical tape, sticking it directly onto his skin and pulling it tight. He had no neck and a big shiny bald head, and you could see rolls of skin bulging from under the tape.

I arrived at the line-out and was getting myself ready when Boris called over in his loud Kiwi voice, 'Hey, Marler. I like your hairdo, mate!'

I was mortified. For fuck's sake, he was complimenting me on looking exactly like him! The lads thought it was hilarious. 'Hey, Marler, bitch. Loving your hair.' I got that for weeks.

I was always much happier with my mohawk. I embraced it and really went to town, like the time I dyed it a bright rusty-red colour and had the word 'Headworks' shaved into my scalp.

Headworks was the name of my mate's barber shop in Heathfield, which had become my regular haunt.

'Do you mind?' he'd asked. 'It'll be good publicity for us.'

'No, mate. It's all fun and games. Do what you want.'

Before that I'd had 'Jolly Hog' and 'Sausage' shaved on either side of my head. I did that for my Quins teammate Olly Kohn, to help promote the Jolly Hog sausage company he set up with his two brothers after he was injured. Why not, if it helped a mate out?

In April 2011, Quins were playing Leicester Tigers again, and I was up against the Argentinian international Marcos Ayerza, one of the top looseheads in the world. His nickname was 'El Toro', The Bull, because of his strength and the ferocious way he played the game. He looked invincible. I aspired to be like him and I was desperate to gain his respect. To do that I planned to throw him off his game, and I hoped my dazzling Headworks and mohawk combination would help wind him up.

I saw the perfect opportunity in the second half, when we were going into a ruck. This was it. It was time to wave the red rag – or at least my red mohawk – at the mighty El Toro.

I got up close, wrapped my hand around Ayerza's throat and got his head in a bit of a lock. Then I grabbed him by the red and green scrum cap he always used to wear, which ripped a bit. That's what pissed him off, and he squared up to me. I could hear the ref shouting, 'Take your hands down! Take your hands down!'

We let go of each other but then Ayerza dropped his nut on me, cracking it into my face. I looked at the ref, as if to say, *Have you just seen what he did?* But my fuse had already been lit and I started unloading punches. Ayerza whacked me back. Of course he did. That's what any player would do in that situation. You have to show you won't be pushed around by anyone, especially not by a crazy young pup.

The match was being televised. 'Red hair, red cap, red mist,' the commentator was saying. 'Is the red theme about to continue?'

It was. We were both shown a red card, meaning we had to attend a disciplinary hearing because our behaviour had fallen below the standards expected by the RFU.

I couldn't believe it when I was told the hearing would take place at the Royal Courts of Justice in London. 'Why am I going to the Royal Courts of Justice for throwing a punch in a game of rugby? This is fucking nuts!'

My Quins team manager Conor O'Shea explained the whole process and the 'plan of action' we would take.

'Plan of action?' I replied. 'It was on live TV. There's footage of me whacking him. Shouldn't I just take the rap?'

Conor was adamant that we needed a plan, and an important part of it was that I needed to shave my head and wear a smart suit and tie.

Fucking hell. Not this again. 'Surely they're judging my behaviour, not my haircut?' I said.

Conor wasn't budging. I had to look the part, to show respect to the panel.

What the fuck? I just didn't get it.

I felt nervous when we went into the hearing. It was strange to see Ayerza in a suit rather than a rugby kit. Everyone looked immaculate and very serious as the details of the altercation were picked over by the panel.

My heart started racing. I suddenly felt like I was in a proper court room, facing a real-life trial, which I hadn't expected at all.

We all had to wait outside while the panel decided our punishment. It took ages, and I was sweating and fretting as I ran over everything that had been said. Although I'd started the whole thing and had ripped Ayerza's scrum cap, according to the rules of rugby he had committed the more severe offence by nutting me. We were equally culpable for the fisticuffs that followed, so on balance I was going to get the lesser punishment, wasn't I?

Wrong. Ayerza was handed a four-week ban reduced to two weeks, on account of his good disciplinary record. Meanwhile, I was handed a two-week ban but guess what? It stayed at two weeks. We'd ended up with exactly the same punishment despite Ayerza's offence meriting double the penalty. My disciplinary record was not as good as his – I'd had a recent sending off – but even so, surely this wasn't fair?

'What the fuck?' I said to Conor. 'How's this happened?'

He looked at me in exasperation, shaking his head.

'What? What's wrong?'

'Joe, we told you to shave your head and wear a suit and tie, but did you listen?'

No, I didn't. I didn't like being told what to do and I'd kept the eye-popping mohawk and Headworks combo. I didn't think my image would make any difference to the outcome of my case, but from the look on Conor's face he clearly didn't think I'd done myself any favours. Not only that, I didn't own a suit so I'd worn a blue checked shirt, a pair of chinos and some working boots. It was the smartest outfit I had in my wardrobe and looked perfectly acceptable to me. I wasn't a lawyer or club official. I was a 20-year-old rugby player, wasn't I?

Conor had bitten his tongue on the day because it was too late to do anything. Now he wasn't so restrained. 'Do you seriously not get it?' he said, clearly irritated.

'No. I seriously don't. I just don't understand.'

I knew some of the boys at the club were thinking what a dickhead I'd been not to heed Conor's advice, but every snooty 'Really, Joe, what were you thinking of?' only made me more determined to stick to my guns and show everyone what I was made of. In hindsight I accept the RFU handed me a fair judgement despite how I looked, but now I'm older and wiser I can also see things from Conor's point of view. What was the point of looking like a rebel when I was facing a disciplinary hearing?

*

It now seems that I was ahead of the curve with my mohawks because all the boys are into their haircuts these days. Forwards and backs, everyone has caught up. OK, they may not be channelling my 'I'll show you posh gits what I can do!' attitude, but most players now buy into Gavin Henson's 'look good, play better' mindset.

Having a haircut is part of the whole ritual and routine of the rugby week, and the sports psychologists and motivational experts are all for it. Every Thursday or Friday you go to the barbers and have your hair done for the game on Saturday, so that you feel your best when you walk on the pitch. Even the big dogs like Owen Farrell, George Ford and Jamie George go in for the weekly trim, to make sure their lines are neat and they look as sharp as they intend to play.

On tour with the England squad, Kyle Sinckler and Anthony Watson will usually get a couple of barbers in and set up a make-shift salon in someone's hotel room for all the boys to use. Sink will do anything in his power to put on his best performance and is a big believer in the psychological benefits of looking good.

During the World Cup in Japan we were staying in the hot springs resort of Beppu. Sink got a hairdresser to come over from Tokyo – about a four-hour flight – because he didn't trust any of the small-time local barbers to do his skin fade just the way he liked it. The guy said he would charge a flat fee of 13,000 yen – the equivalent of about £100 per player. Most agreed – me included – even though it seemed a bit steep.

Dan Cole wasn't having it. 'I'm practically bald, mate,' he told me. 'I can do my own, but can you just go around afterwards with the clippers, make sure I've not left any stragglers?'

'Fucking hell, Coley. What a tight-arse!'

He came to my room and I made a performance of placing the towel round his shoulders, calling him Mr Cole and asking if Sir was happy. I wasn't letting him come near mine – I could only imagine the pleasure he would take from messing it up.

We went back to the makeshift barbers to see how Sink was getting on. 'Fucking hell, what's happened?' I asked. Sink's head had been ruthlessly shaved up the sides and it looked like he'd had a bowl cut on top. 'He should have paid *you* the 13,000 yen!'

Coley was smug that he'd saved money and ended up with a better haircut than Sink. We all ribbed Sink for days, but we were careful not to go too far. After all, we had a World Cup to play in and we all knew that you had to be in a good state of mind to do your best.

One of our security team took himself out for a haircut when we were staying in Sapporo. It should have been easy for him to find a quality barber on any street corner, but he failed spectacularly.

'Fergus, mate, what the fuck happened to your eyebrows?'

'Is it bad?'

'Bad? You could say that. I mean, you haven't fucking got any.'

He explained that the language barrier had let him down.

'What? Surely when he started whipping your eyebrows off you could have just said, "Stop." You didn't need to know any Japanese for that!'

It was early days and Fergus had no eyebrows for the rest of the tournament, so the poor guy had the piss ripped out of him for weeks.

James Haskell is another player to fall foul of a barber's blades. He turned up to training one time, back in the UK, with a patch shorn out of the side of his head. Suspiciously, it was in the shape of a perfect rectangle.

'What happened, mate? Looks like you had a stinker.'

'Yeah, his clipper guard slipped. It went down to a zero. Can you believe it?'

The England boys didn't believe it, and we kept badgering him. 'You sure, mate? Barbers' guards don't just slip. Was it some back-alley joker? Want us to go and have a word?'

'No! No need to do that.'

'Look,' I said, putting on my best sympathetic voice. 'I've had Jolly Hog and Sausage written on the side of my head. Remember that? If you've done something stupid, you know you can tell me.'

He was still not saying, but I wasn't giving up. I was determined to get to the truth. 'Wanna know another dumb thing? I was once offered £10,000 to dye my mohawk bright green and shave Paddy Power on my head. It's true. I was such an idiot I nearly did it, right before an England game. Can you imagine? We all do silly things …'

I'd reeled him in at last, and Hask finally confessed to asking the barber to shave #ELITE into the side of his head. We all pissed ourselves laughing.

'What happened?' we asked. 'Did you change your mind?'

'Er, something like that.'

It was hilarious. He'd clearly bottled it when he saw the finished result, then he got the barber to shave a patch out to cover up the mistake.

*

Ahead of the 2019 World Cup a newspaper ran a feature about the players' striking hairdos, which just goes to show how far we've come. To my surprise I was first on the list. Hair stylist James Johnson said I looked 'distinctly British and manly', with my bushy dark beard and 'half-attempt of a fashionable quiff'. I was quite pleased with that. We all need a little ego boost from time to time and it made a change not to be criticised for my appearance. Though what they didn't know was that the quiff was Hobson's choice. After years of abusing my hair with dyes and bleach, it was all I could muster.

Danny Care and I regularly talk about our thinning hair and receding hairlines, and we've got a secret code going on. When it rains during a game you can see my scalp through my thin lid. It happens to him too, so we give each other a little wink. 'Slick it over a bit, mate. That's it.'

These days there's no shame in a rugby player having a hair transplant. Procedures and outcomes – good and bad – are all discussed in the changing room, but the secret stays there. Nobody wants to draw attention to the Hellraiser stage, do they? No, you have to bide your time. But here's a tip. When a player suddenly starts wearing hats and bandanas in every Instagram post for months on end, it's probably a sign that a new thatch will soon be unveiled.

Not everyone has been so complimentary about my beard over the years. During the Six Nations in 2013 Sir Clive Woodward called me out in a newspaper column for having a beard that wasn't aerodynamic enough. I was shocked. He said stubble was fine but not long beards like mine, not if you wanted that all-important cutting edge.

'He couldn't have watched me play,' I said. 'My game is not based around my pace, is it? Having no beard would not make any difference to my big arse plodding around the pitch!'

A fulsome beard didn't do French international Sébastien Chabal any harm, and he played as a number eight as well as a lock and a flanker. The French named him *l'Homme des Cavernes* – Caveman – because of his long, wavy beard and ferocious tackling.

He had an illustrious 16-year career, was one of the most iconic players of the 2007 World Cup and was such a popular figure that the media wrote about the Chabalmania he left in his wake. If he'd bought into Sir Clive's way of thinking, who knows how his life would have turned out. I often say you should not change for anyone, and he's the proof.

Other players didn't come off as well as me in that World Cup hairdressing feature. The Russian Andrey Garbuzov was criticised for his long, unbalanced bowl cut. 'I recommend using a ceramic bowl to complete this look as plastic can sometimes warp in the dishwasher and would result in a wonky haircut all over,' the hair stylist said, suggesting it might be 'the handiwork of his wife or mother'. Fucking hell, that's a bit harsh, isn't it? Russia didn't make it out of the group. Did the hair play a part? Or the public criticism of it? I wonder what Martin Johnson made of it all.

French player Maxime Médard also made the list, due to his seventies sideburns. I'm always jealous of the French players because whatever they do to their hair or beard they always look suave and sophisticated. I don't know what it is. I mean, if you put Médard's barnet and mutton chops on Joe Launchbury and got him to say, '*Bonjour,*' I can't see him having the same sex appeal.

Jack Goodhue entered the rugby haircut hall of fame at the World Cup, and rightly so for pulling off his magnificent mullet. When the All Blacks beat Ireland in the quarter-final, New Zealand Prime Minister Jacinda Ardern wrote on Instagram, 'That's a brilliant win ... for the All Blacks and mullets everywhere.' What a hero. And Jack Goodhue wasn't bad either.

Faf de Klerk was another poster boy of the tournament. He first caught my eye in 2018. I was on the pitch when he drove a monster tackle into Nathan Hughes in the mid-year Tests in South Africa. Faf is 5 foot 8 and 12-and-a-half stone; Nathan Hughes is 6 foot 5 and knocking on 20 stone. It's not often a scrum-half comes out on top against a number eight, but Faf's blond hair flowing behind him turned into a superhero's cape that day. He drove Nathan back 20 metres, got up without a spot of mud on him and gave his hair a cheeky flick. It was a sight to behold. He'd just melted one of the biggest blokes on the pitch.

When South Africa won the World Cup he wore a pair of budgie smugglers as he kissed the trophy and he looked fantastic. We can all learn from Faf.

Never underestimate the power of hair. Pick a great look, make it your own and wear it with confidence. And if a manager tells you it looks fucking stupid, don't listen. Unless, that is, you're going to court to face a disciplinary panel.

2

MIND GAMES

I was 11 years old, playing my first ever game of rugby.

'Joe's a big lump,' my mate Matt's dad had said to my dad the week before. 'Why doesn't he come down and have a go?'

'Why not?' I'd said, shrugging, when it was put to me. 'Should be a laugh.'

The club Matt's dad had invited me to play for was Eastbourne Sharks Under-12s. You had to bring your own ball, there were three-man scrums, 12 players on each team, playing on half a pitch, and you weren't allowed to push.

The manager asked me to put in a tackle, show him what I could do.

'What? You want me to whack in? OK. I can do that.'

I melted the other kid the first time I tried it. Probably went in a bit too rough but the manager seemed to like what he saw. I loved it. The physicality, the confrontation, beating the other kid. Bring it on.

'You can go at full-back, Joe,' the manager said. 'Last line of defence. So when everyone else has missed the tackle you can steam in.'

Full-back? I knew next to nothing about the game but that didn't sound right to me. My mood sank, straight away. Why ask the fat kid who can't run fast to tackle the fast ones who break through all the other players?

I won't get anywhere near 'em, I thought. *This is a joke.*

By the time the game kicked off I was seething. There were lots of parents standing on the sidelines. I didn't want to look stupid in front of them, but how was I going to catch the sprinters?

'Look at that lad – he's the size of a bus!' I'd heard one of the dads say, sounding impressed. I'd never been admired for being fat before. It had all started so well, but now I was going to make a fool of myself and I was fuming.

Right from the start we were getting pumped, and that had a lot to do with me. Just as I'd thought, I was too slow, getting nowhere near the opposition. *Why's he put me here? I thought this was gonna be a laugh and it's shit!*

Another whippet-fast opponent was hurtling in my direction. I had no fear about tackling him. Having him smashing into me didn't scare me at all. I was pushing ten stone, there was plenty of cushioning and I enjoyed the physicality of battle. But I knew when he was ten metres away that I had absolutely no chance of catching him and my head was going down fast. I just wanted to come off the pitch, call it a day. Punch someone. Preferably the manager.

'Go on, Psycho, get him!'

What the—

'Go on, Psycho, get him! Go on, Psycho, get him!'

The chorus was coming from the sidelines. I looked over to see Matt's big brother Dan standing among the parents, who were all looking at me. He'd obviously told them what my nickname was back in my neighbourhood in Heathfield. All of the mums and dads were chanting at the top of their voices, clapping and whooping and goading me to make the tackle.

'Go on, Psycho, get him!'

I felt a surge of adrenaline. It was another red-rag-to-a-bull moment. I had to live up to my name, show them what I was made of. I launched myself at whippet boy and put in the biggest and hardest tackle I could. It was a turning point in the game. The more the parents chanted, the harder I went in, time and time again. Now we were the ones pumping the opposition.

'Go on, Psycho, get him!'

The buzz I felt after the game was fantastic. Sure, it had been kind of embarrassing to be called Psycho so publicly. Imagine parents doing that today. No chance. Part of me was pissed off at Dan for telling everyone my nickname, but how could I complain when it had made me play out of my skin? I felt fantastic, proud of myself and desperate to do it all over again. Who'd have thought my size would have brought me a reward like this? I could hardly believe it. I wasn't just the fat loser after all.

I didn't realise it at the time, but that was my first taste of rugby psychology. The parents were pulling my chain, making me fight back. It showed how a shift in a player's mindset can change the way he plays the game.

★

You can't ignore the power of mind games in rugby. It can make the difference between lifting trophies or drowning sorrows, being man of the match or dumped in the sin bin. But it's a dark and mysterious art. You need to know the rules and learn from the best.

Martin Johnson gave a masterclass in how to out-psych an entire team when England played Ireland away in the 2003 Six Nations. Ireland were hoping for their first Grand Slam in 55 years, but Martin Johnson was not leaving without the trophy. When he walked out for the pre-match ceremony, he led the England team to the wrong side of the red carpet and refused to budge.

'None of us are going to move, and, if anyone does move, I'll kill them,' he hissed to the boys when the officials tried to move them on.

After a stand-off the Ireland players lined up on the same side, making one long line with the England players. The red carpet didn't stretch that far, which meant Ireland president Mary McAleese had to muddy her shoes by trudging along the turf to shake hands with the Ireland players. It was a brilliant piece of sports psychology. I would have loved to be there, seeing the Irish boys seething before the whistle. It put England in the driving seat before the game had even started, and they won by a thumping 42–6.

In the Six Nations in 2015, England were playing Wales away. We were standing in the tunnel of the Millennium Stadium and we got wind that Wales were trying to stitch us up by sending us out early. When the officials told us to go onto the pitch Chris Robshaw, our captain, refused. The crowd was baying for blood, it was freezing cold and the Welsh boys were still tucked up in the warm, taking their time. Robbo had smelled the wind. This was psychological intimidation. If we were waiting out there for ten minutes they'd have got one over on us mentally.

'We'll go out first, but only when they're ready to come out,' Robbo said.

He stood firm and we all followed suit. It was tense and awkward and absolutely brilliant. I was loving the drama but everyone wasn't enjoying it. I clocked George Ford in front of me. He was only a pup and he was looking uncomfortable, wishing this wasn't happening.

We could hear the crowd from the tunnel and the atmosphere was intense. I was thinking about how we got thrashed in this fixture in 2013, even though we were going for the Grand Slam, and failing that we only had to lose by six or fewer points to win the championship. It was a horrible ordeal. The memory made my blood rise and boil, made me want to come out fighting more than ever before.

I was 22 years old in 2013, and I had an absolute stinker and blamed myself, with good reason. What happened scarred me, made me question my ability and fear for my future career as an England player.

I'd been up against Adam Jones, one of the best tightheads in the world. I could still vividly remember the massive weight of him coming down on my neck and the speed he came at me. He was a 20-stone master of his craft and I was a 17-stone novice, soaked in sweat and wet behind the ears. I was in awe of him and wanted to show him what I was made of, but that only made it worse when he dominated me. I caved under the pressure and he completely bent me in two, pushing me back with ridiculous ease and winning penalty after penalty against me.

It's hard to describe how crushed you feel when you are having the air physically squeezed out of you in the scrum. You're fighting for breath, gasping under the weight of your giant opponent. When you're going backwards too, your spirit starts to break. It's unbearable. I was shrivelling, right there on the world stage, feeling like the Wicked Witch of the West when Dorothy throws the bucket of water on her and she melts away. Gone, just like that. I couldn't see how I would come back from that.

The fans played a part in the psychological warfare that day. I wasn't prepared for the noise when I came out of the tunnel. The roof of the Millennium Stadium was shut and the sound of the crowd was mind-blowing. Some of the seats are so close to the pitch you can hear every word they shout, which I hadn't experienced before.

'You shithouse! Go back home, you prick!'

The Wales fans were ten times more hostile than any I was used to. It was a perfect storm. I was intimidated before we kicked off and out-psyched in the scrum. After the game I was close to tears. *That's me done,* I thought. *My England career's gone – they'll never select me again.*

Now this, two years on. My first game back in the Millennium Stadium and we were in the tunnel, standing our ground against the Welsh intimidation. I was feeding off the pressure this time instead of giving into it. Enjoying the hostility of the crowd and embracing it. Feeding off the psychological game our opposition was playing instead of wobbling and wavering. It comes with experience and you have to learn to do it.

Robbo pushed it right up to the wire before agreeing to go out. 'If they're not out in two minutes we're coming back in,' he warned. They followed us out.

I was feeling cocksure and played a good game. Doing well in the scrum, holding my own, feeling powerful, my brain firing under the white-hot pressure – I was right on top of it. Eyes everywhere, judging the angle of my body, the split second I needed to give that extra push.

I badly wanted the victory and it all came together. We beat Wales 21–16. A fantastic victory for us. I was absolutely ecstatic. It felt like payback for their attempt to manipulate us, and of course I wanted to lay the ghost to rest from the game two years earlier.

Who knows what part psychology played in our victory that day. Maybe we all just played better and we would have won even without the psych-off in the tunnel. It's impossible to say. There's never a guarantee when it comes to mind magic – it's about as reliable as a ouija board but you can't blame a team for trying a few psychological tricks because sometimes they pay dividends.

*

It's the night before our World Cup semi-final clash with the All Blacks in Japan.

'Anyone want to talk about anything? Got any thoughts?' It's Owen Farrell – Faz, as we call him – trying to get the chat going among the boys. There's no management or coaches around. It's just the boys, meeting up as we always do before a game, to chew the cud and talk through any issues. 'No? OK. I've got something. The Haka. What are we gonna do about it?'

'What d'you mean?'

'I was chatting with the boss. He reckons we should come up with a plan.'

I'm liking the sound of this. The Haka's a war dance after all, and it's right that we respond somehow, show the Kiwis we're ready for battle.

'Why don't we try and surround them?' says Ben Youngs. He suggests forming a semi-circle, the ends of which would go up to the ten-metre line, which is as far as we can go.

'Great idea,' I say. 'I'm in.'

Faz is nodding, so are most of the boys. That's that sorted. A semi-circle it is. Simple, effective. Crack on.

'What do you mean, exactly?' says Tom Curry.

Luke Cowan-Dickie is also scratching his head. 'How do you mean, a semi-circle?' He's a details man and wants more of an explanation. 'Who will give the order, and exactly where will each player stand?'

'Fucking hell, boys, it's not difficult,' I say. 'Just get in a semi-circle in front of them.'

Tom Curry still doesn't get it, bless his heart.

'Do you not understand the concept of a semi-circle?'

'Yes, but how is it going to work exactly?'

Ben Youngs brings out a flip-chart. Using noughts for the All Blacks and crosses for us, he marks out our positions on the field. There's the triangle shape for the All Blacks in their Haka formation, and we're in a big, wide semi-circle facing them.

'Which one is me?' says Cowan-Dickie.

'Any of the England players!' I say. 'It doesn't matter, mate. As long as we all form the semi-circle and face them down.'

Everyone's on board and we're getting excited, remembering other challenges to the Haka.

Wales in 2006, demanding their anthem 'Land of My Fathers' be the last piece of ceremony before kick-off, prompting the All Blacks to perform the Haka in the Millennium Stadium changing rooms. Wales again, two years later, forcing a spine-tingling stand-off by refusing to follow tradition and walk away when the Haka ended. A fantastic piece of sporting theatre.

The French team of 2007, winning the toss for which strip to wear and insisting the All Blacks wear their grey second strip in the World Cup quarter-final. Then the French revealing red, white and blue jerseys and advancing as a united tricolour.

Ireland in 1989, linking arms in their green jerseys and pushing up right under the noses of the All Blacks, before the ten-metre rule came in.

Nobody mentions the fact that New Zealand ended up winning three out of those four matches – France were the only team to come out on top. That's the trouble. Piss off the Kiwis too much and they'll end up pumping you by 40 points. But you've gotta have a go, meet challenge with challenge.

*

Fucking hell, we'd better play well, I thought as we walked out on the pitch. Mind you, I wasn't starting. I could piss the All Blacks off and then leave the other boys to deal with the reaction. I'd be safe, sitting comfortably on the bench, drinking my cup of tea and watching it all unfold.

My heart was beating like a drum when we sang the national anthem. This was the World Cup semi-final. One of the biggest games of my life, against the All Blacks. I was going to have to play out of my skin. We all were. I could practically hear my blood pumping and I was telling myself to take things one step at a time. Get the Haka out the way then focus on the game.

You couldn't make up what happened next. I was on the end of the row when we went in to form the semi-circle. Some of the boys were still confused and struggling with the concept, and the semi-circle was looking more like a V-shape. At least I think it was, because it wasn't like looking at the noughts and crosses on Ben Youngs's flip-chart anymore. I was pushing forward further and further, to make sure my end of the semi-circle was in the right position, as close to the All Blacks as we were allowed to go.

The ref started ordering me not to breach the ten-metre rule. I looked back to see how the boys were getting on and realised I'd left them behind. There was too big a gap between me and the rest of the team, but I'd committed so I kept going.

The ref started talking to me again.

'Pardon?' I replied, looking at him in bemusement as he told me I'd encroached within the ten metres. It was way too late to change course now, though. I'd look like a fool, lose the psychological advantage I was going for. I looked back again at the boys to see this fantastic wide V-formation. It didn't matter that the semi-circle hadn't happened. We'd done what we set out to do. We looked amazing. A force to be reckoned with. Faz was smirking, which was an added bonus. We'd told the All Blacks we weren't taking any shit.

It set the tone for the game, and when Manu Tuilagi scored after two minutes it felt like all the stars were aligned in our favour. I wasn't starting – I had no issue with that – and watching from the bench I was feeling the hope and the energy, drinking it in. The All Blacks had not lost a World Cup match since the 2007 quarter-final, but we dominated them. We were faster, stronger, more disciplined in attack, more fearsome in defence.

When I came on in the second half I was full of confidence, riding the crest of the wave with the team. Wanting and deserving to be part of this win, I held my nerve and did my job well.

We won 19–7, one of the best victories we'd ever had over New Zealand. We'd beaten the All Blacks – the best team in the world – in the World Cup semi-final. It felt like it couldn't get any better than that. The euphoria was incredible. Winning the World Cup would be better than that, of course. But we'd played an absolute blinder. The game of our lives.

Here's the question: did we out-psych the All Blacks, out-play them or a bit of both? We'll never know. Their head coach, Steve Hansen, told us afterwards that they were glad we had embraced the challenge, as the Haka is a war dance that calls for a response. They appreciated the fact that we not only challenged them, but did so in a dramatic way. I don't think they knew we cocked it up, but never mind that.

I spent the next couple of days wondering if I'd get fined for encroachment. It seemed laughable to face a fine for what I did. The Kiwis were crazy-eyed, chanting intensely and looking like they wanted to rip our heads off as they performed their Haka. What did I do to threaten them? I put my big toe accidentally out of line and managed to look like a big buffoon on the world stage. It was even more embarrassing given that I'd taken the piss out of some of the other boys for not understanding the concept of the semi-circle.

In the end the squad was fined £2,000 and the bosses paid. Money well spent, in my opinion.

★

Dishing out sneaky little physical taunts during a game is another way of messing with your opponent's head. Sneaky being the operative word.

'No leadership, no ideas. Not even enough imagination to thump someone in the line-up when the ref wasn't looking.' That was J.P.R. Williams's verdict on Wales losing 28–9 against Australia in 1984. He knew the psychological power of a surreptitious blow and he knew the most important rule: don't get caught.

The sly foot-stamp is a favourite among players during televised games. When the scrum stands up and there's a bit of handbags, the cameras are always focused on faces and upper bodies, never the feet. It's the perfect opportunity to go after your opponent's toes. The trick is to do it slowly, treading on the foot and then very gently applying pressure. Not so much as to do any damage or provoke a cry that draws attention from the ref, but just enough to take their breath away and make them think, *Ooh, you bastard.*

The stud scrape's another popular option. I've not done this myself but I've had it done to me, so I know the technique. Again, you go in gently. Then you lift your studs off the ground and slyly scrape them down the side of the ankle – but not enough to draw blood. Same with nipple tweaks. A subtle, irritating squeeze is the order of the day; digging the nails in hard or excessive yanking is not. Pulling leg or arm hair follows the same rule. You're not looking to give them a free waxing. With all of these, you're aiming for that 'ooh, you bastard' response that makes them take their eye off the ball, lose it a little mentally or see a flash of red mist.

One of my favourite tricks is to untie an opponent's shoelaces at the bottom of a ruck. Nobody's expecting that. I love the look on the opponent's face when he realises what's happened and thinks, *Is this player so shit at rugby he has to resort to this?*

It makes me giggle, partly because there's some truth in that. I'm not a skilled player, but so what? I don't mind admitting it. I used to have more mobility as a pup, the ability to carry the ball and tackle, but I don't have that now. When you're a loosehead prop, size and strength are your weapons and scrummaging is your only skill. That's how it's always been. Anything else is a bonus.

Annoyingly, Mako Vunipola is breaking the mould. Not only is he a world-class scrummager, he can tackle 20 times a game, lift 20 times and do all the running too. 'Mako, mate,' I say. 'Why are you doing this? You've made things twice as hard! Couldn't we all just stay as plodders and cave dwellers and leave all that running to the thinner and quicker boys?'

I'd like to blame Mako for the fact that I resort to untying shoe-laces to gain an edge, but that would be unfair. I'd do it even if I was as skilled as he is. It's the pettiness of it I enjoy, pissing a player off with something so daft and trivial. They can't complain to the ref. He hasn't seen it and isn't exactly going to dish out a yellow, is he? The player just has to grit his teeth and refocus on the game, and who knows what that mental interruption might have done to his play?

*

Some players take things way too far. Nastily and grossly so. Remember the rugby-league player John Hopoate, who wore a rubber glove and stuck his finger up three players' bums in 2001? In his defence it was claimed that he was trying to slow down the game and provoke his opponents into striking out at him in order to win a penalty, but he was found guilty and banned for 12 weeks. How did he even come up with that tactic? Surely he knew it was a completely shit idea?

I always thought I understood all the boundaries and knew exactly how far I could push my luck. Especially when it came to the rugby player's favourite wind-up of all – giving a cheeky tweak to a player's meat and two veg.

Players have been flicking each other in the balls and tackle on and off the pitch for as long as anyone can remember. Every rugby player knows that. Exeter Chiefs used to have a ritual. If a player scored a try, all 14 of his teammates had to touch him on the knob as a celebration.

When I was touring with the Lions in 2017 a couple of the lads would always flick me in the groin when we were going down the tunnel. It became a custom, a bit of silly laddish bonding. Like slapping someone cheekily on the arse, because you're comfortable enough with each other and you know you can.

When you do it to your opposite number on the pitch, however, it's all about winding him up, gaining a psychological advantage. You never go in hard, never inflict pain. It's that 'ooh, you bastard' response you're after again, just like a nipple tweak or a sneaky shin scrape. You want to mess with his concentration, get under his skin. I've had it done to me countless times.

The night before we played Wales in the Six Nations in March 2019, we had our weekly meeting without the coaches and managers. As usual, it was a chance for the boys to swap views and discuss the upcoming challenge, the thinking being that the more open we are with each other off the pitch, the more comfortable we'll be on it.

'What do we think Wales are gonna bring to the table?' The senior boys were leading the chat. Faz, George Ford, Ben Youngs.

We picked over what happened the year before, when we lost a tight game at the Millennium Stadium. Alun Wyn Jones expertly baited Kyle Sinckler. He's one of the best players in the world in his position, but Sink was giving away penalty after penalty. And when a scuffle broke out Alun Wyn Jones laughed in his face. That was a turning point, a big sucker punch. Sink looked like the Incredible Hulk, about to burst out of his shirt. He gave another penalty away and was taken off. It was a lesson in rugby psychology from a master of the art. It's in Alun Wyn Jones's DNA to perform wind-ups like that. That day he'd shown perfectly how to pick on the right player, play the right mind games, avoid the referee and win.

'How are we gonna stop Alun Wyn Jones going after one of the young hotheads this time?'

We split into small groups and talked it through. The atmosphere was quite intense, and whenever that happens I like to bring the charge down a bit.

'Listen,' I said. 'We're at an advantage here. We know Jones will bring his nausy self. We know he'll probably be looking to wind up Sink again, or one of the other young pups. Don't worry about it. Forewarned is forearmed. I've got this.'

They all looked at me. 'How?'

'I don't know yet, but I promise you now, I will out-Alun-Wyn-Jones Alun Wyn Jones. I will get him. Do not worry about a thing.'

There were mumbles from some of the boys about how we should be focusing on our own performances.

'Agreed. But winding people up is part of my skill set. It's one of the few things I can bring to the game. I'm not gonna go for him, but I'll be ready for him. Trust me.'

When the game kicked off I had no more of a plan than I had the night before. We'd already got wind that the Italy game – our last of the tournament – was off because of coronavirus, so I was making the most of it, enjoying the moment and feeling quite relaxed. Who knew when we'd play again? And depending on if or when the Italy game took place, maybe this would even be my last-ever England game.

When it all started kicking off after ten minutes or so I was miffed. The scuffle was holding up the game. I'd been enjoying myself and I wanted to carry on, so I wandered across the pitch to the melee to see what was going on.

Can't we get on with things? I thought. *Why is this taking so long? If we were playing ice hockey, a goon would throw a glove down and we'd all be allowed to have a fight and then crack on. If only I could ice skate …*

I saw Alun Wyn Jones go into the melee again. There was more pushing and shoving. It was getting boring now. Something had to give because the game needed to get back on course. *Fuck it. I'll intercept him. I'll play Jones at his own game, do something to distract him.*

I'd been on the piss with Jones during the Lions tour in 2017 and had got to know him quite well. We'd had a funny night out in Queenstown when the pair of us, along with my good mate Dan Cole, ended up in a 24-hour burger place called Fergburger. It was packed with teenagers and backpackers. We didn't want to be recognised, but the New Zealanders are so obsessive about their rugby that they knew all the Lions players.

'I know, let's pull our caps down a bit,' I suggested, in my far from sober state. 'Nobody will clock us if we do that.'

We all tugged at our caps then burst out laughing. How were the peaks of our little baseball caps going to hide three enormous rugby players? We weighed nearly 60 stone between us and stuck out like three not-so-wise monkeys among all the trim young students and travellers.

Back on the pitch, I decided on the way to distract Jones from the scuffle and get the game back on track. *I'll just do something silly and make him laugh,* I thought. *Simple.*

I walked calmly in and gave his tackle a gentle tickle. It was something he did to me once on the Lions tour. Not on a pitch, of course, but off the field, at the end of a game. A lot of the lads did it to each other, giving a little flick of the balls as a way of saying, 'Hey, mate. How you doing?' I wasn't in the least bit worried about how he'd take it. I knew he'd laugh.

Alun Wyn Jones did not laugh. He just looked at the touch judge as if to say, 'Sir? Urgh!' It was more for the officials' benefit than because he was really bothered.

The situation was defused and we played on, at last. We won the game 33–30 and the Triple Crown was ours. Fucking brilliant! I paraded around the pitch afterwards, drinking in the glory, having played well. I didn't have a care in the world.

The team manager, Charlotte Gibbons, came up to me at the end and gave me a cuddle. 'Congratulations,' she said, 'but are you prepared for what's going on?'

'What?'

'You tickling Alun Wyn Jones's bits. It's gone wild.'

'Really? No, surely not. It was nothing. Whatever ...'

I was off to the changing room to have a drink and sing a victory song with the boys. I checked in with my wife Daisy and the kids and saw that my mates had sent me screen shots of my tickle on Jones.

'What have you done this time?' they asked. They were laughing about it. Of course they were. It was insignificant and it would give everyone a giggle and then go away.

After the match I had a pint with Jones and he wasn't worried at all, which didn't surprise me. Why would he be? It was only later that he tipped me off that he was under pressure from World Rugby to make a stand. They want to grow the sport, get it out to a wider audience, and it seemed they didn't have a choice but to respond after the way things rocketed on social media.

It had become a huge story. Headlines everywhere, #fondle-gate trending on Twitter. Some saying it was genius, others that I'd committed an assault. *What the fuck?* Even Gareth Thomas – openly gay – was getting trolled online after joking during his commentary that if it had happened in his day he'd never have retired.

I hoped for a misconduct charge, a slap on the wrist for inappropriate behaviour and a short ban. That was dim of me. World Rugby did not have rules about touching another player's tackle, so they used the rule for 'grabbing, twisting or squeezing the genitals', for which the shortest ban was 12 weeks. In the end I got a 'reduced' ban of ten weeks, after making an apology.

The ban was a blow. That's putting it bluntly. Clearly, I shouldn't have done the deed in the first place. But I also couldn't believe I had failed so spectacularly to abide by the biggest unwritten rule in the dark arts of rugby: don't get caught.

Instead of applying everything I knew about the psychological tricks on the pitch, I had been gazing around like an idiot, looking at the screen that plays the live footage while I slowly tickled Alun Wyn Jones's nuts in an international game that was being broadcast around the world. Why, oh why? Huge lesson learned.

★

A few carefully chosen words can change the course of a match. I'd experienced it for myself as a kid called Psycho, and I used to love watching recordings of Muhammad Ali when I was growing up. His sledging and trash-talking were so smart that he'd beat his opponent before they even stepped in the ring. I was in awe.

'Joe Frazier is so ugly that, when he cries, the tears turn around and go down the back of his head.'

'I've seen George Foreman shadow boxing and the shadow won.'

I lapped it up. Ali was the boy, a master craftsman conquering the world with pearler after pearler, each delivered with incredible poise and skill.

The cricketers have always had sledging down to a fine art too. Glenn McGrath to Zimbabwe's Eddo Brandes: 'Why are you so fat?' Answer: 'Because every time I shag your wife she gives me a biscuit.'

Raman Subba Row to Fred Trueman after spilling a catch between his knees: 'I'm sorry, Fred, I should have kept my legs together'. Reply: 'So should your mother.'

There are so many belters, whole books have been written about cricket sledging. Rugby can't compete. But it's not that we aren't as quick or witty – or as foul-mouthed or politically incorrect. With innings that can go on for hours, there's a lot more opportunity in a game of cricket for a carefully crafted sledge – and a killer comeback – than there is in the middle of a ruck or a scrum during a muddy, violent 80-minute blood bath.

We still have a go. Ali didn't blaze the trail for nothing. And if out-psyching the opposition verbally might help you win the game, bring it on. I've learned a lot about sledging over the years. Gypsygate taught me precisely, and painfully, how not to do it. We'll come back to that later. But here's what does work, in my humble experience.

RUGBY SLEDGING DOS AND DON'TS

Weird 'em out.

'You know what, you've got the most beautiful, sexy blue eyes,' fierce South African lock Bakkies Botha said to Welshman Mike Phillips during a Lions match. Botha then held his gaze and blew him a kiss, which completely messed with Phillips's head. I play a different weird card going into a scrum. When the ref says, 'Crouch,' I make eye contact. It's eight on eight, man on man. It's intense and I should be frothing at the mouth, but I'm not. The ref says, 'Bind,' and I start to sing, usually Tina Turner or Adele. 'Someone Like You' usually does the trick.

Don't be shy.

My fiftieth cap, against Scotland in 2017, and I was feeling perky in the tunnel at half-time, when we were 30 points up. Before the game Tim Visser had told the press we were 'pretending' to be more confident than we were, and I thought it was time to retaliate. I was sandwiched between Richie and Jonny Gray – all six foot nine and six foot six of them – when I took the bull by the horns: 'Oi, lads. Any danger of you lot turning up out there? It feels like a training session.' Madness, really. But we won 61–21.

Do your homework.

Quins were playing Wasps away when I heard Chris Robshaw yelling something to Joe Simpson that instantly threw him off his game: 'Come on, Skimmo. Hurry up and put the ball in!' The nickname 'Skimmo' hailed from Simpson's school days, when he gained a reputation for skimming the crumble off the pudding and leaving the apple. How Robbo found out about it was a mystery. Genius.

Don't poke the bear.

Quins were up against Montpellier at home when Dave Ward decided to start gobbing off in the scrum, trying to speak in French. He was murdering the language and they were furious. They started to push harder and harder. The baiting had backfired on us and we were going in reverse, fast.

Target your audience.

I was up against a sharp young gun in a Quins game. 'No spray, no lay!' I started to sing at the top of my voice. 'No aftershave? You go with Dave.' And then, 'Smell like a scrummer? The night's a bummer.' I belted it all out, deadpan. He was losing focus fast, wondering how a receding old plodder like me knew all the chat you get from the toilet attendants in a nightclub.

Don't be a dickhead.

Quins were playing Wasps when one of our young lads started calling a senior player a shithouse. The response? 'Sorry, mate, I can't hear you. My ears are covered by my 70 England caps. You got any?' Or there's the other old favourite, asking a player to turn around so you can read his name on his shirt because you don't know who he is. Arrogant rubbish like that never works – you just look like a pompous dick.

Don't pick on the ref.

'You wearing those boots for a laugh?' I asked Andrew Small, as he had fancy white boots on instead of the usual black. My piss-take was picked up on the ref mic, as was his wittier retort: 'Yeah, I paid for mine, though.'

★

Rugby sledging is a dying art, unfortunately. I hate to see it, but professional players are too focused on doing the job now. Not all of us, obviously. But the boys with the skills can't lose concentration for a second, and they're too afraid to say anything to the opposition in case they can't back it up.

Me? I'm going to crack on. Sledging when I'm bored. Sledging when I'm pissed off. Sledging when I fancy throwing down the gauntlet and forcing myself to rise to the challenge. Sledging for sledging's sake. It's in my blood. After all, where would I be without the parents who shouted, 'Go on, Psycho!' all those years ago?

3

NICKNAMES

I was 19 years old, away in Ireland for a Quins match. I'd only recently broken into the first team and I didn't know many of the other boys. We were in a hotel in Galway and I was on my own in my room, looking for something to watch on my laptop.

It's hard being the new boy. You have to earn your stripes and there's a fine line to tread. Act too cocky with the senior players and you'll piss them off. Be too quiet and you might be pushed around and ignored. Neither is any good for your game. You need to bond with your teammates, make friends. It doesn't happen overnight and I was feeling a bit out of it.

I had time to kill before our team meeting. I started looking at YouTube, rewatching some videos of Nick Cummins, the crazy Australian player known as the Honey Badger. He's a genius – aggressive, quick, crazy and smart. He inspires me, and I can't get enough of him and the things he comes out with. 'The boys were on it like seagulls at a tip.' 'If I get a gig I'm gonna go off like a cut snake.' 'You're as tough as woodpecker lips.'

When he's asked about his nickname, he replies, 'One of the stories that inspires me, it's documented that a honey badger killed a lion in a one-to-one …'

I was giggling away when my phone rang. It made me jump. I wasn't expecting anyone to call me.

'Where are ya?' It was Olly Kohn, our six-foot-seven, twenty-two-stone lock forward, and the friendliest senior player at the club. They called him Fisherman's Friend because he got on with everyone. I thought it was a kind of mint, so it was a bit of a rubbish nickname, but there you go.

'What do you mean, where am I?' *Fucking hell. Don't tell me I've fucked up.*

'Mate, there's a team meeting. You're late.'

'What? I thought it was later …' My heart was sinking. I slammed the laptop shut and jumped to my feet.

'No, mate. You'd better get your arse down here, fast.'

Fuck's sake! The last thing I needed was to give the boys ammunition to take the piss. I wanted to fit in and to be seen as a grown-up, a professional. I sprinted downstairs, charged through reception and pushed open the door of the team meeting room.

The room was dimly lit. I could see there was a full house of players but they were all reclining in their seats, heads tipped backwards. Had they started already? Was this some weird team-building exercise and I'd missed the memo?

There was a momentary pause and then 20 heads popped up. 'Alright, Croissant!' they shouted in unison, all whooping and laughing their heads off.

I couldn't believe my eyes. Every player had a croissant stuck to his nose. Olly Kohn. Tighthead prop Ceri Jones. Hooker Matt Cairns. All the senior boys were there, giggling along with the younger players.

'We just wanted to look like you, mate,' said Kohn. 'We all wanted a nose that looked like a French pastry!'

It was a huge relief that I hadn't fucked up. I started laughing. Did I care that they were taking the piss out of my huge nose? I'd broken it three or four times already, and each time it set into a slightly different shape. I'd take Croissant. It wasn't a bad nickname. I'd have taken anything, to tell the truth. Choux bun. Brioche. Greggs sausage roll.

I had a nickname and it made me one of them. That's the joy of nicknames. On the face of it the other blokes are taking the piss. But really they're showing acceptance, bringing you into the fold. That's what it's all about. You're worth inventing a name for. You're worth going to a bit of trouble over. You're part of the team, and the nickname will help you bond with the other boys.

I had another nickname bestowed upon me during this period. I'd gone on loan from Quins to Esher RFC when I was still an academy player. All the lads were brilliant characters and liked to take the piss.

'I've got a question for ya,' one of the boys said, looking me up and down.

'What d'you wanna know?'

'Your physique, mate. I'm just thinking about it.'

This was going to be some wisecrack about my silhouette, wasn't it? I was well aware that as I'd reached the end of my teens

I'd started to morph from the shape of a fridge into something a bit more complex.

I decided to get in first. 'What about it, mate? I know I look like a melted wheelie bin. You got a problem with that? I'm a prop. I'm meant to look like this.'

He laughed at my little joke. 'Yeah, mate. Melted wheelie bin. I like that. But it looks like you've been on the gear.'

'What?'

'Steroids, mate. A hunchback is a common sign. You've got a bigger hunch than Quasimodo.'

I knew I'd developed a hunch on my back from pumping weights to build the muscles in my neck and shoulders. Not to mention the hours I'd spent bending into a scrum and lifting and tackling 20-stone men. But steroids? I'd never touched them.

'Are you joking? If I was on the gear, don't you think I'd have gone to town on it and got a six-pack as well? Got myself properly shredded instead of having a rubber ring bulging over the waist-band of my shorts?'

'Nice try. But maybe that's how you're hiding it, mate.'

'Bollocks!'

'Whatever you say, Quasi Marler.'

Quasi Marler? Fucking hell, that was cruel. But touching too, in a weird way – even when the boys spent an entire train journey to a match singing 'Quasi Marler' to the tune of 'Bomboleo'.

'Leave it out, boys!'

'Quasi Marler! Quasi Marler!' They were really going to town, clicking their fingers, putting on a Spanish accent and belting the tune out at the top of their voices.

I took it. For one thing, the more you react, the more abuse you get. But mostly I accepted it for the same reason I embraced Croissant. Having a nickname meant I was in the gang. I felt connected to the team, part of the club. I was a character worth inventing a name for.

*

Rugby players have always given each other nicknames – it's part of the history and tradition of the game. After all, the sport came out of public schools and the upper-class world inhabited by boys called things like Spunky or Lumpy or Bunter or Biffo.

Growing up, I loved the player nicknames that needed no explanation. Bald, wide-eyed Keith Wood was the Raging Potato (or Uncle Fester). Tighthead Duncan Bell: Ding Dong. Brian Moore, a master of taunting and aggressive play, was Pitbull. Dimple-chinned Will Carling was Bumface and lightning-fast Jason Robinson was Billy Whizz. You didn't need to be inside the changing room to understand where the names came from, which helped you feel connected, like you were in on the joke.

Fun Bus might have been my favourite nickname from this period, mostly because Jason Leonard was my childhood idol. A juggernaut on the pitch and a legendary drinker and socialiser off it, he took the game seriously but somehow not too seriously. I thought all props should be like him. The nickname was coined after he came on the pitch with his red shirt stretched around his barrel chest. 'You look like a London bus,' Martin Bayfield said. Fun Bus was born and the name stuck. A fantastic nickname for a fantastic character.

During the summer of 2004 I was partway through reading Jason Leonard's autobiography when my local club, Heathfield Rugby Club, invited him in to open a new pitch. I couldn't believe it – I'd watched him win the World Cup the year before.

Fucking hell, I'll get him to sign my book! I thought, gobsmacked that Fun Bus was coming to my little East Sussex village. The only autograph I'd ever collected before was from Phil Collins's drummer, whose dad lived round the corner. Who knew Phil Collins needed a drummer? I thought he *was* a drummer.

Anyway, what were the chances of JASON FUCKING LEONARD coming to Heathfield and signing my book? Apologies. I should say JASON FUCKING LEONARD OBE, as he'd quite rightly been honoured since that glorious World Cup triumph. He was recognised as one of the nation's great sporting heroes, and he was an absolute colossus in the eyes of a young prop-in-progress like me.

The club put on an exhibition game and Fun Bus kicked it off, playing about five minutes. I was a blancmange-like 14-year-old, wobbling with nerves and puppy fat, as I looked up at him in awe and asked him to sign my book.

'Yes, son, 'course.'

I didn't say anything coherent to him, though I had a million questions I wanted to ask. *If only I was old enough to have a pint with him, see him live up to his reputation*, I thought. *What would it be like to be in a pub with the legendary Fun Bus?*

The moment was gone. The next kid in line was thrusting an autograph book at him. Would I ever get a chance like that again?

Fast-forward three years. I was at Quins, just starting out in the academy. There was a mentor system in place, pairing academy youngsters with ex-pros who've played in the same position.

'You're being mentored by Jason Leonard,' Collin Osborne, head of the academy, told me.

'JASON FUCKING LEONARD?'

'Yes, Joe, but I think you'll find his name is just Jason Leonard.'

'He's my hero! Fuck me!' I was catapulted right back to being 14 years old again.

'Here's his number,' Collin said. 'Send him a text and fix up a meeting.'

I was staring at my mobile. I had Jason Leonard's phone number in my contacts and I was going to send him a text. What do you even call the man you have idolised for years? Mr Leonard? Sir? Jason? Mate?

I settled for: 'Hiya, Jason. My name is Joe Marler. Collin Osborne gave me your number and said to arrange a meet with you. Is it possible to set something up?'

He messaged back straight away. 'Alright, son, 'ow's things? Yeah, be good to meet. I'll be at the Sun, Thursday next week, this time.'

Fucking hell! The following week I travelled by several trains from East Sussex to Twickenham and found my way to the pub. It was a summer's evening and the Sun was packed out. I couldn't see him anywhere so I went up to the barman.

'Is Jason Leonard here?'

'You 'aving a laugh? He's outside.'

It was my first time in the Sun. I didn't realise he was in there all the time, propping up the bar. The pub more or less belonged to Jason Leonard – still does. There are photos of him everywhere and it's littered with memorabilia, like his first expenses cheque for £15, enough to get him across London to a game when he was still working as a carpenter in the amateur era.

I headed outside, pulse racing. *This is it,* I thought. *I'm finally going to properly meet my idol – have a pint with Fun Bus himself! Is this for real?*

That was when I spotted him, perched up against a car, swaying back and forth with a pint in his hand. If I'd been nervous before, I was shitting myself now. I'd clearly got there too late. The last thing I wanted to do was interrupt his drinking session.

'Er, hi, Jason. I'm Joe,' I started nervously. 'We arranged to meet …'

'Hello, mate. Good. Yeah. Lovely to meet ya, mate. I'll be honest, it's not a good time. Not right now. I'm a good halfway through a session with the boys.'

'Yeah, yeah, of course. Maybe we can arrange it for another time?'

'Let's do that, son.'

Disappointing, yes. But I was still buzzing. I'd seen a glimpse of Fun Bus in action, even if I didn't get to have a drink with him.

I met Jason – yes, I'm calling him Jason now – a few days later, at a little place round the corner from Twickenham Stadium. It was early, he was slightly less intoxicated this time and we had coffee rather than beer.

'What can I tell ya, son?' he started.

'Er, what advice can you give me?'

I hoped he'd say, 'Work hard and play even harder,' or something along those lines. I wanted a green light to uphold some of the amateur-era traditions in the professional world of rugby.

'Believe in yourself, son,' he said. 'Never forget, you're 'ere because you're good enough. If you want to make it to the top, you 'ave to be prepared to go to dark places, mentally and physically.'

I nodded. I hadn't expected that.

'And enjoy every minute,' he went on. 'Because you're a long time retired.'

I was surprised he made no mention of the social side of rugby, which was stupid of me, when I look back now. Why would he? Fun Bus was his own walking advert for the rugby social. His name said it all.

★

These days I have the privilege of being on the scene when nicknames emerge and evolve. I hear first-hand the stories of how they've come about. Fancy a tour of rugby nicknames? Come aboard the nickname bus.

JOE LAUNCHBURY – SLOSH, SLOSHBUCKET OR BISCUIT

Back in 2016, Dean Benton, the England strength and conditioning coach, got us training with giant water packs on our backs. They were half-full to make us unstable, so we worked our core. Joe Launchbury already had a reputation for being clumsy – he has the biggest arse in world rugby and was forever knocking things over – and with these water packs on we all felt like we had a big clumsy arse like him.

'Your arse is like a permanent slosh bucket!' we laughed. 'Is this what it's like to be you, Sloshbucket?'

He hated it, which made us use it more.

'Oh, Slosh!' we all cry now whenever anything hits the deck or gets broken, regardless of whether it's his fault or not.

'Can't you stop using it?' he moans. 'The joke's over. It was years ago.'

No, we can't. Because Slosh's big arse is the gift that keeps on giving.

When we were doing our altitude training in Italy before the Japan World Cup, Eddie Jones arranged for us to have a day trip to Venice.

'That'll be fabulous,' we all said. 'It'll be lovely to go on a gondola, sit in St Mark's Square.'

When we arrived at our destination after a hot and sticky bus journey, we were not in Venice at all, but instead a small town on the outskirts. We were all feeling cheated until someone explained that Eddie had organised this trip as a thank you to the town because the Italian international Fabio Ongaro was like a king there.

'Fair enough. That's a nice idea.'

The locals couldn't do enough to make us feel welcome. Local dignitaries came out to meet us and a meal was laid on for us in a traditional village hall. Lovely.

We arrived for the meal and were invited to 'Take a seat, please!' My face dropped when I looked at the spindly wooden chairs set around the table. *Will I be able to fit my fat backside into there?* All the bigger boys had the same reaction.

'We'll be fine,' we said, wedging ourselves in gently. 'We'll manage. Might take us a minute or two to pull ourselves out again, but we'll smile through it.'

We couldn't make a fuss, could we? The locals had gone to so much trouble, making us a very strong anchovy-paste dish as a special treat. We tucked in politely, determined to make a good impression for Eddie's sake.

Partway through the meal there was a creaking sound. The boys looked around the table to see where it was coming from.

Slosh! It had to be Slosh, didn't it? Sloshbucket was sweating, looking like he wanted the ground to swallow him up. The chair was straining under his weight. We could hear it groaning. Then it happened.

'*Mamma mia!*' one of the dignitaries cried, rushing to help him.

Slosh was sent sprawling onto the floor, the wooden chair smashed to smithereens under the weight of his giant Sloshbucket arse. He was bright red in the face and very apologetic, which made the whole thing even funnier. I picked up one of the broken legs and said, 'Should keep this as a souvenir, mate.'

Slosh was spitting tacks that I was taking the piss at a moment like that, but he couldn't react in front of our hosts, who were all clearing away the mess, telling him not to worry and that they'd find him another seat.

'I'll get it framed. You'll thank me when you have your testimonial ...'

'You're a wanker!' he hissed.

I also have my own personal nickname for Slosh – I call him Biscuit. He's developing a bald patch on top of his head. It's hard to spot, seeing as he's six foot five, but he's been done by the Spidercams in stadiums, which have a habit of zooming into scrums when you're bent over and have nowhere to hide.

'I feel your pain,' I tell him. 'I'm in the same boat. Maybe we could look into a two-for-one deal on hair plugs?'

'Wanker!'

Why Biscuit? Because his bald patch looks exactly like a digestive biscuit.

He hates the nickname intensely, so I use it as often as I can. I like to creep up behind him, stretch up high with my phone and take a close-up photo of his bald patch, which I then send to the England players' group WhatsApp chat.

JAMES HASKELL – THE UNFLUSHABLE TURD, RIG CITY

Despite being embroiled in a number of off-the-pitch controversies over the years and falling foul of various regimes, the Unflushable Turd has repeatedly bounced back.

'Not you again. Thought you were toast this time.'

'No, mate. The Unflushable Turd is here again!'

He coined his own nickname and he loves to use it.

'Ta-dah!' he said, bursting into the England training camp in Japan. 'I'm here! The Unflushable Turd is back!'

He'd retired from professional rugby but Eddie Jones had brought him over to do some gym sessions for the boys. He brings so much energy and raises spirits in the team, which is why managers have always found it hard to get rid of him.

The Unflushable Turd is also known as Rig City, another self-appointed name, as he supposedly has the 'best rig in world rugby'. His words, not mine.

CHRIS ROBSHAW – ENGLAND PLAYAHHH

I was one of several Quins youngsters, along with Chris Robshaw, Nick Easter, Ceri Jones, Danny Care and Ugo Monye, out on the beers in Biarritz back in 2011, after a European game. We were all up for going on to a club, but there was only one venue in town and it had a big queue to get in.

'Don't worry, boys, leave it to me,' Robbo said in his upper-crust voice. He was the perfect man for the job and everyone trusted him to handle the situation perfectly.

We all watched as he strode to the front of the queue and approached the doorman with a charming smile on his face. I wondered if he would speak to the guy in French – it's the sort of thing Robbo would do, being the well-educated man about town he is.

But Robbo didn't speak French. Instead he started pointing to himself and talking very slowly and purposefully to the doorman. 'England playahhh,' he intoned, sounding like Prince Charles on steroids.

The doorman was unimpressed. We all were, to put it mildly. The smiles had slipped from our faces. I wanted to crawl under the nearest hedge.

Robbo, however, was oblivious to our embarrassment. He ploughed on. 'England playahhh,' he repeated, pointing at an open-mouthed Nick Easter.

I wasn't sure if the doorman was confused or annoyed, but he definitely wasn't buying into it.

Still Robbo didn't change tack. 'Welsh playahhh,' he said, pointing proudly at Ceri Jones, who was examining the cracks in the pavement.

'Non,' the doorman said sharply, shaking his head.

'Non, non, non,' Robbo retorted, choosing now as the time to start speaking French. 'Academy playahhh!' He was pointing at me this time.

We didn't get into the club. Of course we didn't. But all was not lost. At least we'd got a nickname for Robbo out of it, who's been called 'England playahhh' ever since.

GEORGE KRUIS – SHNOOZE OR SHNOZ

His nickname is Shnooze because his chat is so boring it makes you fall asleep. That's the theory, at least. The name was bestowed on him years ago, and once it stuck, poor Shnooze couldn't get rid of it. The boys love him, but every time he tries to engage in a bit of banter someone turns it round on him and tells him he's being boring, even if he's not.

I prefer Shnoz, a nickname he earned when I went out for dinner one night with him and Justin Tipuric. They've both got huge noses and, for once, I was enjoying not being the man with the biggest nose in the room. And I said as much.

'Hang on, who said you haven't got the biggest nose?' Tipuric said. 'Who decided that?'

I called the waitress over. 'This might be a strange request,' I said, 'but can you do us a favour?'

She looked a bit sceptical. 'It depends what it is,' she said cautiously.

'Can you examine our noses and then tell us who has the biggest shnoz?'

She looked relieved that that was all the three huge-hootered, burly blokes were asking of her, and she happily gave each nose a solid assessment.

'On balance,' she said. 'It has to be his.'

Shnooze looked crestfallen while we cheered.

'Well done, Shnoz!' we teased. 'You won, mate! Good for you, Shnoz!'

MARK LAMBERT – SMUG PIG

I was 18 years old and doing a bit of stretching after training at Quins.

'What did you have to eat last night?' one of the other academy boys asked.

'Domino's Two for Tuesday. What about you?'

'Oh, I had sole.'

Never heard of it. 'What's that?' I asked.

Before the other lad could answer, I heard this exasperated 'Pfff!' from across the changing room. 'You don't know what sole is?'

I looked over to see Mark Lambert staring at me in disbelief.

'It's a fish!' he spluttered.

'Alright, mate. I know what a battered cod is. I've just never heard of sole.'

Lammy was a few years older than me, infinitely better educated and he spoke with a cut-glass accent. Was I intimidated? No. His nickname was Smug Pig long before I arrived, and now I knew why. Not only did he act all superior, he had a reputation for really, really enjoying his food.

More than a decade on, the nickname is still going strong. Smug Pig has become one of my best mates at the club, and I love a bit of sole now.

DAN COLE – COLAR BEAR

'What d'you think of the training, Coley?'

'Shit, mate.'

'Which bit?'

'It's all shit.'

'Can you be more specific?'

'Passing's shit. Tackling's shit. Running with the ball. All shit.'

'Do you just hate rugby?'

'No. I like scrummaging. Why don't they just make scrummaging a separate game?'

That's what you have to put up with, all the time. He's the grumpiest man in rugby. His nickname is Colar Bear because with his bald head, white stubble and yellow eyebrows he looks like a polar bear, an animal renowned for being miserable.

'What d'you think of your nickname, Colar Bear?'

'It's shit, mate, and can you stop talking to me?'

'Why?'

'I'm nearly on 10,000 steps on my Fitbit and I'm trying to concentrate.'

We're in a hotel in Japan and he's walking round in circles like a caged bear, appropriately enough, as he tries to hit his daily steps target. When the Fitbit vibrates he's ecstatic. We're playing in the World Cup but this is what's made his day. That's Colar Bear all over.

MANU TUILAGI – CHIEF OR LITTLE CHIEF

We call him Chief because of his Samoan heritage, but only when his big brother Freddie isn't around. The oldest of Manu's five rugby-playing big brothers, Freddie is a world-class legend and great to drink with. He often comes on the beers with us, and always corrects us when we call his little brother Chief.

'You mean Little Chief,' he says, giving the Tuilagi hard-man stare.

Nobody argues. Not even the Chief. Sorry, Little Chief.

MAKO VUNIPOLA – SNORLAX

The name has nothing to do with snoring. I've roomed with him several times and I'm the only one who snores – very loudly. Mako sleeps like a baby, for what seems like 22 hours a day. On one occasion, in Japan, I nudged him because I thought he was dead.

That's why he's named after the Pokémon who's famous for sleeping and eating and not much else. Mako only gets up to eat and train and occasionally play *FIFA*. Or dance. And he also lives in a sleeping bag. OK, it's a quilted jacket that goes down to just above his ankles and has a big hood. He's had it for about eight years and, come rain or shine, it goes on top of everything – shorts, jumpers, fleeces. Why? I have no idea. He's over 19 stone, so he's already a man with a healthy protective layer on him. Trust me, I know. I'd boil to death.

RORY BEST – SIR BEST

Besty was made an OBE for his charity work in 2017, the year we both toured with the Lions in New Zealand.

'Charity work? Not for keeping the booze industry afloat?'

Big mistake to take the piss. Besty started to insist that he wasn't going to carry his own bags now he was an OBE, and he ordered me and James Haskell to skivvy around after him. We decided to have a laugh with it, christened him Sir Best and even strapped him in a makeshift sedan chair and carried him around like royalty some days.

WILLI HEINZ – BEANS

Some people like to call him 57 after the old Heinz '57 varieties' advertising slogan, but I prefer to call him Beans. Nothing to do with Heinz beans. I'd call him Beans if his surname was Jones because he's got a head shaped like a baked bean.

BILLY TWELVETREES – 36

You have to say his surname in an Irish accent to get it. His old man was called Kevin Fentiman, and when he married Billy's mum, Beverley Twelvetrees, he broke with tradition and took her name because he was a tree surgeon. He took it for his business too, renaming it Twelvetrees tree surgeons. It would have been rude not to. It's a fantastic name, and '36' always gives people a laugh when they work it out, even if the nickname is hardly used.

COURTNEY LAWES – SPIDEY

It feels like he has eight arms when he tackles. That's it.

MATT CAIRNS – THE BOLLOCK

Another simple one. He has a shiny, bald head that looks like a shiny, bald bollock. He's been retired for eight years and is a successful businessman nowadays, but I still insist on using it.

ELLIS GENGE – BABY RHINO, WHICH IS SELF-EXPLANATORY

ELLIOT DALY – BRIEFCASE

He got the name after turning up at his first Wasps training session in his Whitgift private-school uniform, carrying a briefcase. Bless his heart.

★

A word of caution as we disembark the nickname bus. Just because you know a person's nickname it does not give you the right to use it. Tread carefully, or it might turn into the opposite of a cosy bonding experience.

After we'd just beaten Scotland in an ugly game during the Six Nations in 2016, their director of rugby, Scott Johnson, came over to me and Colar Bear at the after-match dinner.

'How's the Beaver getting on?' he asked.

'Who's the Beaver?' we replied.

'Eddie, of course. That's his nickname. Do you boys not use it?'

We clearly didn't. We'd never heard it used once, and Eddie had obviously decided not to bring it into the England camp.

'Ask him about it.'

We weren't sure. Eddie was new in the job. We'd never experienced the hardcore, volatile Eddie we'd heard so much about and we didn't want to. What if he took exception?

'Typical English cowards,' Scott Johnson goaded.

That pissed me off. The gauntlet had been thrown down. I'd do it – when the time was right.

I'm not stupid. I did a bit of homework first, to make sure I wasn't being stitched up. It turned out the nickname Beaver had been given to Eddie when he played for his first club, Randwick in Sydney, where he was known for his burrowing style of play. Nothing wrong with that. Nothing to be ashamed of. The nickname had been in use for 20-odd years. Everybody used it, apparently. Everybody except his new squad of England boys.

It was the morning after we won the Grand Slam, beating France away. I'd been partying in Paris all night and hadn't yet been to bed. I wandered into the hotel restaurant, where breakfast was being served, and walked straight up to the buffet. I was still half-cut.

I saw Eddie Jones arriving at the counter. *Nicknames,* I thought, looking at the pile of croissants in front of me on the counter. *Now's a great time to talk to Eddie about his nickname!*

I sidled over, plate in hand, perusing the eggs and mushrooms. 'So, Eddie,' I said, as casually as I could muster. 'What about Beaver? Shall I call you the Beaver?'

''Scuse me, maaate?' He only ever called me 'maaate' when I'd done something to annoy him.

'Er, the Beaver. It's your nickname, isn't it?'

There was a sharp, awkward silence and Eddie fixed me with a frown. It felt like an eternity waiting for his response. I'd clearly overstepped the mark. What was he going to say now?

He took a breath and looked me straight in the eye. 'Boss will do.'

Just three little words, but that told me, didn't it? Ever since then it has only ever been boss.

4

INJURIES

'I fancy a change,' I said to Daisy, leafing through a car magazine.

'Really? I thought you loved your truck.'

'I do, but I'd like something a bit fancier.'

I'd been touring with the Lions and was feeling like Johnny big bollocks. I'd had a sponsorship agreement with a VW dealership for years. They'd change my car every 8,000 miles, and I'd gone through about 14 Golfs and was now driving an Amarok truck.

Daisy was right. I did love the truck. It was comfy and roomy and reliable, and I had no complaints about it at all. But I'd never owned a sports car in my life, and it felt time to put that right.

'What car d'you drive?' is the question you always get asked by kids when you give a talk at a school or they come to look round the club. They expect rugby players to be like Premier League footballers, earning squillions and driving top-of-the-range Lamborghinis and Ferraris, with garages stuffed full of Bentleys and Bugattis. You can see the anticipation in their eyes as they wait to hear your answer, and it's always a shame when you have to burst their bubble.

'Oh, I don't drive a car, actually. At the moment I'm driving an Amarok truck.' You can almost see the tumbleweed blowing across the room. Even the teachers look a bit disappointed.

'What's an Amarok truck?' the child asks.

'It's, er, like a pickup truck. You heard of a pickup truck?'

'Yeah. My dad used to have one. Ages ago.' The disappointment in the voice comes through crystal clear. I've lost the audience, right there.

There are a few flash Harrys around, boys who like their cars and don't crush kids' dreams the way I do. Henry Slade and Luke Cowan-Dickie like their Porsche Caymans and Anthony Watson owns a beautiful black Maserati Ghibli. But generally speaking, rugby players' cars are a bit of a let-down.

This is especially true of cars owned by props, because the flamboyance of a player's car tends to diminish in relation to how far forward his position is on the pitch. You only have to look at Harry Williams, Exeter Chiefs' tighthead prop, to see my point. He drove a 1999 red Nissan Micra for more than a decade before giving it to one of the academy players and switching up to a 2001 burgundy Toyota Land Cruiser. Good for him, I say.

But sometimes it's good to break the mould and have a bit of a splurge. My hero Jonah Lomu famously loved his cars. A Nissan Patrol with a $100,000 sound system. A Hummer, a Lamborghini and a 1967 Chevy Camaro street car. That man had style.

'I've made up my mind,' I said to Daisy. 'I'd like a Jag.'

'A Jag?' There was a momentary pause. 'You'll look like a twat in a Jaguar.'

I knew she had a point, but I couldn't resist. My career was going well and I wanted a piece of the action. I searched around and found a good finance deal on an F-Type Jaguar, the kind Jack Nowell now drives.

'What d'you reckon, Dais? I thought I'd go for white.'

'White? You're going for white?'

'Yes. Why not? If you're gonna have a sports car you might as well make a statement. Don't you like it?'

This time she resisted repeating that I'd look like a twat, but her face said it all. 'It's a beautiful car,' she said, 'but, er, are you sure you want white?'

'Yes! It's the only colour to get. It's a fantastic-looking car.'

Daisy rolled her eyes, but I'd made up my mind. I'd been a professional sportsman for a decade and I was finally having a sports car.

When I picked the Jag up I was so excited. Daisy came with me and watched as I got in the driving seat. And she watched. And she watched. It took me a little bit of time to adjust the seat and get myself comfy because it was low-slung and much less roomy than my big-boy truck. But it was gorgeous. Leather interior, all the toys, fantastic sound system. I loved it.

We'd only gone a couple of miles down the road from the showroom when Daisy started asking if I was OK.

'I'm fine!' I said. 'What d'you mean?'

'You look a bit squashed, that's all.'

'No, no. It's just that you're used to seeing me in the truck. You've got to get used to it, that's all.'

Daisy watched me squash myself into the car the next morning, before I went to training. It was like forcing a sweaty red Jelly Baby into a Tic Tac box, but I had to get on with it, stand by my decision. How could I admit to Daisy how uncomfortable it was after we'd splashed out so much money on it? I'd have to stick with it.

'Have you hurt your back?' Daisy said the next day, when she saw me walking stiffly round the kitchen.

'What? Oh, yeah. Just the usual. Training, you know.' I was fobbing her off as I didn't want her to worry, but my back was sore and stiff and had been getting worse – ever since I got the Jag. How could I tell her that? Wasting money was one thing, but putting my back on the line was another thing altogether. I had to look after it, as a rugby player's back goes through quite enough as it is.

One time, when I was a youngster at Quins, I was a bit over-zealous in a training session and ran straight into Nick Easter, catching him off guard. I sent him flying, which sparked a lot of whooping and piss-taking from the other players.

'Been bulldozed by a pup?' they laughed, loving the fact that one of rugby's notoriously powerful hard men had been floored by a kid.

I apologised to Nick, who picked himself up and dusted himself down.

'Fair play,' he said. 'Don't worry.' I think his ego was a bit bruised but no harm was done. We cracked on and I didn't think any more of it.

The next day one of the coaches told me he had the readings from the GPS pack I'd been wearing in training.

'See here,' he said. 'This is the point where you crashed into Nick Easter.' He showed me the data. 'This reading shows us that when you made contact, it was the same impact as a small Nissan Micra crashing into a wall at the same speed.'

'A small Nissan Micra? Are you saying that's not good? Should I be hitting like a big Nissan Micra?'

'No, Joe,' he laughed. 'A small Nissan Micra is more than good enough. Nick Easter hit the deck; what does that tell you?'

Now I know that a rugby player's body goes through the equivalent of about 30 car crashes a game. Subjecting your body to brutal physical punishment is all in a day's work, and injuries are an occupational hazard. Broken noses, mashed-up ears, torn ligaments, fractured bones. It's par for the course and you have to get used to it.

I've lived with varying degrees of pain ever since I became a professional rugby player and I'm not afraid of being hurt. You can't be. I enjoy the physicality, always have. It's in my DNA. I'm prepared to accept that I'm heading into a series of mini car crashes. It's what I train for. It's why I build the muscles in my neck and shoulders and everywhere else. I need to be able to charge like an ox with as little fear and as much strength in my body as possible. Without that mindset, you can't play the game.

However, when you're not on the field you don't want to cause yourself any extra physical harm, which takes me back to the Jag …

I knew I'd made a mistake getting the Jag. It wasn't just the difficulty I had wedging myself in and out of it. I didn't enjoy the attention I got when I drove it. I'd clock other drivers admiring the shiny white bodywork when I pulled up at the lights, then they'd look at me and narrow their eyes. *What's that thug with the black eye driving a Jag for? Why's that fat-boy wrestler driving a slick Jag?*

Some didn't even admire the car. They'd look directly at me with a look that said, *You're a Jaguar wanker!* I hated it. I wanted to disappear inside my anonymous pickup truck.

We had a league game against Northampton on the Saturday and I was driving to the Stoop to get on the coach with the rest of the boys. On the way there my back was aching more than ever and I was really pissed off.

This car has really got to go. I can't have this. What if my back goes in the game, all because I wanted a sodding sports car?

I pulled into the car park and there were several of the boys also arriving. Danny Care, Chris Robshaw, Will Collier and Adam Jones all clocked me. It was the first time they had seen me in the Jag. *Here we go,* I thought. I tentatively levered myself out of the car. There was no way of doing it with any panache.

'Alright, Marler? Wanna borrow a shoehorn? I might have one in my kit bag!'

'Very funny,' I said, trying to laugh it off.

'Think you're a big dog now, do you? Got more money than sense?' There were a few whistles too.

Again, I laughed it off. Normally I'd come back with something, but the last thing I wanted was for me and my Jag to be in the spotlight for a second longer.

I straightened up and my back immediately felt much better. *That's a relief, I've got away with it,* I thought, walking round the car to get my stuff out of the boot. *Sit in a comfy seat on the coach and I'll be absolutely fine for the match.*

As I went to open the boot I glanced down and noticed that one of my laces was undone. I bent down casually to tie it up, like you do.

Whoaaaaah! What the fuck? There was an agonising pain in my lower back and then I felt a spasm, shooting right up my whole back. My back had gone, completely. The pain was so intense I hit the deck.

The boys were slow to respond, as they thought I was winding them up.

'Lads,' I wailed. 'I need the doc!'

'What? You're actually in trouble?'

'Yes! What the fuck do you think I'm doing on the floor? Get the doc, quick!'

The spasms were unbearable and I was frightened to move. 'I need painkillers, right now. Get me painkillers!'

'OK, mate, we're on it. Someone's gone to get the doc. What happened?'

'Dunno. I just stepped out the car and bent down to do my shoelaces up.'

'Fucking hell … the Jag?'

I knew what they were thinking: *Maybe you should get a van, mate. Something better suited to a man of your proportions?* If I hadn't been in such trouble they'd have been pissing themselves laughing by now.

The doc gave me a couple of Diazepams but I didn't take them immediately, as I just wanted to get home. I drove the Jag back in agony, ruing the fact I lived 71 miles away. It was a terrible idea, but it wasn't as if any of the boys could have given me a lift. They all had to get to the match.

When I arrived home I struggled like mad to get out of the Jag. Daisy came to the door to see me doing a very good impression, in reverse, of Leonardo DiCaprio in *The Wolf of Wall Street*, when he's attempting to crawl, wide-eyed and legless, into his white Lamborghini. The only difference was that he was drugged up and I was out of my mind with pain. Daisy helped me onto the sofa and gave me a look that said, *That'll teach you to be a Jaguar wanker!*

I took the painkillers and some muscle relaxants and watched the game on TV, high as a kite. The Jag was gone the next day, traded in for a nice, roomy and anonymous VW Caravelle. I've never looked back.

★

I shudder when I think of some of the injuries players have suffered. The 'fucking hell, that must have hurt!' factor that makes your guts shrivel and your stomach drop to your feet.

I'll never forget Danny Cipriani doing his ankle in when he got badly trapped at the bottom of a ruck when Wasps were playing Bath back in 2008. I was watching from home and I can still remember the horror that shot through me. Danny was sitting up, holding his calf, yelling in agony, his foot turned at a right angle to his leg. Injuries like that have the potential to end careers, though thankfully that wasn't the case with Danny.

I had the same sickening feeling when Leicester's Rob Hawkins had his arm broken by Northampton flanker Calum

Clark, coming into a ruck in a match in 2012. For a moment it was like watching professional arm wrestlers, but then Clark bent Hawkins's arm so far back it hyperextended and snapped. 'I'm in agony,' Hawkins shouted.

Rugby players are renowned for their high pain threshold – I have one, I don't know anyone who doesn't at the top end of the sport – so when a player shouts something like that you know it's a bad one.

I can remember when the England Under-21 prop Matt Hampson dislocated his neck and severed his spinal cord in a scrummaging accident during a training session back in 2005. He was paralysed from the neck down. It was a tragic accident and very close to home for me, but even when something as bad as that happens you have to push the fear away.

I know how dangerous the sport is and it's my choice to carry on. I love the game. It's my career, my livelihood. I was born to be a prop, that's how I feel. The prop life chose me, not the other way around. I've got the perfect body for it, and what else would I do with a physique like mine? I admit it, I also have the thuggish, reckless streak you need. The mad glint in your eye, the adrenaline rush when you're about to slam hard and fast into 20 stone of bone and muscle and sinew. Fight not flight, every time.

Bring it on!

You want to do it, even though it's going to hurt like hell. You'll rip your skin open, pull your joints out of their sockets. You'll be in agony for days afterwards, unable to move your shoulder or your hip. Maybe you've bitten a lump out of your tongue, taken a gouge to your eye. Sometimes you do damage you don't even notice at the time because your whole body has been through the mill and you've no idea what's hurting the most. You've been pummelled in a ruck. Squashed in the scrum. Trodden on with spikes. Barged by a six-foot-eight man of steel. Taken out in an illegal tackle and dumped on the ground, bloodied and bruised and concussed. Yet still you want to go out and do it all over again.

I can't explain why I want to do it. It's how I'm built, how I've been for as long as I can remember. The Psycho kid who wasn't afraid to take on half the neighbourhood. The teenager who had fights in the street, always front of the queue with his fists and his attitude when it all started kicking off.

Bring it on!

Daisy has learned to put the fear out of her head too. What else can she do? You can only worry when you have something to worry about. How would you live your life otherwise?

Some injuries are so freakish or gory it's easier to put them out of your head, because surely they could never happen again. I'm thinking of South African Nick Schonert, the Worcester prop, who was caught with a stud in his face in a match against Saracens back in 2015. It sliced him from his ear to the edge of his mouth, and he needed 40 stitches in the gaping gash. It was just 'unlucky', he said afterwards, which was something of an understatement. Studs can cut when they're a bit worn or scuffed, but a slash in the face like that belonged in a *Saw* movie.

That incident took me back to the iconic photo of J.P.R. Williams playing for Bridgend against New Zealand in 1978, his cheek cut open after being stamped on by the All Blacks prop. This image of him with blood covering half his face became emblematic of the brutality of the amateur era. Williams's dad gave him 30 stitches – father and son were both doctors – and he ran back out and played on. That was how the amateur-era boys rolled.

Remember All Black Wayne 'Buck' Shelford? He was booted in the nuts so hard his scrotum ripped open during the now infamous Battle of Nantes game, against France in 1986. Ouch. He also lost four teeth. Buck played on, not even realising he had one testicle hanging out. How? I might have a high pain threshold, but I don't understand that one. I'd be crying like a baby. He went back on the pitch after the team doctor eventually stitched him up, only to be hit on the head and concussed. (I bet the geezer who booted him in the nuts didn't get a ten-week ban for it.)

I understand the hunger to get back on the field. Not with my nuts hanging out, of course – no chance – but I know what it's like to be so keen to play a game that you'll push on regardless of injury.

When I had the honour of playing a match for the Barbarians in 2019, I was carrying a shoulder injury and felt like it was hanging by a thread. 'Doc, can you put some painkillers in for me?' I asked, because there was no way I was missing that game.

I've done a similar thing with concussions too, having been knocked out more times than I can remember. 'How many fingers have I got up? Who's the Prime Minister?' The docs always used to ask the same questions after giving you the smelling salts, and I'd memorise the answers and rattle them out even when my head was still swimming because I was so desperate to get back out and play. The rules have changed now and you're automatically off with a concussion. It's a sensible precaution but, if you feel OK, I don't see why you can't just play on and be monitored.

There's no helpful medical data available on what happens to a professional rugby player's body in old age, or whether there's an increased risk of dementia. That's because the first players of the professional era – the ones who had most of their careers post-1995 – are still only in their forties and fifties. In a way, we're like crash test dummies, but I accept the deal.

Rugby is a brutal contact sport, and we know this when we sign up to it. Make the game 'safe' and you have no game left. I don't agree with changing the rules so that tackles have to be below nipple height to protect the player's head. You're then tackling closer to the knees, which is going to lead to an increase in concussions to the player doing the tackling.

Lifting in line-outs damages your shoulders – both of mine are fucked – but how do you get around that when line-outs are a crucial part of the game? Similarly, we all know how catastrophic it can be when a scrum collapses and a player like Matt Hampson suffers a life-changing injury, but how can you play rugby without a scrum?

The one improvement that could be made would be to structure the season better. I'd prefer to play 12 games a year instead of 30 to 40, and have a career that lasts until I'm 38 and a body that isn't destroyed at the end of it. I'd take the pay cut tomorrow to do that, but it's not going to happen.

All the major clubs are in debt and would like to raise the profile of the game and grow the sport. How do you do that and see to player welfare properly? It's a catch-22, and we're now seeing players retiring in their twenties who should have had longer careers.

Take Alex Corbisiero, who played in my position for England. His knees were shot to shit when he retired at 27. I'm sure I wouldn't have played as many times as I have for England if it wasn't for his injury struggles and early retirement.

Then there's Sam Warburton, the consummate professional who took his health incredibly seriously yet was only 29 when he announced his retirement because of a string of injuries. If he was allowed to play fewer games and not give his body such a relentless battering he might still be playing now, and that is very hard to take.

★

Back in 2017 I was tackled side-on in the first half of a Quins game against Worcester, taking a knock to my left calf. It felt pretty innocuous and I played on, thinking I'd maybe just torn the muscle a bit.

'Strap it up, mate. It's only a tight calf,' I said to the doc afterwards.

It wasn't until the following week, when we were up against Sale Sharks at home, that I realised there was a lot more to it. It was an ice-cold day, the pitch was rock hard and I started my warm-up. I'd barely run all week because of the weather and the frozen pitches, and now my left leg wasn't having any of it. I persevered for a bit, telling myself I could run it off, but it was no good. My leg was killing me.

Fucking hell, I can't play. I was really pissed off. No one wants to admit he can't play. It's showing weakness. Ridiculous really, but that's the mentality and I fully buy into it. Not only that, the Six Nations was starting in three weeks and I desperately didn't want to miss out on that.

I was sent for an X-ray. The doctor explained that I had a compartment fracture – I'd broken my leg. I was gobsmacked. 'But I played until 80 minutes last week. What's going on?'

The doc was scratching his head too. 'I can't explain how you played on. I can only tell you that you have a fracture and you need to rest and recover.'

I was told I'd need five weeks to fully recover, which would rule me out of England's opening game of the Six Nations, against France. 'How fucking unlucky is this?' I fumed. 'Why did this have to happen?'

'Stay positive, it helps with recovery,' Eddie Jones texted when I told him the news.

I worked hard on my physio exercises every day, and I also started guzzling blue-top milk. Two pints in the morning and two pints every evening.

'Did Pask tell you to do that?' the boys asked.

'No, I just thought it was a good idea. Milk's full of calcium and that's what we need for our bones. Isn't it just the obvious thing to do?'

They seemed surprised by my answer.

My recovery went quicker than anyone expected. So quick, in fact, that I was named in the team's starting line-up for the France game and was asked to do some media. The journalists inevitably wanted to know how I'd managed to mend a broken leg in just three weeks instead of the predicted five.

'I've just been doing as much recovery work as I can,' I said. 'Oh, and drinking full-fat milk.'

The journalists were even more surprised than the boys and went crazy for this. 'Seriously? Full-fat milk has got you back on your feet in record time?'

'What's so surprising about that? If you're a kid and you break a bone, doesn't your mum make you drink milk? It's not some secret cure. It's not magic. It's just good old-fashioned milk. Surely everyone knows milk is good for your bones?'

I also praised Phil Pask for his part, but of course JOE MARLER RECOVERED FROM BROKEN LEG BY DRINKING MILK was the story that made the news the next day. And as a result, dairy companies and farmers from all over the UK started to get in touch with me. 'Thank you so much for supporting the milk industry, Joe. We'd love to send you some samples of our milk as a token of our appreciation.'

It started arriving by the gallon and Daisy began to wonder if we'd ever have to buy the white stuff again. We were loving it, but I realised I'd missed a trick. 'At the next press conference I'm going to say it was red wine that got me through. Malbec, to be specific.'

I think Eddie Jones must have had the same idea when he mentioned red wine in a press conference in South Africa the following year. After he'd had a bit of an altercation with a fan, the press got wind of it and asked Eddie what it was about. He replied, 'It was nothing, mate. I was just asking what the best red wine in the region was, that's all.'

After that wine companies and vineyards started sending him bottles of red left, right and centre. I texted him and said, 'Well played', adding that I really should do the same next time the opportunity arose. 'Much as I love milk, I like a drop of red even more,' I added.

At 5am the next day there was a knock on my hotel-room door.

'These are for you.' It was someone from the hotel, delivering some of Eddie's freebies to me.

'Cheers, mate,' I texted him. I wanted to add, 'Why the 5am call?' but I didn't want to appear ungrateful. The red was well worth getting out of bed for, after all.

*

I don't lean on physios and recovery as much as some of the boys. It's the quick guys – the Ferraris, as we call them – who like to make the most of the massage table. The wingers and outside centres, the Jonathan Josephs and Jonny Mays of the rugby world – they're the boys who like a good rub. They need a massage to help them feel relaxed and it's an important part of their post-match routine. Let them hog the massage table, I say. I'd rather just have a shower and chill out in the changing room with a can of lager.

Ice baths are something else I leave to other boys. I just don't like them.

'Why not?' Chris Robshaw asks.

'Because they're fucking cold, mate!'

Robbo swears by them. He's one of the most professional players I know. He does ice baths every single day and is appalled that I shun them. 'You really should try them, Joe. They're excellent for recovery. It could even improve your game.'

I'll do anything to stop Robbo enticing me into the ice. 'There are as many studies saying they don't make a difference as there are papers claiming they improve recovery,' I say, very seriously. 'It's a placebo effect.'

'Really? Where did you hear that?'

I never give any evidence because I don't have any. I just make random stuff up to fob him off.

Stretching is something else I can't get my head around. I hate it. Dean Benton, the England strength and conditioning coach who'd made us train with water packs on our backs, asked me what I did before a warm-up.

'*Before* a warm-up? I walk to the warm-up session.' What kind of a question was that?

Deano also tried to make the team do stretching every night. 'Forty-five minutes, that's all,' he said.

'Forty-five minutes of stretching? No. I'm not doing it. I can't do stretching. I've never liked it.'

'What do you mean you can't *do* stretching?'

'I'm just not flexible.'

'Yes, Joe. That's because you don't stretch.'

I could barely even lie down, let alone stretch, thanks to the hunch in my very rigid back, but Deano was very encouraging. I realised he was starting to sound very much like I do when

I'm trying to get my kids to eat vegetables. I felt sorry for him and gave in.

Every stretch was a struggle but Deano was very patient and I managed to get through the session. Just. *Never again,* I thought when I went to bed that night.

The next morning I woke up in absolute agony, my back spasming like billy-o. I was livid. *What did I tell him? It's that sodding stretching. I knew I should never have done it!* It took me quite a while to get myself out of bed. As soon as I managed to put some clothes on – wincing and cursing as I did – I headed downstairs.

Deano saw me staggering down the corridor of the hotel. 'Mate, what happened?' he asked.

'You fucking stretched me – that's what happened!' And with that I went in search of the team doctor and a large dose of painkillers.

★

Noses are the worst things to break on the pitch because the medics just get a roll of tape and stick it round your whole head and across your nose, flattening your ears and anything else in its path. It's brilliant to see on other people, but if it's you it's happening to, you just want to say, 'Nah, you're alright. I'd rather come off the pitch than look like a cross between Hannibal Lecter and Voldemort.'

My nose gets broken at least once a year. Quins did a video of me when I played my two-hundredth game for the club, one of those moving montages that overlaid pictures of me through the years. I think you're meant to look at it nostalgically and think, *Ah, look how much I've grown up each season.* But what struck me was how my nose got more and more bent and misshapen in each photo. *Fucking hell,* I thought. *I've actually had a bit of a tough paper round here.*

When you break your nose the doc normally shoves a couple of tampons up your nostrils to stop the flow of blood. Or at least that's what they look like. The doc once pulled out something a bit different. The two cotton-wool rods were longer than the usual ones – much longer.

'What are you doing with them?' I said through a mouthful of blood.

'They're going to stem the flow of blood.'

'Yeah, I thought so. But where the fuck are they going? I know my nose is big, mate, but there's not enough room in my nostrils for those big boys.'

He explained that they would go in at an angle, rather than straight up the nostrils.

'It's not going to be very comfortable but it'll do the job. So get yourself in position. That's it, Joe. Angle your head back a bit and we'll do it on the count of three.'

He counted, 'Three, two …' and then rammed them into my face without the 'one' as doctors like to do, to catch you off guard.

And catch me off guard he did. The shock of it was like having my sinuses pierced and I threw up all the blood and gore that was in my mouth, completely splattering the doc. His face was a picture and by now I was trying hard not to laugh. And by trying hard, I mean I was pissing myself laughing.

★

Ears are another body part you have to be prepared to sacrifice. Props have to accept that cauliflower ears are going to replace our lovely, normal ears sooner rather than later.

I don't know why they're called cauliflower ears. If I saw a cauliflower that looked like either of my ears on display in a shop, I'd take it to the counter and say, 'I'm sorry, this is disgusting. Nobody's gonna eat that.'

Cauliflower ears come about through years of rubbing against other players' heads and getting whacked with their knees, fists and elbows. The first sign of damage is when blood builds up between the cartilage and the tissue surrounding the ears, making them swell. When it started to happen to me, my ears blew up like big balloons. It was horrific. I'd have the blood drained out – the doc pulling out about 20 or 30 millilitres of blood each time – and then I'd put Blu Tack in place to encourage my ear to return to as normal a looking shape as possible.

I also tried taping my ears and wearing scrum hats to protect them, but they didn't work. Scrum hats are soft, for starters, and how's a bit of tape going to save you? I've said for years that we should wear hats with cups over the ears, like water polo players do, but it's too late for me now.

As time goes on you can only drain so much blood from your ears. What's left congeals and hardens and you get a build-up of scar tissue. That's where I am. My ears are solid enough that my kids can hang off them with no fear of them flapping or moving in any way. They love it, and so do I.

A Bath player I often come up against had plastic surgery on his ears recently.

'They look wonderful!' I said when I realised he'd been under the knife.

'Would you go for it?'

'Maybe. But only when the kids are too old to swing off my ears.'

He laughed, but I was being very serious.

It's a shame I couldn't turn my ears into a bit of a quirky trademark, but the crown for the most famous cauliflower ears in rugby has already been bestowed on the head of Graham Rowntree. He had massive ears before he started his rugby career, and his massive ears turned into massive cauliflower ears. He loves 'em and there is no way anyone could ever challenge him for that iconic look.

★

Sometimes the treatment for an injury turns out to be much more of a challenge than the incident that caused it. In the middle of the 2013–14 season I fell awkwardly on my hip in a Quins game. It turned out I'd torn my labrum – the soft cartilage that helps the ball of the hip sit and move properly in its socket. The ball joint was jagged too and was catching all the time, giving me a lot of grief.

I was referred to see a top hip specialist in Manchester. The Quins physio, Richard, came with me and was sitting in the room when the doctor examined me.

'Right, Joe. Can you drop your trousers?' the doctor said.

'Yeah, sure.' I took my trousers down, no problem.

'And the rest, please.'

'What? You want me to take my undies off too?'

'Yes, please. If you don't mind.'

I wasn't expecting this. *What is this, doc?* I thought. *It's the ball of my hip, not my balls that need looking at.* But I didn't really mind, even with Richard sitting there. I'm used to nudity. It comes with the territory.

I still wasn't bothered when the doctor got me to move into different positions and tell him how the joint felt. He made a couple of notes and then started pulling on a pair of surgical gloves. I didn't like the look of this.

'Now, then,' he said. 'All I need to do is push up through one of your testes so I can feel your pubis.'

He made it sound very mundane, which I suppose it was, to him. But I wasn't going to argue, was I? I could see Richard in my eyeline, which was a bit disconcerting. I looked away as I felt the gloved hand do what it had to do.

'Can you cough for me, Joe?'

'Yes!' I squeaked.

'Excellent. All done.'

I breathed a sigh of relief and started reaching for my undies, but before I had even got one leg in, Richard piped up: 'Er, do you mind if I try that?'

I looked at Richard, only to see that he wasn't addressing me. Oh no. I was only the man whose testes he wanted to manhandle. He was directing his question to the doctor.

'Hang on a minute, Richard, why are you asking the doc? It's not his nut sack we're talking about!'

'Oh,' he said, looking a bit embarrassed. 'I just assumed you'd be alright with it, Joe.'

'Yeah, but while I'm here it would be nice to be asked!' Richard was quite new and was keen to learn. Of course I wasn't going to say no, but still. 'Anyone else?' I asked. 'Is there anyone out in reception who might want a go too? Want to go outside and ask?'

To be fair, I'd probably given out mixed signals to Richard. Back at Quins, when we were deciding if I should see a specialist, he'd asked me to come into his office for a quick meet after training. He spat his tea out laughing when I sat down at his desk naked from the waist down.

So I was examined twice in the specialist's office, and then there was a discussion about the pros and cons of me having an operation. We all decided against it, on the grounds that if I had surgery in my early twenties I'd increase the likelihood of needing a hip replacement in my forties or fifties. The alternative was to have a steroid injection at a clinic in London, to help settle the joint down.

There was, however, one large drawback. 'It's a big needle, Joe,' the doctor explained.

'How big?'

'Well, big enough to get through your hip and into the ball and socket joint.'

Great. With the size of my hips that'll be about eight inches long, then. I might be fearless on the pitch, but needles? Urgh!

I was booked into a clinic on Harley Street and this time I went on my own. I had to strip in a side room and put on a gown. The gown wasn't big enough to meet at the back and my arse was on display.

I was nervous as hell about the procedure. The thought of the giant needle going into my hip turned my stomach. *Just think of the alternative*, I told myself. *It's not a hip replacement. It's just a needle.*

Two friendly middle-aged nurses were looking after me, and they did their best to make me feel comfortable and keep my nerves at bay. 'How are you today, Mr Marler? If you'd like to lie down on the bed, on your back, we'll get everything ready for the doctor.'

I did as I was told and lay flat on my back, the gown covering my body. It was a bit chilly in the room, but I didn't mind that. I preferred it to being too warm.

'Just try to relax,' one of the nurses said, smiling. 'It really is a simple procedure. We do it all the time.'

'Thank you.'

Both nurses were lovely, and I appreciated their kindness. I felt very safe in their hands. One explained that she was going to prepare my right hip: 'I'll just need to lift the gown a little on this side, so the doctor will be able to get in.'

She started lifting the gown, flicking it up to expose my hip and then … *What the fuck?* She was way too heavy-handed, and instead of just revealing my bare hip she exposed my manhood to the room.

I felt myself blush. *Never mind. They've seen it all before.*

'Ooh, sorry about that, Mr Marler,' she giggled.

Giggling? Why is she giggling? I looked at the other nurse. She had tilted her head to one side and was raising an eyebrow. 'Bit cold in here, isn't it, Mr Marler?' she said.

I went bright red and started giggling myself. What else could I do but laugh it off? 'Yeah, actually, do you mind turning the air con off?'

Decency was restored by the time the doctor came in to carry out the procedure. The needle really was at least eight inches – and completely unaffected by the cold – but I was past caring by now. I just wanted it over and done with.

I've been able to manage fine with my hip ever since, and it's just as well really. That experience put me right off having any more treatment. Giant needles are one thing, but being called a tiny penis by the nurses? No thank you.

5

DRINKING

We were in Wellington, during the Lions tour of 2017, and we midweek boys – those not playing in the Test team – had a few days off.

'Let's go out for a bite to eat, relax a bit,' said Rory Best. Which really means 'let's have a piss-up'. About 14 of us were up for it, and Besty suggested a nice little Italian restaurant he'd scoped out, not far from the hotel.

'Sounds good,' said George Kruis, looking a bit shell-shocked. 'I could do with drowning my sorrows.'

The Test team had lost against the All Blacks on the Saturday, and poor Kruiser had had a stinker of a time. In the team review meeting he'd come in for a hammering. Rob Howley, the attack coach, was presenting the meeting, and as usual he played clips from the game so we could all discuss aspects of play and look at how we could make improvements. We're all used to the format.

When a clip is played, the initials of the player involved appear on the screen. The first clip that came up was tagged GK, and it showed Kruiser dropping the ball. Fair enough, it happens to us all and you just have to put your hand up and say, 'Yes, I made a mistake. Yes, I can see how I could have done things better.' Kruiser took it on the chin.

Then the next clip came up. This one was tagged GK too. Rob Howley explained how 'the player' could have got himself in a better position. The lads were starting to titter because you could see clip number three lined up, also with the initials GK. 'Not you again,' the boys were saying. 'Aren't you gonna give someone else a chance?'

When the next clip and then the one after that also came up with GK in the corner we started to feel bad for him. 'Fucking hell, Kruiser's getting it in the neck.' The coach hadn't done it to deliberately shame Kruiser. He'd simply picked the moments in the game when he saw a point of discussion, and they all happened to involve poor old GK.

The coach kicked off a lengthy discussion about the forwards picking and going close to the New Zealand line, and how we should get the backs to come in and run a short line to help share the workload.

Kruiser was looking thoughtful, no doubt working out what he could contribute to redeem himself. When the discussion was over he saw his moment. 'Do you think it would be possible,' he said, 'when we're picking and going quite a lot, if we got a tighter line from the backs, maybe, and they could share the workload a bit?'

'You can't have been listening to anything that's just been said,' Rob said, shaking his head, clearly exasperated. The rest of us looked at the floor and cringed for Kruiser. The poor guy had obviously been so focused on getting some credibility back after appearing in all the clips that he'd zoned out of the lengthy discussion while he tried to come up with something useful to say.

Rob turned his attention back to the screen. The next clip was ready to go, and we could all see it had GK tagged on it, yet again. Rob decided to put the dog down, and he called an end to the meeting.

We reconvened in the team meeting room that evening, and the team was announced for our game against the Hurricanes in two days' time, on the Tuesday. Kruiser was on the bench, which was no reflection of what had gone on in the previous game or the review meeting. He was a Test team player and we were the midweek boys, the 'shags'. He'd only play if we really needed him to because the boss would want to save him for Saturday's Test match.

The Hurricanes game was a cracker, played to a full house in the main Cake Tin stadium in Wellington. The atmosphere was incredible and all the boys were going hell for leather, particularly Courtney Lawes, who was playing out of his socks.

'Here, you seen that?' It was Dan Cole, whispering in my ear before half-time.

'No, mate. I'm blowing out of my arse here. What am I supposed to be looking at?'

'Courtney. They're taking Courtney off. You know what that means, don't you?'

'No, mate. What does it mean?'

'It means they're going to play Courtney in the Test on Saturday. They're saving him.'

Kruiser came off the bench to replace Courtney, and at that point he must have known he wouldn't be playing in the Test team on Saturday. *Fucking hell, poor Kruiser.* How had he gone from enjoying the biggest honour in his career to date – playing for the Lions first team – to being humiliated in the team review meeting and then having to play a midweek game with all the shags while he watched Courtney move into pole-position?

It was no surprise to anyone when Kruiser jumped at Besty's suggestion of going out that night. No wonder he needed to drown his sorrows after the few days he'd had.

The Italian restaurant Besty had found was ideal. It had a private dining area at the back – well, it was more of a glorified garden shed – but it suited us down to the ground. We could have a few beers and a enjoy a good craic without bothering anyone else, which is not always that easy when you've got 14 loud and thirsty rugby players in a group.

We hadn't even parked our backsides when Rory called the waiter over. 'Can we have 14 beers, please?'

'Sure.'

'And can you do us a favour, mate?'

'Of course.'

'Bring another 14 beers over in 15 minutes? And just keep 'em coming. Every 15 minutes.' Besty was setting the pace. We were obviously putting our big boy pants on tonight.

The piss-taking started straight away. 'Oi, Kruiser, what d'you think we should do about the backs sharing the workload a bit?'

The beer was flowing and Kruiser was letting off steam. He didn't mind the ribbing. Every clip was relived. Every sharp intake of breath when we saw GK on the screen recounted. 'Fucking hell, Kruiser. Talk about a fall from grace!'

He was laughing it off, having a good time. Good on him.

When the food arrived Besty asked the waiter to bring the beers every ten minutes, quickly followed by every eight minutes. Then we were onto shots and shorts, songs and games. I can't remember the finer details, or even what shots and songs and games we did, but I do remember how I felt.

Looking around, I felt so lucky and grateful to be there. It was absolutely brilliant to be out enjoying the company of so many great players from the four Home Nations, getting to know them on a completely different level. I'd battled against some in games against Scotland, Wales and Ireland, but now my rivals were my drinking buddies, my mates. Iain Henderson, Dan Biggar, Justin Tipuric, Leigh Halfpenny, Greig Laidlaw. Besty and Coley, of course. It was a great crew. The night summed up the Lions' values. I didn't want it to end; I don't think anyone did.

'Can we get another round of shots?' Besty asked.

It was only about 10.30pm but the owner said no, he was shutting up shop.

'Fair enough, can we get the bill?'

We all started talking about where we could go next, but Wellington isn't known for its nightlife and Besty had done well to find this place. We'd have to make do with drinks back at the hotel.

When the bill arrived Besty asked me to sort it out. I was just trying to work out what £2,500 divided by 14 was when someone suggested we have one last little adrenaline rush in the restaurant: 'Who's up for credit-card roulette?'

The first voice I heard was Kruiser's. 'No, no, no, no, no!'

I'm not into that kind of thing normally, but as soon as I heard how opposed Kruiser was I wanted to play. So did lots of other boys.

'Come on. It'll be a laugh,' I said. I took off my hat and it was passed round for everyone to put their credit card in. I then checked to make sure nobody had cheated and been a tight-arse. Fourteen cards. Perfect.

I asked a waitress to come and pick the cards out one by one. Before she started I took my time explaining the rules, trying to create as much drama and tension as possible. 'When a card is pulled out the name will be read out. If it is yours you must not cele-brate. You must take your card back and politely say, "Thank you very much." The last card out pays the entire bill. Is everyone clear?'

Kruiser still wasn't happy. In fact he was positively grumpy. But it was too late now, the game was on.

It didn't take long for the tension to start mounting. And by the time it got down to the final four I was starting to feel the pressure, because my card was still in the hat. As was Kruiser's. Of course Kruiser's was in there! He'd been on a trail of destruction all week and this would cap it all. Hero to zero. Surely it couldn't happen?

Before long Kruiser and I were the last two standing. I was trying to work out if I actually had £2,500 in my account to pay the bill.

'Look, mate, shall we split it? Go 50/50? I'm happy to do that. What d'you reckon?' I wasn't being completely selfless. He'd be doing me a favour if my name was on the bullet and I didn't have enough cash in my bank account.

'What d'you say, Kruiser? Want to split it?'

He looked really pissed off. 'No,' he said, obviously hoping his run of bad luck could not go on any longer.

'You sure?'

'I'm sure.'

He was looking nervous, blowing out air.

'Honestly, mate. Let's just split it. I don't mind.'

'No. We've come this far. Let's finish it.'

The suspense was intense when the waitress pulled out the penultimate card. 'The name's a bit faded,' she said, squinting in the dimly lit room. 'I can't quite make it out.'

We all held our breath, waiting for the moment of truth. 'Is it G something?' someone asked.

'No, not G, sorry. It's a J. Yes. It's definitely J. Is it J Marler?'

I tried not to break into a smile. I took my card, put it in my pocket and the whole room erupted.

Fuck me. Poor Kruiser. His mistake was to say no to the game in the first place. The grumpy man always loses. That's what I've learned after playing this game on a few different occasions. You have to embrace it, join in wholeheartedly and then fate will look kindly on you and shower you with good fortune. It's the power of attraction, I'm convinced of it.

★

Though Kruiser probably won't believe me, I'll always remember that night more for what it meant to me than for what it did to

Kruiser's bank balance and his already dented pride and reputation. It epitomised why drinking and rugby make a great cocktail. We've all dined out on that story so many times. Beer is bonding. Wine binds you together. Shots and shorts and drunken singing make shared memories. You can't quantify how that translates onto the pitch, but those things matter. And it's all good fun and games.

As a teenager I was captivated by tales of legendary drinkers from the amateur era, and I rued the fact that I'd missed out on being part of all that. How fantastic would it have been to be one of those men who played international rugby as a hobby? Miners, farmers, doctors, solicitors. Priests and pilots. Turning up to play an international game after a week at work and a night in the pub. That's what they did. A few pints on a Friday or Saturday night then go out and play for England in front of 50,000 at Twickenham the next day.

Jason Leonard, one of the lucky ones who got to play in both eras, was playing for England when the sport turned professional in 1995. A part-time nutritionist was brought in and the players were asked to record their weekly intake of food and drink, to see what improvements could be made.

Fun Bus dutifully kept a tally of his pints of lager, which came to 28 for the week.

'What exactly are you up to to consume 28 pints in a week?' the nutritionist asked, horrified.

It wasn't complicated, he told her. 'It's 20 pints on the Saturday and 8 to settle the head on Sunday.'

It was another age, a magical time to be a rugby player. Some of my favourite drinking stories come from Lions tours from decades ago, when teams travelled by ship and were away from home and living the dream for months on end. I'm not endorsing the bad behaviour, you understand. I don't hanker after breaking the law or putting anyone in danger, but I love these tales.

After one of many drunken nights out during the 1938 Lions tour of South Africa, Irish lock Paddy Mayne went hunting in the early hours and returned to the hotel with a dead antelope over his shoulder. A dead antelope? Imagine what would happen if Coley and I went out for a few pints and brought a dead antelope back into Pennyhill Park.

The Johannesburg *Sunday Times* labelled the 1968 Lions the 'worst-behaved team ever to tour South Africa'. One of their stunts was to make a bonfire out of some of the team's blazers on the tarmac at Kimberley Airport, after what was politely described as an 'airborne cheese and wine party'. Who wouldn't want to have been there? And I don't even like cheese.

On the night of the Lions' victory over South Africa in the second Test of 1974, Willie John McBride is said to have stood in a smashed-up hotel foyer in his underpants, pipe in mouth, surrounded by a dozen drunken Lions, all out of their tree. The hotel manager – soaking wet after one of the boys used a hose to put out a fire started in a stack of empty beer boxes – was understandably doing his nut. 'What seems to be the problem?' McBride said innocently.

Irish hell-raiser Willie Duggan and his partner in crime Moss Keane partied so hard when the Lions toured New Zealand in 1977 that the local press reported their leaving a trail of 'empty beer crates, broken hotel doors and false fire alarms' in their wake. Before home internationals in Dublin, Duggan and Keane would drag the whole team to a bar run by Sean Lynch, a former Lions prop, for a 'few pints', which usually meant six or seven.

'I always had the philosophy,' Duggan said, 'that if you took 30 players out for a night and made sure they were well pissed before they went to bed at 3am, then got them up at 8am, trained the bejaysus out of them, then you would know who was up to lasting 80 minutes in an international.'

My philosophy is that you can go out on the beer, but you have to stay out of the public eye because, like it or not, you're a role model as a professional player. Most importantly, never, ever miss training or any other commitment you have at the club as a result of going out on the beers. You have to turn up on time and put in the work, whatever you did the night before. If you feel shit and have a hangover, that's on you. You made a choice, and you have to push through and take the pain and punishment the next day.

*

I had a call from the coach Pat Lam, asking me if I fancied playing a game for the Barbarians.

'Fucking hell, of course I do!' It was a huge honour to be invited. It had been on my bucket list since I was a teenager, along with playing for the Lions and representing my country.

What rugby fan hasn't seen the clip of Gareth Edwards's incredible try in 1973, when the Baa-Baas beat the All Blacks? I'd watched it countless times. I'd seen my hero Jonah Lomu play in a Barbarians match against England at Twickenham when I was a kid. I was in the rafters and all the players looked like ants, but it was still an unbelievable day out. I couldn't wait to pull on the black-and-white hooped jersey and claim a little piece of history for myself.

OK, cards on the table. When Pat Lam called me, the first thing I thought about was what would happen off the pitch. The Baa-Baas are a relic of the amateur era, a throwback to the old-school traditions. A club whose players are expected to drink every bar dry with a ten-mile radius of wherever they play. Everybody knew that. I'd laughed in 2013 when the Barbarians put themselves on a booze ban after being beaten 40–12 by England, so they could do better in their upcoming clash with the Lions. Marco Wentzel and Schalk Brits didn't last a day – they posted pictures of themselves drinking wine at the races in Hong Kong within hours. I wanted to taste some of that tradition for myself.

*

Day one of my week with the Barbarians in May 2019. Pat Lam made it clear that we could let our hair down from Monday to Thursday, but that we had to stay off the booze on Friday and Saturday so we were good to go on Sunday. There would be as many as 60,000 watching at Twickenham, he said. 'We don't want to embarrass the jersey.'

I had an incredible time from the word go. We did a little bit of training, and every night the drinks and treats were flowing. Wining and dining in fantastic restaurants like Benihana and Scalini. Staying in Park Lane. Eating kebabs at 5am with the hardcore Kiwis John Afoa and Colin Slade. Toulon owner Mourad

Boudjellal turning up uninvited and getting four of his players to sing 'Pilou-Pilou' – France's version of the Haka – at the top of their voices in a posh Covent Garden restaurant. A magician from *Britain's Got Talent* to entertain us. A fancy-dress karaoke contest, in which the Welsh hooker Richard Hibbard and I dressed as gorillas and sang Phil Collins's 'In the Air Tonight'. Pierre Schoeman and Finlay Bealham – both obsessed with wrestling – jumping out of a cupboard like two excitable kids, and Finlay smashing through a table full of beer bottles in the middle of our dire performance. I could go on, but it's exhausting just recalling all the shenanigans. I was blown away by it all and savoured every moment.

When I was on my own I started to think about the effect this week was having on me. I don't mean physically. I knew exactly what was going on there: my liver was being taken by surprise on a nightly basis. I mean mentally and emotionally.

I'd announced my retirement from international rugby in 2018. It was the second time I'd done it – I'd retired and unretired in 2016 – and one of the reasons was that I was struggling to see the point of it anymore. Why put myself through it? All the touring, being away from home, missing out on so much family time and not seeing my kids grow up

I thought I'd be better off focusing on my career at Quins. That was enough. It paid the bills. I could still manage that, and what choice did I have? The only other job I'd ever done was cutting grass for my uncle's turfing company when I was 16. Going up and down a field all day on a solitary mower for £50 a day. I couldn't go back to that, could I?

The truth was that I'd fallen out of love with the game. Rugby had started to feel like a job, not a passion. It was the same shit, just a different day. Dealing with the spotlight, the physical aches and pains after every game, the constant pressure to win, the feeling that you had to be dull and serious and pristinely professional in order to succeed. All of it had started to get me down, and sometimes I got so bored on the pitch I was thinking about what I was going to have for dinner when I should have been foaming at the mouth, in the zone and desperate to win the battle.

But something magical was happening to me during my week with the Baa-Baas. It was changing my way of thinking. Reminding me why I loved the game, how much fun it was to be a rugby player and how ridiculously privileged I was to get to play alongside phenomenal players from all over the world.

★

'How you feeling, bud?' Richard Hibbard, the Welsh hooker, asked me as we walked out of the tunnel at Twickenham. I'd played against Hibbs for a few years and always thought he was a bit of a helmet. He'd melt me in tackles and there was just something about him I didn't like, though I couldn't say what. At the start of the week, when we all sank a few pints to help break down the barriers, he admitted he'd felt the same about me. He'd thought I was an arrogant little wanker. Fair enough, lots of people do. But as it happened, once we got chatting we got on like a house on fire. And in the true spirit of the Barbarians, we'd had a wonderful bromance going all week.

'Not great,' I said. 'Never felt so nervous.' It was a blistering hot day and we were playing against a load of England young guns –

the Under-23 side. The reason I was nervous was because I'd never had a full week on the piss before a game like this. I was hazy and hungover. You could smell the fumes coming off me. Hibbs was in a similar state – we'd even had a few beers together the night before, the Saturday, which was naughty of us – and we both spent the match asking the ref for a water break every five minutes just to have a rest.

We lost the game 51–43. Do I look back with regret? Not one bit. I had the time of my life. And that's the ethos of the Baa-Baas, right there. The point is to enjoy the camaraderie of the game without the pressure of having to win. And that's exactly what I did.

Cards on the table time again. I'd sneaked in an extra drinking session that week with Eddie Jones, on the Friday night. Eddie had been randomly checking in with me ever since I announced my retirement. It was always in a text and usually included his go-to emoji – a glass of red wine. We'd had a pretty good relationship ever since he became the England boss at the start of 2016 and I respected him a lot. I think he respected me too, for being honest about how I felt and stepping away from the team when I knew my heart wasn't in it.

He knew I was playing for the Barbarians and got in touch that week. 'Where you camping with the Baa-Baas? Let's catch up. Red this week?' He suggested Friday at the Anglers in Teddington.

Yes, I was supposed to be off the booze on the Friday night. No, I wasn't going to stick to that. This was Eddie Jones, and I wasn't going to say no to Eddie. I might have been in retirement, but you don't burn your bridges, do you?

I knew myself well enough to realise that I might change my mind about playing for England again, as I had in the past. I didn't know why my mood swung like that. I just knew it did – and that it might again.

When I arrived at the Anglers the first people I saw were the managers of the England Under-23 team we were playing on Sunday. I didn't want them to see me with Eddie, did I?

What the fuck? I'm not exactly a packet of peanuts. What do I do now? Then I clocked the whole team of young guns, sitting down to have a meal together. *Is Eddie messing with me? Is he getting his own back because I've retired twice on him?*

'Anglers no good,' I texted. 'England XV here. You stitch me up?'

'No. Meet me at the Lensbury. Club bar.'

When I got to the hotel bar Eddie was sitting in the corner with two glasses of red on the table, plus a bottle of Merlot ready to go. We chewed the fat for a while before he said, 'If you wanna come back, you can. But you have to want it.'

I loved to hear that. Not just because my week with the Baa-Baas had reignited my love for the game, but because it showed that Eddie knew me. He understood why I'd stepped back, and that it was important to me to want to play. I was never going to just turn up and take the pay cheque. I had to have my heart in it.

'Thanks, mate,' I said. 'That's very good to hear. Can I think about it?' *If I go for it I might get to play in the World Cup in Japan,* I thought. *Fucking hell. Do I want that?* I didn't know the answer. We were already on our third bottle of red, about to order a fourth.

'If you do come back into the squad, there's no guarantees you'll make the team. I've got Mako, Genge, Ben Moon.'

'Understood.'

At the end of the night I watched Eddie leave while I sat there thinking, *Maybe this is something I do want to do. Maybe I should have one more roll of the dice – try to put the demons of 2015 to bed?* Something like that, anyhow – maybe the words didn't flow quite as well as that after hammering the Merlot so hard with Eddie.

When I came off the pitch after the game on Sunday I knew what I was going to say to him. I was in a completely different frame of mind to the one I'd been in when I quit the England team the previous year. *Fucking hell, I LOVE this game,* I thought. *It gives you so much, and I want so much more.*

I texted Eddie. 'I may not have done much to impress you in the Baa-Baas game but I'd like to work my tits off for you. What are you saying?'

He replied straight away: 'See you in five weeks.'

Before my return to the England camp the *Sun* ran a story: RIOJA N ROLL. ENGLAND STAR SINKS SIX GLASSES OF RED WINE WITH EDDIE JONES AS HE ASKS FOR WORLD CUP SPOT BACK.

'He made the approach to us that he wants to play,' Eddie was quoted as saying. 'And you can't help miss him. He is the ugliest player on the field so is easy to pick out.'

You have to put up with Eddie chucking in a cheeky insult. It comes with the territory. But I took exception to what else he had told the reporter: 'Six glasses of red wine he had – though I'm teetotal!' Cheeky fucker!

DRINKING

The first thing I did when I went back into the England camp was to ask him why he threw me under the bus like that. 'Were you taking the piss?'

'Mate,' he said, a glint in his eye. 'It was there in black and white. You were drunk and I was sober. The press don't lie.'

Eddie may be a cheeky fucker, but he knows the value of sharing a drink like no other manager I've played under.

★

In honour of Eddie, his red-wine emoji and commitment to social-ising with his players, I've compiled my fantasy drinking team, Marler's Malbec XV. Here goes:

FRONT FIVE

1. DANCE CAPTAIN Mako Vunipola.

His drinking is as heavy as he is, and he's also the unexpected king of light entertainment. He's a brilliant dancer, and by that I mean he's truly awful, but he has the balls to go for it on the dancefloor. His Peter Andre coming out of the water is a sight to behold.

2. FALL GUY Rory Best.

A legendary drinker who went all out to turn the 2017 Lions tour into an eight-week stag do. On one occasion we wheeled his bed outside the hotel, and he was so drunk he slept in the street, oblivious to it all. My wife stopped accepting my calls because I FaceTimed drunk so many times. It was Besty's fault, I swear. You always need someone in the team to blame for leading you astray. Even if it's not entirely true.

3. MINDER Dan Cole.

I love a sappy, negative drinking session, and you're always guaranteed that with old Colar Bear. He has a sensible head and is a great minder too. When I went AWOL in Japan at the end of the World Cup, he tracked me down on the streets of Tokyo at 5am, fed me, cleaned me up and made sure I didn't miss the coach to the airport. I'd be lost without him, literally. Possibly still in Tokyo.

4. SECURITY Olly Kohn.

He's an awful drinker (and dresser) but he's incredibly well organised and always has the night planned out. He also makes a great personal security guard. You need a heavier unit than you in case there's any trouble. At 6 foot 7 and knocking on the door of 22 stone, he's the perfect head of security.

5. ACCOMPLICE Joe Launchbury.

You've heard of hollow legs on big drinkers, but that's nothing on the sloshbucket arse of this very capable drinker. We share a love of red wine and he likes to stay the course, like I do. A great drinking pal.

MIDDLE FIVE

6. RACONTEUR James Haskell.

No drinking team would be complete without Hask. He holds court like no other player I know, and even though you've heard all his stories a million times he tells them so well they still make you laugh. He's also a DJ, so if things go flat you can always get him on the decks to liven up proceedings.

7. WARDROBE Will Skinner.

When he was captain at Quins he dressed up as Bumblebee from the film *Transformers*. He'd spent weeks making the costume from scratch and the attention to detail was mind-blowing. Until that night, my best effort had been daubing myself in blue body paint and trying to pass myself off as a Care Bear. I'd copied the idea from George Lowe, but he was shredded while I had my muffin top hanging over my underpants in the bars of Kingston. Skinner raised the fancy-dress bar to another level, although he did also get into a fight with the Australian lock Justin Harrison that night. In fact he knocked Harrison out. Quite a feat for a man dressed as Bumblebee.

8. HEADMASTER Nick Easter.

Has to be the drinking team leader, even though he's a tight-arse. Old school, revered and charismatic, Nick Easter is as big a leader off the pitch as he was on it. He gives all the orders, expecting the youngsters to fetch the drinks and find the next bar while he focuses on necking his next pint. When he retired there was as big a void at the bar as there was on the pitch.

9. MASCOT Danny Care.

He calls himself the Talisman, and with good reason. He leads the charge on the pitch and he's the same on the piss. A ball of energy, he gets everyone going and picks boys up if they're feeling down. He's like a shot of adrenaline on a night out and I love going on the beers with him. Every drinking pack needs a Talisman.

LOOSE HEAD

10. SPONSOR Nick Evans.

A great bloke, a real chilled character. He's also a gazillionaire and is prone to random acts of generosity. I arrived late at a do in Fulham once to find the bar lined with about 50 drinks, a Jägerbomb shot balanced on the side of each glass. He'd bought one for every person in the bar because he wanted to video the domino effect when the shots landed, one by one, in the glasses. I love crazy stuff like that. Plus, you always need someone to compensate for the tight-arses in the group.

BACK FIVE

11. ECCENTRIC Jared Payne.

I met Jared on the Lions tour in 2017. A quiet Kiwi, he barely said two words until he came up with an idea for a drinking game. 'We should all climb a tree with a box of "stubbies",' he said. 'And whoever drinks the whole box of beer first is the winner.' 'Can you go back to not talking?' I said, scratching my head. We didn't do it, but I'd welcome Jared on board now. I like a weird drinking pal, and better still one who thinks outside the box.

12. THERAPIST Jordan Turner-Hall.

Danny Care's partner in crime, he's another really good bloke who likes to lead the charge. But what I especially like about Jordan is that he's always up for a deep-and-meaningful conversation. If you've got something emotional going on, he's your go-to guy.

13. GAMES MASTER Ollie Devoto.

Ollie knows all the drinking games inside out, including all the rules and all the songs. During the Six Nations in 2016, when he was yet to be capped, he taught the squad a load of new games. Any other young pup would have been rinsed for sticking his head above the parapet, but Ollie's knowledge and commitment were so good he won everyone over – and made a lot of players fall over too.

14. HEALTH AND SAFETY Jack Nowell.

We were in Auckland during the Lions tour when we decided to play a game called 'fire pussy'. The idea was to build a little fire out of empty boxes, and the first person to worry it was getting out of hand and put it out would be the 'fire pussy'. Jack was the first to bottle it, stamping it out in a frenzy of panic when the flames started to build. The boys took the piss, but in hindsight he saved our necks. We were indoors, in the team room in our lovely hotel, which now had a smouldering black hole in the middle of the carpet.

15. DIEHARD Alex Goode.

A player with awesome staying power. When Saracens beat Leinster to win the Champions Cup in 2019, Goode went straight out on the piss in the kit he'd played in. His epic bender lasted three days and was charted on social media. 'Boots on, strapping done, gum shield in – we are moving,' he tweeted as he headed to the next drinking destination. Respect to him. He'd earned his place in the rugby drinkers' hall of fame.

HEAD COACH

John Kingston, my first Quins head coach. To my delight and surprise he turned up at our first rugby social dressed as Mrs Doubtfire. Fully kitted out, immaculately made-up, he was the spit of her. I couldn't believe my eyes. And the attack coach had come as SuperTed, complete with swishing red cape. It was brilliant and a massive moment for me. *Yes!* I thought. *It's not them and us. This is fantastic!*

I'd been so worried about fitting in at a prestigious club like Quins. I was convinced I was at a disadvantage because I wasn't posh enough, well educated or rich enough. Seeing our well-spoken, middle-aged head coach turn into Mrs Doubtfire was a game-changer. What did I have to worry about? We were all in this together.

REFEREE

Has to be my favourite ref, Romain Poite. Firstly, he loves a glass of wine. Secondly, he's laid-back and chilled. And thirdly, he's a French policeman, so he'd be handy to have on our side if we were to get into trouble.

MANAGER

No contest. It has to be Eddie Jones, of course. He's been the biggest advocate for boozing I've ever worked under. He believes in its magical bonding powers like no other manager, and I'm with him all the way on that. Cheers, boss.

6

TEAM BUILDING

'Dean Richards wants to see you in his office first thing Monday morning.'

My heart sank. It was only Thursday. I knew what this was about and I started sweating and fretting. How was I going to cope, waiting four long days to face the big man and hear my fate?

Dean Richards was Quins' director of rugby, but he wasn't just that. He was also a hard man and legendary drinker of the amateur age. I'd lapped up stories about him over the years. How he and Brian Moore had stepped off the plane in Australia before the 1987 Rugby World Cup, the former wearing a Ronald Reagan mask and the latter a Mikhail Gorbachev. How 'Deano' drank and smoked and played cards until the early hours with old-schoolers like Jason Leonard and Jerry Guscott when they toured together back in the day. Then there was the time he clouted Ross Kemp on a night out, saying, 'Take that. Your brother's not with you now!' Ross Kemp looking at him and thinking, *Does he really believe I'm Grant Mitchell?*

Dean Richards understood the social side of rugby like nobody else, but he was still going to throw the book at me, wasn't he? I was a minnow. Seventeen years old and just three days into my career as a professional rugby player. And the trouble was, I hadn't just gone out and had one too many. Things had turned out far worse than that.

The night had started so well. One of the managers had taken a group of us youngsters out for a meal in Kingston, so the new boys like me could get to know some of the other academy players. It really broke the ice and we had a great time, and when the manager left us to it we took ourselves off for a few more drinks.

Bring it on! I was living the life, out on the town with the boys, feeling like a proper grown-up rugby player. Most of the group decided to call it a night early doors, but a few of the boys were up for going on to some more bars and then a club.

'You in, Joe?'

'Me? Course I am!' I couldn't believe that anyone would not want to stay the course on a night out like this. Or on any night out.

The club was already buzzing by the time we arrived, and it didn't take long for us to get into the swing of things. I was having a great time, enjoying a few shots at the bar, when I heard that one of the other boys had got into a fight. It was Mickey Pointing, a player who would become known for his massive chest and short T-Rex arms. I immediately put my drink down and ran to see what I could do to help. That's when things started to unravel.

I can't recall how exactly, but I ended up on the floor outside the club, getting completely filled in by a couple of giant bouncers. My shirt was ripped in the scuffle and when I came up for air I was on my own. All but one of the other boys in our group had buggered off at the first sign of trouble. It was the posh boys who'd scarpered, which did nothing for the class divide I was already wary and resentful of. *Posh wankers!*

I got to my feet and was working out how to get back to my rented house when I saw a blue flashing light. Then a very tall police officer appeared. He stepped out of his van and walked towards me. *Fucking hell, am I being arrested?*

I was. My stomach lurched as the police officer grabbed me and pushed me, shirtless, into the back of his van. The engine started up and the van began to move slowly. I was trapped behind a grille, feeling like my whole world was ending. *It's my first week as a professional rugby player. This can't happen!*

The van then stopped abruptly and the police officer got out and came and sat in the back with me. 'Right, son,' he said calmly. 'Are you able to find your way home from here?'

'Huh? What's going on? Am I off?'

'Yes. You're 17, aren't you?'

'Yeah.'

'So the nightclub shouldn't have let you in in the first place. They don't want to press charges. Go home, son.'

I couldn't believe my luck. I'd got away with it, or so I thought. Now Dean Richards had obviously heard about the incident. Why else would he be calling me in to his office? Oh yeah, another thing I knew about Dean Richards was that he used to be a policeman, when he played in the amateur era. That's right. A policeman.

I had a hell of a weekend, worrying myself stupid. He was going to sack me, wasn't he? I'd be dismissed on Monday morning, the only professional rugby player in history to be sacked after just a week. I was already envisaging packing my bags and saying goodbye to the other academy boys I shared the house with. I could see it all. The train ride back to Heathfield, tail between my legs. Having to ask my uncle for my old job back, cutting grass for his turfing company.

When Monday morning finally came round I was absolutely shitting myself. By now I'd heard on the grapevine how the news had filtered back to the club. The police officer who arrested me was the son of one of the Quins managers. He'd let me off to avoid bad publicity for the club, but he'd grassed me up to his dad.

I was done for. I was convinced of that. I'd thrown away my whole career and I would never get a professional contract anywhere ever again.

Dean Richards had set his office up like one of those official police interview rooms you see in TV dramas. 'Take me through the night,' he instructed, fixing me with a steely gaze across his desk.

Talk about a squeaky-bum moment. 'We had a meal,' I said. 'And after that we went to a bar.'

'How many drinks did you have?'

'I had a pint in the restaurant, or was it two? Then another pint in the first bar.'

'First bar?'

'Yes, and we went on to another bar after that.'

'What did you have in there?'

'Another pint or two, and a shot, I think. And then we went round the corner and had a couple in the pub ...' I tried to stick to the truth as best I could. I didn't know how much he already knew about our movements on the night. 'We moved on to another bar, I think. And that's when we decided to go clubbing.'

'What did you drink in that bar?'

'Er, not sure. Maybe a couple of beers. A shot or two. Sorry, I can't remember exactly.' It felt like an eternity getting to the end of the list of bars and pubs we'd visited. By now I could see he was absolutely furious.

'Take me through what you drank in the club.'

'I think I had a Jack Daniel's and then a shot, maybe. There was a promotion on. I think I might have had two shots, actually ...'

I thought he might explode with rage. 'So, let's get this straight. You think, as a professional rugby player, it's appropriate to have 15 to 20 alcoholic drinks on a Wednesday evening?'

'No, no, I don't,' I squeaked. 'I'm sorry. I'm really sorry.'

'Now, take me through the fight.'

Fuck. This is what's gonna do for me. I did my best to explain what happened, but the truth was that I couldn't entirely remember. The one thing I was clear about was that I went to help my new mate Mickey Pointing. 'I left the bar of the club when I heard there was trouble and went to see what I could do to help. My mate was already in the scrap and I reckoned he could do with a helping hand.'

'Let's get this straight. You went to help one of the other academy boys, did you?' It was like I'd waved a magic wand. Straight away, the anger melted from his face.

119

'Yes, I couldn't just leave him ...'

'Good, I like that, son,' he said, nodding approvingly. 'And the other lads scarpered, did they?'

I didn't want to tell tales. 'Er, I'm not sure, I didn't see them again.'

It might have been wishful thinking on my part, but I was sure I could see Dean Richards thinking, *Those posh little fuckers buggered off and left you.* There was even a hint of a smile on his lips now.

'Well,' he declared. 'I'm impressed with you. Your actions show you have a team mentality. I like that, I really do. You've got to bond with the boys if you're gonna play well together. You've got to be a team player.'

I couldn't believe it. I was getting away with it after all, and I'd even been praised by the big boss himself. He didn't even mention the fact that I'd been picked up by the police – it was obviously not an issue any longer.

'You can go now, son. But keep off the beer in the week, d'you hear?'

'I do hear. Loud and clear. I understand. Thank you.'

I didn't stay off the beer in the week. In fact I carried on going out drinking at least three times a week in Kingston, always ending up in a club, though making sure never to end up in a police van again.

Still, I learned a big lesson from Dean Richards that day. My junior coaches and managers had told me all about the importance of being a team player, that a team performed better when all the boys looked out for one another. What young rugby player hasn't been given that chat?

But Dean Richards rammed the message home with a sledge-hammer. Team spirit was vital. Team spirit had saved my bacon. He made sure I would never forget it.

★

There's no magic formula for building team spirit. Even the All Blacks can't explain the secret to their phenomenal success. Their famous 'no dickheads' policy can't be it. After all, their scrum-half Aaron Smith was caught having sex with a woman in an airport toilet and he carried on playing, didn't he? Maybe they changed the rule to 'no dickheads *unless you're the star player*'.

In their quest for success the coaches will sign you up for all kinds of team-building exercises, and they love anything military-themed. Remember Kamp Staaldraad, the boot camp set up for the South African Springboks in preparation for the 2003 World Cup? The team was ordered to climb into a foxhole and sing their national anthem while ice-cold water was poured on their heads. They also had to crawl naked across gravel and kill and cook chickens, but not eat them. Horrendous insanity. How's that going to help you win the World Cup? It didn't, of course – the Springboks were eliminated in the quarter-finals – and when details from the camp leaked out it was widely condemned.

'Look, lads,' one of the boys should have said. 'Let's all refuse to do it. They can't sack us all, can they?'

I did my first army training camp at Aldershot when I was a youngster at Quins. It meant dressing up in camouflage gear and working alongside real-life army boys on codded-up rescue missions, to improve our leadership and communication skills. It sounded ridiculous and a complete waste of time. I was scratching my head as to why a prop like me needed leadership and communication skills. My job was to push like a tank, not command one.

It didn't start well. I hated suits of any kind – never wore them – and the camouflage uniform was especially unforgiving. How was I going to get into character when I looked like an obese Action Man?

'What's the point of this?' I moaned to my mate Chris Brooker. 'What's this got to do with rugby? Even in a World Cup final, it's not a matter of life and death, is it?' I was genuinely baffled.

The main exercise was a role-play that involved rescuing soldiers from a helicopter crash in a hostile environment. Once we'd rescued the injured soldiers we had to take them to an exclusion zone. It was a boiling-hot day and it was absolutely knackering carrying these big blokes on stretchers.

'Friend or foe?' It was a Quins boy, the hooker Joe Gray, relishing his role as an officious soldier. He stopped us in our tracks and demanded an answer. 'Who goes there? Friend or foe?'

He was deadly serious and very convincing in the role. Not a flicker of the Grayzer we knew. 'Are you for real, mate? This isn't an audition for *Saving Private Ryan*, you know.' Brooker and I were pissing ourselves laughing, but Grayzer still didn't crack.

'Friend or foe?' he demanded again, this time even more forcefully. 'Answer the question!' he barked. 'Are you friend or foe?'

That was it, we were gone. How could Grayzer stay in character like that when we were laughing our heads off and this situation was so fake and surreal? Then another over-zealous character intervened and told us we had to turn round and take our stretch-ered soldier on a different route. That was game over for us.

'You're joking, aren't you? We're already sweating like pigs. We're not gonna drag this stretcher any further than we have to, mate.' We flipped the guy into the undergrowth, leaving him for dead, and ran off giggling like a pair of naughty school kids. 'Fuck that for a game of soldiers!' I was enjoying myself for the first time all day, even though we both knew we'd get it in the neck at the debrief.

We weren't wrong. We were absolutely carpeted. 'We were *very* disappointed in team B,' the army officer said, looking appalled. 'You left a soldier behind. It was almost as if you didn't take the exercise seriously.'

He glared at us once he'd said his piece, while we sat there biting our lips, trying not to giggle. *How can we take this seriously? It's not real and how does it transfer to a rugby pitch?*

I thought the whole team-building day had been a complete waste of time – until I got to the club the next day and spotted Joe Gray heading to the team meeting room. 'Morning, Grayzer. Friend or foe?'

'Piss off, Marler!'

'Morning, Grayzer,' said the next boy who clocked him. 'Friend or foe?'

The story had done the rounds and every single player greeted Joe Gray the same way. He was so pissed off it was brilliant. We didn't sharpen our leadership and communication skills on the day, but Grayzer's catchphrase stuck and was trotted out regularly for about eight years, until he left the club.

I've long since stopped asking, 'What's the point?' with these team-building exercises. It's best to just go with the flow, hope you have a laugh and that something sticks. I've come to the conclusion that the shitter the experience, the more you get out of it. Rugby boys love sapping, and if we're taking the piss out of the situation and moaning to each other we're bonding, aren't we?'

*

You always learn something about the other boys on a team-building exercise. Before the 2015 World Cup the England squad did a day of riot training with the Met Police. I was struggling with the thinking behind this. *I know rugby's a tough game, but Twickenham Stadium's not exactly a riot zone, is it?* But there wasn't a peep out of me. Like I said, you learn to roll with it and hope something sticks at the end of the day.

We were all kitted out in full riot gear and started off with a one-kilometre run to warm up. Half the boys had been given the wrong size boots – me included – and it was agony running with my size twelves squashed into a pair of size tens. I hate running even in trainers, and I was struggling and cursing from the start, trying not to lose my temper. *Not many people get to do stuff like this,* I told myself. *I should stop being such an ungrateful whinger. Try to make the most of it.* But I was finding it hard to turn my mood around.

After the run it was into the simulated riot. Not only did we have to do more running, we had to dodge fake Molotov cocktails and carry riot shields, which are a lot heavier than they look. *This is shit,* I thought. *How am I gonna play in the World Cup with mangled feet?*

A couple of the other boys were having a stinker too. Kieran Brookes and Marland Yarde were struggling so much that they ended up ditching their riot shields. What happened next? Chris Robshaw – England captain at the time – went back for Kieran's shield and Tom Wood picked up Marland's. No fuss. No drama. Just instinctive acts of support for teammates.

I wound my neck in at that point and finally saw something to smile about. As ludicrous as some of these things seem when you embark on them, we were left in no doubt as to who'd be there for us when things got tough.

*

I saw a surprising side to Courtney Lawes when the England squad did an assault-course camp at the Royal Marines Commando Training Centre at Lympstone.

We knew it would be tough, and I knew I was going to get pissed off as soon as we were given our orders. No amount of talking to myself about making the most of this opportunity was going to make a difference. Even if it went better than expected, I knew I'd get wound up at some point because I always did. If these marines pulled rank and started barking orders at me I'd have to challenge them. I couldn't be bossed around like a kid at school; it's just not in my nature to bow to authority. It never has been, which explains why I spent large chunks of my secondary-school education in the weird wooden box compartments we had under the stage at Heathfield Community College, in isolation and serving detention for bad behaviour.

Courtney, on the other hand, is as laid-back as they come. You wouldn't know it from the way he plays rugby, but he's so relaxed he's practically horizontal. I'm sure he would never have been sent to the wooden boxes if he'd been a classmate of mine. Nor would he have had a devilish glint in his eye when he became hyperactive and disrupted the class, throwing ink up the back of the teacher's white shirt as he wrote on the board or goading the other kids to hum when the teacher's back was turned and then stop when he turned round to face the class.

No, I can't imagine chilled-out Courtney doing anything like that. It would be more trouble than it was worth to him. We were put in a team together, which was great news. *When I start losing the plot he'll be a good foil to me,* I thought.

The main exercise involved carrying massive jerrycans filled with water up hills and over moorland – for three kilometres. It only took ten minutes before I snapped. 'This is fucking nuts! We're gonna have to ditch the water. Come on!'

I could tell the exercise wasn't making Courtney tick, but true to form he stayed as cool as a cucumber. There was a truck following us and we were being monitored. When I attempted to empty out the water from my jerrycan I got a dressing down from a furious officer.

I was pissed off that the truck was there and I'd been rumbled, but level-headed Courtney didn't turn a hair. 'Aren't you pissed off?' I asked.

He shrugged. 'You know what,' he said matter-of-factly. 'I just can't do this anymore. My feet are gone. I'm gonna tell them.'

'What? You serious, mate?'

He was. Deadly serious. I watched in astonishment as Courtney politely explained his dilemma to the angry officer who'd just torn a strip off me. Surely he wasn't going to buy this?

Fuck me, it worked. Mr Cool got in the back of the truck while the rest of us mugs spent the next hour and a half breaking our backs. I'd look behind from time to time, totally discombobulated and wishing I had some of Courtney's sangfroid, thinking how much easier life would be if I did.

There he was, happy as could be, playing on his phone with blister plasters stuck on his poor little feet. Total respect, mate. To this day I've no idea how he pulled it off.

★

Sometimes you look back on an event and think, *That set the tone. It was obvious how we were going to perform after that.*

As the World Cup in 2015 approached, head coach Stuart Lancaster decided to take us out to Denver for some high-altitude training. *Bring it on,* I thought. *I'll go anywhere you like, mate.* I'd have agreed to go to the Sahara Desert at that point, dropped off in my undies to practise squats in the burning sand. Anything would have been better than dying of boredom at the England training camp in Surrey.

When the squad had first assembled at Pennyhill Park in Bagshot, we'd all gone, 'Great. Home World Cup. No travelling for us. We've got the advantage.' It didn't work out like that. Cabin fever set in very quickly. We were spending way too much time just looking at each other, stuck in the same gym or mundane training session, getting breakfast, lunch and dinner together and then doing it all over again. The atmosphere was subdued. Stale, even. Boys were retreating to their rooms to play computer games. I'd call home and complain to Daisy that it was like *Groundhog Day.*

I didn't like to bleat. I was in the England squad, preparing for the World Cup and living in a luxurious hotel. How could I be whining about it? But it was dire, and I felt lonely.

I'd never been to Denver. I Googled it and it sounded wonderful: 'Denver, Colorado, where urban sophistication meets outdoor adventure.' It was known for its music scene, craft breweries and for being close to the Rocky Mountains. Bye, bye, Bagshot.

Denver was bitterly disappointing. The part we were staying in felt like an area you'd pass through on your way to somewhere better. And after the intense training, which consisted mostly of mind-numbing drills, the only place to go was a coffee shop. We didn't bond as a squad. I felt isolated and bored all over again, just in a different climate. There was no escape. It was like being in a pressure cooker with no valve.

You could hardly blame Stuart Lancaster for choosing somewhere so safe. He'd taken on the job as England boss in the wake of the 2011 World Cup, when members of the squad had been caught in a bar where dwarf-tossing was taking place. The players were going on the piss all the time. It was a national embarrassment and Lanny had quite rightly taken steps to restore credibility when he took over.

At least he recognised that we needed some form of entertainment during the week, and one day he arranged to take us white-water rafting.

Get in! This'll be a great laugh. I was chomping at the bit, desperate to get out of the training camp and have some fun. All the boys felt the same. But even before we got to the river my enthusiasm began to wane.

TEAM BUILDING

'Quiet please, boys. Settle down. Make sure you listen carefully to all the health and safety rules and the regulations ...' Lanny was a PE teacher in Wakefield when England won the World Cup in 2003. Did he think he was back there, taking a load of kids on a school trip?

He was sharing one raft with the coaches, the team doctor, our lovely kit man Dondo and a media guy. Meanwhile, all the boys were divided between a few other 12-man rafts. I was sitting next to James Haskell. 'How are we gonna spice this up?' I said, giving him a nudge.

'Only one thing for it,' he said, nodding over at the raft full of managers and staff. 'I'll get in their boat and throw them overboard.'

I burst out laughing, slapping him on the back. 'Good for you, mate. Lanny included?'

'Yeah, why not. Of course. I'll flip the whole boat, give the whole lot of them a soaking!'

Everyone was giggling. 'Bet you don't do the boss,' we all said, knowing how to wind Hask up. 'You wouldn't dare dunk Lanny in the river.'

'Wouldn't I? Just you watch me.'

We got going. For a white-water experience, it was pretty sedate. 'How are you, boys?' Lanny shouted over as we drifted calmly over to his raft. 'Everyone enjoying themselves?'

'Oh, yes. Isn't it lovely? Great fun!' I gave Hask another nudge. 'You gonna go for it, mate?'

'Yeah. I'm going in!' In a flash, and to cheers from all the boys, Hask leaped from our raft straight onto the staff raft, stood up tall and began rocking the boat. They barely had time to react before he started picking off men to throw overboard. The doctor and media guy were his first victims. They tried to cling on but they were no match for Hask. At 6 foot 4 and 18-and-a-half stone, he looked like King Kong chucking lolly sticks in the water.

Splash! There went the doctor. The poor guy was spitting out river water and gulping for air. Splash! There went the media guy, trying desperately to cling on to his glasses.

'Wahey!' the boys were goading and laughing. It seemed rude not to offer Hask some encouragement. 'Who's next?'

None of the staff left in the raft was laughing. It was very obvious this stunt had backfired, but the Unflushable Turd was living up to his nickname. Hask was in too deep and he had already grabbed his next victim.

Splash! There went our loyal kit man. I felt a pang of guilt as I saw old Dondo bobbing in the water like a cork, clutching desperately to his lifejacket. Whenever you left your training jacket in a heap on the side of the pitch, he and the other kit man, Reg, would always fold it up neatly and leave it with your initials displayed. They worked their socks off for us and really cared about us. *Bless his heart, this should not be happening,* I thought. It was like watching one of those *You've Been Framed!* clips, where canned laughter is played over footage of toddlers smacking their heads or grannies falling off pontoons.

Some of the boys were still cheering Hask on, still hoping that this was all just crazy high jinks after all. And true to form, Hask was irrepressible, still rising to the bait. He was going for the big prize now. Fuck me, Hask was closing in on a stony-faced Lanny. He had the boss by the lapels. Was he really going to dunk him in the drink?

We all watched intently. I was dying for him to do it, even though I knew it would go down like a lead balloon. Lanny looked Hask straight in the eye and wagged his finger under his nose. Clearly, the boss wasn't having it. He wasn't going to play ball. 'James,' he shouted sternly. 'Don't you *dare*!'

We all held our breath. What was Hask going to do? He'd bet us he'd throw the boss in and he wasn't one to go back on his word.

'James!' Lanny was looking at him, unblinking, and Hask was staring back, not sure which way to go. Hask likes to win and has balls of steel. But this was England's head coach, and at the end of the day nobody wanted to cross him too badly, however shit his training drills were.

'Don't you dare, James!' Lanny repeated, more sharply this time. 'I mean it. Don't you *dare*!'

That's when Hask finally caved, taking his hands down and leaving Lanny in his seat. The game was up and Hask clambered back into our raft.

'You bottled it, mate. You fucking bottled it!'

'What was I supposed to do?' Hask was spitting feathers that he'd gone to all that trouble and ended up being ridiculed. I must admit, I was lapping up his frustration almost as much as I'd have enjoyed seeing Lanny getting chucked in the water.

The farce wasn't over yet. The three men thrown overboard had been carried down the river. We'd been told not to worry if that happened, as there were plenty of pit stops and the river was well patrolled. They'd get picked up. At least that was one blessing.

At the next stopping point you had the option to switch to a canoe. *Why not?* I thought. *Bit of variety might make this more interesting.* You had to have a long-winded safety talk before you took a canoe, so I was out of the water for quite a while. But when I finally got going I was loving it, picking up speed as I navigated my way down the river.

What the fuck? I spotted a body casually floating past me. Twenty minutes had gone by since Hask had dumped the three men. Surely they'd been picked up by now? Clearly not. It was the doctor. 'D'you wanna hop in or hold on to the canoe till we get to the bottom?' I said.

'Oh, yes please, Joe,' he said gratefully. 'Thank you very much.'

Before I got close enough to help him, I spotted the media guy. 'You alright, mate? Wanna hand?'

'Oh, yes please, Joe,' he called. 'Thank you very much indeed.'

The pair of them looked overcome with relief as they prepared to cadge a lift on my canoe. But then I spotted Dondo bouncing along forlornly in a torrent of white water. 'Dondo! Wait there, mate. I'll come and rescue you.'

I paddled straight over to Dondo and hauled him on board, leaving the doctor and the media guy still adrift. 'Sorry, lads, needs must!'

It was a two-man canoe and Dondo was having the seat. No question. Apart from anything else, that doctor had shoved a needle so far into my finger one time it must have numbed the bed it was resting on. *That'll teach him!*

'But, Joe, wait—' they started. But it was too late. With Dondo on board the canoe picked up speed and they were left in our wake. There's a pecking order in every team, and sometimes you've just got to do what you've got to do.

I look back on that day and wonder if the die had been cast. Were we always going to have a disastrous World Cup after that lacklustre event and all the boredom and monotony of the Surrey training camp? I don't think that's as crazy a leap as it might sound. The rafting trip said a hell of a lot about the vibe in the squad. Everything was a bit awkward, a bit off balance. People were trying their best but somehow the atmosphere never quite felt right. The cogs weren't meshing. We looked nothing like a World Cup-winning team. Nothing at all.

And we weren't, of course. We made the history books as the first host nation to bomb out of the World Cup at the pool stage. It's an event in my life that I still struggle to process and which did a lot of psychological damage to me. I was mortified, demoralised, absolutely distraught that our campaign ended so disastrously. It made me question everything. How could I carry on after such a humiliation? What was it all for? Why bother?

'Sorry, lads, it wasn't our time,' Lanny said in the immediate aftermath. 'It wasn't meant to be.'

I didn't blame Lanny. I still don't. If we'd won we'd proba-bly have said how well he managed us, how it was right to keep us wrapped in a bubble and how brilliantly the rigorous training drills paid off.

'When head coach Stuart Lancaster faced down an excitable James Haskell during a daring white-water rafting experience in

Denyer, he looked every inch a World Cup-winning manager,' the media guy might have written.

*

Eddie Jones does things very differently. His focus on team bonding was a huge factor in how well we played in Japan. Quite simply, we wouldn't have got to the World Cup final if he hadn't melded us together the way he did.

Eddie's all for allowing the lads to enjoy a good social and for letting us decide what we do. Within reason, that is. Nobody wants a repeat of what happened to Nick Easter at the 2011 World Cup, when he did a bungee jump in New Zealand before a pool game and had to pull out when his back went into spasm.

We've done all sorts under Eddie. Beach volleyball, paddle-boarding, bowling, dodgeball. Swingers club in London is a popular choice, which is not what it sounds – it's a really cool indoor crazy-golf course. Darts is a hit too – the boys love a good night out at the Flight Club in London, where the dartboards are electronic so no need for any adding up. A fabulous night of darts preceded England whacking Ireland 32–20 in Dublin in the 2019 Six Nations. I missed it, unfortunately, because I'd retired from England duty at the time, but Eddie was buzzing about how the squad had bonded at the oche.

Fast-forward to Japan eight months later and you've got Elliot Daly and Jamie George – the boys who run the social commit-tee – wandering around Tokyo Disneyland in Mickey Mouse ears with Joe Launchbury and Ben Youngs. I skipped it – it didn't seem right to go without my kids. The boys were gone so long that we wondered if we should send out a search party, and they were still on a huge high when they eventually came back to the hotel, looking more like lads on holiday than rugby players in the thick of a World Cup campaign.

The same vibe was going on all around the camp, encouraged by Eddie. I was enjoying it, and despite being away for months on end I didn't feel anything like the loneliness I experienced back in 2015, on home turf.

Midway through the pool games, Eddie allowed me to leave the squad for a night out with my old mate Olly Kohn, which I really appreciated. I got heat from the team for leaving – it's not the done thing – but I had Eddie's blessing and nobody could argue with that. He knew I had no family out with me and he thought it would do me good to see one of my best mates. 'Just make sure you meet us the next day for training,' he said.

I had a lovely dinner in Tokyo with Kohnan, his parents and the ex-Saracens prop Dave Flatman, now a sports pundit. Afterwards Kohnan, Dave and I went to a real rugby nause bar – the type of place rugby fanatics love to gather – and in there we ran into three big ex-Australia players, Wendell Sailor, Lote Tuqiri and Justin Harrison. The last time I'd seen Justin Harrison was when I was a kid at Quins, when Will Skinner (dressed as Bumblebee from *Transformers*) knocked him out cold at our fancy-dress party. I reminded him of it and he laughed.

The next day, when I was back in the camp, I told Eddie I'd seen some of his old players. 'Fuck,' he said, looking horrified. 'Mate, are those three still as loose as they were?'

Justin Harrison had once been banned for admitting cocaine use. Lote Tuqiri had been accused of cheating on his wife and Wendell Sailor's reputation had been marred with various indiscretions, including drug use, road rage and public drunkenness.

'It was all fine, mate,' I said.

'Good. You should have tried fucking patrolling them as their coach!'

That was it. Eddie was as cool as a cucumber. I didn't need nannying and I appreciated the trust he had in me to have a good night out and turn up the next day, no harm done.

I'm a person who needs a certain level of social contact. I don't want it all the time. I like to retreat into my room and wallow on occasion. But I can't spend too much time alone and I can't stand being bored. I need to interact, share a laugh with the boys, enjoy the buzz of a bit of banter and have different things to try my hand at.

Coley and I had our own little two-man social club going. We rub along together well and it's not an effort. You can't be 'on' all the time, can you? And even though he can be a miserable bugger who rarely cracks a smile, his dry sense of humour means we always have a laugh.

We went to a couple of themed cafes, which the Japanese are big on. The hedgehog cafe was creepy. It stank of wee, and how are you supposed to pet a hedgehog? We tried an owl cafe next, but Coley became animated, which was odd.

'What's wrong, mate?' I asked.

'Nothing. What do you mean?'

'Look at you.' To the untrained eye there was nothing wrong with Coley. He was very alert and lively, looking around at the owls just like all the other customers in the cafe. But it was a dead giveaway to me. 'You hate them, don't you?'

'What?'

'You're scared of them, aren't you?'

He nodded. 'How did you know?'

★

Coffee culture is growing in rugby because we have to find ways to socialise that don't involve getting pissed. We had two top-end coffee machines installed in our hotel, and it turned out that Jamie George, Elliot Daly and Manu Tuilagi were fantastic baristas.

'What would you like on top?' Manu would ask. 'I can do you a swan? A heart? A bird?' I swear some boys didn't even like coffee, but they didn't want to miss out and they joined the queue. Manu would stand for hours making player after player a coffee with a different design on top.

We managed to break a couple of coffee-bean grinders and it took a few days to track down new ones. It hit the boys hard. They were edgy days. We missed the ceremony of coffee-making, of seeing Maro Itoje's characteristic hard stare soften into an appreciative smile when he took a sip of a lovingly made latte. When the machines were back in action new rules were brought in. You had to be vetted by the baristas before you were allowed to use them.

Often Manu would still be at the machine five minutes before training, racing down at the last minute, coffee fumes percolating through his pores. But there was never a question that the coffee culture was interfering with training. It was exactly the opposite.

In one particularly intense session I was in a team with Maro. He has such a powerful aura around him, calm yet ferocious all at the same time, that he seems untouchable. But he was giving away penalty after penalty in the line-out. It happens when you get tired, and we were all exhausted. 'Look, Maro', I said. 'You're giving away too many penalties. Do that for real and you'll get a yellow.'

How did he react? He nodded and took it on the chin, no problem at all. And that, right there, is where team-building comes into its own. I would never have felt able to speak to him like that if we hadn't bonded over coffee with swans and hearts on top.

It's not how team-building was done in the amateur era, of course. Jason Leonard et al would have done a double-take if they'd seen us rattling our coffee cups together. But I know my old boss Dean Richards would have been nodding in approval if he'd seen me with Maro that day. Like he said to me all those years ago: 'You've got to bond with the boys if you're gonna play well together.'

7

RED MIST

You're on a tightrope as a professional rugby player, especially when you're a forward. Not an actual tightrope, of course – I wouldn't last long on one of those with my physique – but you're asked to perform a balancing act every time you run out on the field.

This is what Rugby asks of you: 'I'm a game of intense physical confrontation, Joe. I need you to pump the opposition, dominate them with your power and aggression. Make them feel like they're up against a mad dog, one who's foaming at the mouth and ready to end them. Melt them with your strength and skill. Scare the living daylights out of them.'

Forwards have to be more aggressive than the boys at the back. A loosehead like me is at the sharp end. Head-to-head confrontation is our meat and drink, same for all the boys on the front row. We have to lock horns with raging bulls and we need fire in our belly to do that.

'But, Joe,' Rugby says. 'Don't let the fire get out of control. *You* are in control. Push yourself to the limits of your aggression.

Get yourself on the knife-edge, then stop right there. *Do not tip over the edge.'*

I get this now. Go too far and you end up with a ban. Players get hurt, reputations ruined. It's not what Rugby wants. But how do you ask a rugby player to be threatening and aggressive yet never lose his temper? To put his body through the equivalent of 30 car crashes every game then not react when some sneaky bugger scrapes studs down his shin in the bottom of a ruck?

★

'Put your shoes on!' Mum would say when I went out to play in our cul-de-sac in Heathfield. 'You'll cut your feet!'

'No – I don't need 'em!' I'd slam the front door as I left the house, refusing to listen, even in deepest winter. *She can't tell me what to do. So what if I cut my feet? What does it matter?* That's how I was, right from when I was a very small boy.

The other kids thought I was an oddity, someone to be mocked. 'Joey-no-shoes!' they teased. 'Look at Joe's no-shoes!'

'Come 'ere and say that!' I'd be spitting tacks, ready to wallop anyone who said another word to me about my bare feet, or anything else for that matter. Inevitably, the more I reacted, the more the kids in the neighbourhood took the piss. I was very close to losing it every time they taunted me.

One day it happened, out of nowhere. The red mist descended like a curtain in front of my eyes, completely engulfing me. I snapped and lashed out, kicking and hitting and elbowing my way through not just the kid who called me Joey-no-shoes, but all the others who were standing around laughing and mocking me.

'Psycho!' one of the bigger kids shouted. 'You're a fucking psycho!'

The others jumped on the bandwagon. Of course they did. 'Joey-no-shoes is a psycho!'

I raged around, shouting threats and telling them all that I'd batter them properly if they dared say that again.

'Psycho!' they carried on shouting, running off down the street. 'Psycho! Psycho!'

I was too fat to chase after them so I stood there growling and hurling out threats. 'I'll get you all! Say it again and I'll flatten you!'

Calling me Psycho was like pressing a button that started the Joe show, setting me off like an angry bear. One of my sisters joined in one day, poking the bear, calling me Psycho like all the others. It was bad enough having the kids in the street rip the piss out of me and my bad temper, but my big sister? I wasn't having that.

'Calling me Psycho, are ya?' I went from zero to boiling point in a flash, totally losing control. I picked up the nearest thing I could find and smashed her over the head with it. It was a toy rake, made with proper wood and metal, and I brought it down so hard that it split her scalp straight down her centre-parting.

Both parents gave me the mother of all tellings-off, and after that they decided to send me to karate lessons to give me a channel for my aggression and hopefully teach me some self-control. It didn't work. A couple of weeks in and both my sisters were crying and screaming all round the house because I'd practised my karate moves on them.

Psycho boy needed another outlet. I was 11 years old, but my mate's dad had clocked that I was already the size of an overweight

14-year-old, and with an attitude too. He thought I could probably cut the mustard in an under-12s side. And that is how I ended
up giving rugby a go, joining Eastbourne Sharks.

★

I loved being in the Eastbourne Sharks team. And I definitely loved
it when our South African coach, Will Stadler, took us all on a bus
trip to the Stoop, to watch Harlequins play the South African team
Sharks, the club Eastbourne Sharks were named after. The journey
to Twickenham with my teammates, the anticipation of seeing the
game, looking round the famous stadium – I was buzzing.

I'd watched quite a lot of Premiership matches on telly and
considered myself a Quins fan, but until that day I'd never set foot
in the Stoop. It was wonderful to be in the crowd and I lapped up
the atmosphere. As I watched the game – Quins were losing – my
mind began to wander a bit. I was hatching a plot. I'd decided I
wanted to get some grass off the pitch to take home as a souvenir.

When the final whistle blew I had it all mapped out and I
knew exactly what I was going to do. I shot out of my seat and ran
towards the barriers surrounding the pitch. There were still loads
of players on the field, but that didn't matter, did it? I only wanted
a few blades of grass.

I was just about to jump over when a burly security guard
nabbed me. 'Oi! You can't do that,' he said. 'You're not allowed
on the pitch!'

I saw red, straight away. 'You can't stop me – I only want a
blade of grass!' He grabbed hold of me, and that's when I really lost
control. 'Piss off! You can't stop me! You're just a stupid jobsworth!'

With that the security guard hauled me by the scruff of my neck to the gates of the stadium – the same ones I now walk through every day to work – and booted me unceremoniously onto the streets of Twickenham.

'You're an absolute disgrace to your profession,' I yelled at the top of my adolescent voice. 'Can't even let someone have a sodding blade of grass?'

I was snapping and snarling, frothing at the mouth, exactly like the mad dog rugby wanted me to be. Trouble was, I'd gone too far, hadn't I? I'd tipped over that knife-edge. Worse still, I was on the pavement and not a rugby pitch.

'You've got a lot to learn, Psycho,' my coach told me. He wasn't wrong there.

★

Red mist is an occupational hazard that lurks in the shadows of every game. It loves a world stage, feeding on pressure and thriving under spotlights. The bigger the audience the better, and nobody in professional rugby is immune to its mean and mischievous methods.

France's lock forward Sébastien Vahaamahina had a crazy brain-fug moment in the 2019 World Cup quarter-final against Wales. The Welsh back-row Aaron Wainwright had got hold of the Frenchman, not illegally, when they were coming out of a maul early in the second half of the game. The red mist descended on Vahaamahina and he gave a powerful, straight elbow to Wainwright's head. He was red-carded, France ended up losing by one point after being nine points ahead and Vahaamahina retired from internationals after the game.

The red mist had claimed another scalp. And in a roundabout way it took down the referee too. South African Jaco Peyper was the ref who red-carded Vahaamahina that day. After the game Peyper went out on the town and bumped into a group of Wales fans who asked him to recreate the elbow strike for a photo with their group. It wasn't the red mist, but Peyper must have had something clouding his brain that night because he agreed, posing with a smile on his face as he jokingly pointed his elbow at a fan's head. The picture ended up on social media – of course it did. Peyper was forced to apologise and was told he wouldn't be reffing the England v New Zealand World Cup semi-final. I bet he saw the red mist then.

I'm not criticising him, though. How could I? I've had a couple of bans in my time for hot-headed behaviour and I've also lost the plot in a random moment of madness after a game.

I picked up my first proper red-mist ban in a European Champions Cup clash against Wasps in October 2017, when Will Rowlands held me by the leg and I lashed out and whacked him with my forearm. I hadn't been playing particularly well and I took exception to the fact that he was playing me at my own game, winding me up with a bit of one-upmanship. I didn't see it coming – the red mist was wielding my arm before my brain caught up with my body. I was yellow-carded and ended up with a three-week ban.

It wasn't a good day. After the game, as I was walking towards the tunnel at the Ricoh Arena, a middle-aged Wasps fan leaned over the hoardings. 'You're a disgrace, Marler!' he shouted. 'A complete thug! I hope your parents are proud of you!'

The red mist swirled in like a tornado, all over again. A lot of the fans had dispersed by now and I jumped over the empty bench seats and started clambering into the crowd seats, most of which were also empty. The fan hadn't expected this and he panicked, backing off and running away as fast as he could through the stand.

I kept going, blood boiling as I jumped row after row of seats, trying to chase him down, which was no mean feat in a pair of rugby boots with 21-millimetre studs in them – it was like doing the hurdles in a pair of stilettos. I managed to get to the twenty-fifth row, the man still in my sights, when a security guard who'd seen it all unfold got a grip on me and told me to give it up. I don't think he could believe what was happening. And to be honest, once I'd calmed down as he escorted me back to the changing room, nor could I. The lads were none the wiser and I didn't bother to enlighten them. It wasn't exactly my proudest moment, was it?

Afterwards I thought about what happened to Toulouse's Irish lock Trevor Brennan. He had been warming up to come on as a sub in a 2007 Heineken European Cup pool game when it all kicked off. Ulster fans were taunting him from the stands, so what did Brennan do? He dived into the crowd and gave one of the supporters a good hiding. He was banned for life from rugby, reduced to five years on appeal, fined £17,000 and he never played again. A sobering reminder of just how dangerous the red mist can be.

I had no intention of punching the fan at the Ricoh Arena – I just wanted to teach him a lesson. It pisses me off when people think they can verbally abuse you just because you are a rugby player. I wanted to make the point that I'm a human being, just like everyone else. 'I don't get it right all the time,' I wanted to say. 'But I'm fucking doing my best out here. How would you like it if I started hurling personal insults and shouting about *your* parents?'

A few months later I had my ear trampled on during a tackle in a Quins game against Sale Sharks. It was killing me and pouring blood like a tap. I was fuming. *I know who's responsible for this,* I thought. *I'm going to let you have it, TJ Ioane.* The opportunity for revenge against the Samoan flanker came when we went into the next ruck a couple of minutes later. As I walked over I had my hand over my ear, as if to say, *This is why I'm paying you back, pal.* I deliberately struck him with my shoulder, hard, and for that I got a six-week ban.

Embarrassingly, it turned out that I'd actually got the wrong man. But when you're lost in the red mist you can't think logically at all.

*

South African prop Johan 'le Beast' le Roux took things to a different level when his blood was up in a Test match in 1994, chomping down on the ear of New Zealand captain Sean Fitzpatrick. Le Roux was sent home and given a ban. 'For an 18-month suspension, I feel I probably should have torn it off,' he said. 'Then at least I could say, "Look, I've returned to South Africa with the guy's ear."'

How scary is that? I can understand how a player loses his temper, but not why you'd come out with something as menacing as that after the event, in the cold light of day.

While playing for Bath in 1998, prop Kevin Yates – an England player too – was suspended for six months for biting the ear of

London Scottish flanker Simon Fenn in a Tetley's Bitter Cup match. Fenn needed 25 stitches and Yates, who denied the charge, went to play Provincial rugby in New Zealand after serving the ban. It was a decade before he played for England again. Like Trevor Brennan's story, it's a reminder of how badly your luck can switch when the mist descends.

Biting in rugby tends to be a defensive move, for self-preservation. I'm not defending it, but a rugby bite is typically a reaction to being fish-hooked with a finger in the mouth, nose or eyes or to feeling that you can't breathe properly. That's quite different to the behaviour of someone like Luis Suárez, a persistent biter on the football field for reasons less easy to explain.

I have to hold my hands up and admit that I've dabbled in a bit of nibbling myself. I was at the bottom of a ruck when Quins were playing Gloucester. Their hooker Darren Dawidiuk had his arm wrapped so tightly round my face I thought I was suffocating. I could feel myself losing it, so I nuzzled my teeth into his arm. Not to break the skin, but just hard enough to make the point that I wanted him to get off me, quickly. I'd forgotten all about it until I saw him in the lift after the game.

'Hey, Bab, how's my arm taste, then?'

'Shit! I forgot all about that. Sorry, mate, but I was running out of air!'

'It's alright. We crack on.' The red mist hadn't won that time. Dawidiuk knew the score.

Some players have incredible careers despite being plagued by the red mist. Take hard man Danny Grewcock, for example.

Six-foot-six tall and a black belt in karate, the bans kept coming for him, but his impressive 15-year career for both England and Bath is perhaps proof that, if you can learn how to feed off the fire in your belly instead of letting it engulf you, it can keep you sizzling at the very top of your game. That's the tightrope for you, right there. You have to be close to the knife-edge to hold your own on the rugby field, but it's so easy to lose your balance when someone pushes you too far.

★

Sometimes the most innocuous things can set a player off. Twenty minutes into a Premiership game away to Wasps in September 2017, I was in a maul with James Haskell that was spinning out of control. He pulled me to the ground and I could see he was losing it. *What do I do?* I pulled his scrum cap off his head, just for a bit of light relief. OK, maybe I was poking the bear too. It was a spontaneous move. Hask was a player who liked to dish it out and I was having a bit of a play to see if he would react.

I tucked the scrum cap under my shirt, walked off and then lobbed it onto my side of the pitch so he'd have to go and get it. *This'll be interesting,* I thought.

When I turned round I expected to see a pissed-off Hask muttering, 'Fucking hell, Marler, why do you have to be such a wanker?' But Hask wasn't just pissed off. He was fuming. Absolutely livid. And he was heading towards me like the Terminator.

Chill out, mate, I thought. But he was a long way from chilling out, so I tried to lighten the mood. I lifted my water bottle, pointed it in Hask's direction and gave it a little squeeze, splashing a bit of water in his face.

That was when he really lost it. He was like a man possessed, ready to rip my head off. He closed in on me and grabbed my neck in a death grip, hands like claws around my throat. Other boys started to wade in, pulling us apart. Hask was still absolutely furious, especially when the ref pulled out a yellow card and ordered him to the sin bin.

'But he sprayed water in my face,' he protested indignantly. 'That's not allowed!'

I couldn't help laughing. Death-grip Hask now sounded like a stuck-up public-school boy bleating to the teacher that he didn't deserve detention.

We hugged and made up straight after the game. That's the upside of the red mist – it lifts almost as quickly as it rushes in, and once it's gone you see the world in a much cooler light.

*

Eddie decided to give us an old-fashioned day off the leash when we were doing our altitude training in Treviso in Italy, before the Japan World Cup. We had the following day off, save for a bit of recovery training, so it was the perfect chance for us to let our hair down, enjoy the sunshine and chill out in a beach bar.

'Cheers, mate,' I said to Coley as we supped our beer together. 'How good is this?' We'd set ourselves up at a bar off to the side of the main action, watching the world go round like the pair of cantankerous old codgers on *The Muppet Show*, griping and sniping, heckling and piss-taking, and laughing at our own crap jokes.

Pint after pint was going down. All the locals knew who we were. News of our camp had made it into their papers, and who else could this bus-load of bulky Englishmen be? Some wanted selfies, though Coley and I got off lightly there. The six-packers like Sam Underhill, Anthony Watson and Jonny May were attracting a lot of attention, especially since they'd taken their tops off in the roasting heat. *Crack on, boys,* we thought. They were welcome to the spotlight.

I was loving life. It felt like I was on holiday with my mates rather than away for work. I was in the moment and managing to relax without feeling guilty, which was something I wasn't able to achieve all the time. In fact, I'd had a major wobble while we'd been in Treviso.

One night I had a heart to heart with Daisy on the phone and she told me that Jasper had been upset. He was missing me and not understanding why I was away all the time. 'He said it's the worst school holidays ever,' said Daisy.

My six-year-old boy saying that. The words cut to the quick and I sank hard and fast. Daisy always worries about telling me stuff like that, as she doesn't want to make it even harder for me to be away. She knows I struggle when I'm missing out on normal life and not doing all the things you want to do as a dad and a husband. But Daisy had had a tough week herself. Felix was only six weeks old and, with our daughter Maggie as well, Daisy had been struggling with all three kids on her own. I wished I could be there, even if only to give her half an hour to herself.

I reassured her that she'd done the right thing by telling me what was happening at home. I didn't want her bottling it all up and just soldiering on for my sake. I needed to know what was going on even if I wasn't there to bath the kids and make their dinner.

'We're in this together,' I said, though I'm sure from Daisy's point of view it can't have looked like it, not right then. I'd been away for weeks already and had months to go until the World Cup. It was a long slog and she was the one doing the heavy lifting.

After that phone call I really struggled to keep telling myself I was doing this all for the family. I wasn't, was I? I was a self-centred bastard. This was all about me, selfishly chasing my career, trying to fulfil my dreams. What a wanker, leaving Daisy with a newborn baby and two small children. How hard must it have been for her?

I'd been experiencing waves of guilt ever since that phone call, even when having a coffee with the boys or playing indoor cricket. My mood was so low I felt like I had a permanent lump in my throat, and the only thing that would get rid of it would be to pack it all in, to spit out the words, 'Eddie, I'm retiring again. Sorry, mate.'

'One last shot,' I told myself, trying to keep the focus. 'You're here now. The campaign has started.'

Thankfully, today was different. Today was a good day. My mood was lighter, the clouds had shifted. I was in the sunshine with all the boys around me, and I was getting slowly sozzled.

Me and Coley went to get another drink and were standing up, leaning on the bar, when two local police officers came over. My first reaction was: 'Hang on, how am I getting into trouble in another country?' but they turned out to be fans. We had a bit of banter and when one of them asked me for a photo I was very happy to oblige. He pretended to hand-cuff me for a joke, while telling me, 'You have been a very naughty boy, Joe!' It made a really funny picture, not least because I was half-cut. We were all still laughing about it when I noticed a scuffle had broken out between a couple of the boys. Coley and I put our drinks down and went to see if we could help.

I guess it was no surprise tempers had frayed. The training we'd been doing had been so intense. The temperatures were hitting 36 degrees, with 80 per cent humidity. We were sweating buckets and being sprayed with ice-cold water to stop us dehydrating, and we had to constantly take on water and rehydration fluids. Or in my case, eat ten orange ice lollies in quick succession. All in all, there was a massive amount of steam to be let off.

The incident was contained as quickly as it started, but unfortunately it hadn't gone unnoticed.

The following day Eddie called us in for a review of training. Before we got onto that he completely roasted our arses. He said we needed to look at our behaviour and decide how we wanted to move forward. We deserved it. None of us should have been drunk in public. We all agreed we wanted to pull together and move on, focused on the job we were there to do.

It's funny how things work out. The piss-up in Treviso proved to be a turning point in terms of how well we bonded as a team and how we moved forward. As a group of men we'd shared an experience and the whole squad felt tighter afterwards. We all knew what had happened in 2011, when it all went tits-up for the

England team in New Zealand, with drunken behaviour grabbing the headlines and players embarrassing themselves. Nobody wanted this World Cup campaign to go down that route, and it was clear we were at a pivotal moment. We had to decide if we were going to pull together and propel ourselves forward as a squad or let it all go to shit. Of course, we chose to watch each others' backs and crack on as a team, tighter and stronger than before.

★

Some players behave very differently off the pitch to the way they do on it. Dylan Hartley is as calm as a cardboard box in the team room, but when the lid comes off on the pitch, you find out it's a box of snakes. When he was England captain for a couple of years – 2016 to 2018 – I always found him chatty and sociable and a great leader. To talk to him, you'd never imagine he has one of the worst discipline records in rugby, racking up almost two years' worth of bans during his professional career. Two of his outbursts cost him particularly dear. He lost his place on the Lions tour in 2013 after calling the ref Wayne Barnes a 'fucking cheat' and he missed the 2015 World Cup after headbutting Jamie George in a Premiership semi-final. I have a lot of sympathy for Dylan. He saw a sports psychologist to help him cope with the rest mist, but he still struggled.

Psychology sessions work for some players. Lewis Moody sought help for his temper after brawling with Alesana Tuilagi in England's 40–3 victory over Samoa in 2005. He never had another red or yellow card after that, having learned to look at the ref as soon as the red mist started to descend, which forced him to think about the consequences. Psychologists are all around the game now, on hand to help with motivation, anger issues and with little habits and tricks like the one Moody used.

It wasn't like that when I was starting out, but luckily for me my old Quins teammate Olly Kohn had me sussed. He had my back.

'Stop being a dickhead,' he said to me during a game, when I was gobbing off and arguing with the ref. I got another yellow, and Kohnan had had enough of me. He's someone with a high tolerance level, very accommodating and understanding. I looked up to him and respected him, and his outburst stopped me in my tracks.

'It's not all about you,' he went on. 'Wind your neck in and get a check on yourself. Carry on like this and you're gonna cost us the game. We need 15 players on the pitch and you're putting the team in jeopardy.'

His words really got through to me. I was part of a team, and I couldn't let my heart and my temper rule my head like this. Still, I didn't find it easy to move the dial. Your temper is an intrinsic part of you. Your red-mist filter is something you're born with, something you have to get to know and learn how to manage. That doesn't happen overnight.

*

Sometimes there's more to red-mist moments than meets the eye. You might try to pass it off as a 'moment of madness' – perhaps because you genuinely don't understand it any better – but there are times when bad temper is not the only factor at play.

Come with me back to the Stoop. Quins are playing Grenoble in the European Challenge Cup semi-final in April 2016. It's my first match back after serving a two-week ban and being fined £20,000 for calling Welsh prop Samson Lee 'Gypsy boy' in the England v Wales Six Nations game.

I'd been through a lot since Gypsygate, and on the way to the Stoop that day I was thinking back over the past month or so. I'd made a big mistake with Samson Lee. It didn't matter that his team-mates called him Gypsy boy or that he was proud of his traveller heritage. I'd called him that name with the sole purpose of pissing him off and throwing him off his game. That was wrong of me.

The Six Nations committee handed me a misconduct charge, which I deserved. Far worse was the fact that I was trolled online and accused of being racist, which rattled me to the core and cut me deeply.

Eddie Jones was put under pressure online and in the media to drop me from the England squad. We only had the decider against France to play and we were well on our way to winning our first Grand Slam since 2003. But Eddie's not one to bow to outside pressure and he didn't drop me. That was a huge relief. He put me on the bench to start with but brought me on to play in the second half, and I'll always be grateful to him for that.

The game was one of the highlights of my career. We beat the French by 10 points, the final score standing at 31–21, a win we thoroughly deserved. We played great rugby that day. There was no stand-out moment on the pitch for me, at least not one I can recall. Often my memories of big games are fogged and I can't remember the fine details of tackles or even who scored the tries. The white-hot stress messes with your synapses, I think, and I have to look back over videos to remember what went on, just as if I was a spectator.

But I am proud of the part I played. I know I turned up and did my job well, and if I'd missed out on that opportunity I'd have been absolutely heartbroken.

Not only had England waited 13 long years to win the Grand Slam, we'd got rid of the monkey on our back from losing the home World Cup the year before. I was ecstatic, like all the boys. The beer started to flow as soon as the final whistle was blown and we had one hell of a night celebrating in Paris. I forgot – literally – all about the hideous circus that had followed me around for the past couple of weeks.

After our triumph I assumed I'd be allowed to move on. I'd not really given it much thought, but that seemed the logical thing to happen. It wasn't to be. The party was over in Paris but the trolling over Gypsygate hadn't stopped. In fact, to my annoyance and dismay, it had escalated. It was off the scale.

World Rugby had got involved because of the continued furore over the incident, and it decided that the Six Nations committee hadn't done enough by simply giving me a slap on the wrist with the misconduct charge. I was summoned to a disciplinary hearing in Canary Wharf, where I had to face three top sports lawyers who were flown in from around the world to 'prosecute' me.

It was a surreal and terrifying ordeal, listening to their discussion of other instances of racism at the top level of sport. I didn't recognise myself in the same category as the other offenders – Luis Suárez being one, who when playing for Liverpool repeatedly said 'negro' to Manchester United player Patrice Evra – but I had to accept that was where I'd stupidly landed myself.

It was very hard to listen to. I was sweating and shaking, and at one point it all sounded so gravely serious that I thought I might be sent to jail. Of course, the upshot was my famously huge £20,000 fine, plus the two-week ban. I'd much rather have had a £2,000 fine and a 20-week ban – I was in desperate need of a break and would have grabbed that with both hands – but I couldn't and wouldn't appeal. I'd promised on Twitter that I'd take whatever rap came my way, and I had to stand by my word.

'I'm sorry,' I said to Daisy every single day as Gypsygate unfolded. 'I wish all this would just go away.' As I knew all too well, even at the best of times it was hard for Daisy being married to me. She was doing too much on her own, too much of the time. All because of me and my ridiculous job. Throwing a ball around on a muddy field. Running around in a pair of shorts. Travelling away for months on end. Why was I so selfish, putting my career above being a good husband and father?

Now this. Now I'd brought the whole Gypsygate shit storm down on us, just when I had something wonderful to celebrate and should have been revelling in the glory of the Grand Slam win.

For weeks our lives were turned upside down. If I wasn't ranting and raving as I constantly scrolled through the abuse I was getting on Twitter, I was moody and withdrawn, blaming myself for being such a helmet and seething about the enormous fine. People were slagging me off on the radio and on TV. Every time I looked at my phone it was something else. I was starting to feel like the whole world was against me. There's no textbook that tells a rugby player how to deal with this. I was feeling my way through it – and not doing very well.

'It's OK, Joe,' Daisy would say. 'The most important thing is that I know you're not a racist. All your family and friends know you are not racist, and we are the ones who know you. That's the truth of it. We'll get through it.'

Daisy had rings under her eyes. Maggie was just a few months old and Jasper was two. It wasn't fair. I'd caused so much stress and upheaval and I wasn't helping her the way I should have been. I knew that, but I couldn't lift myself out of it. It was too easy to disappear down rabbit holes on social media. I'd fret and panic and then shut down as I tried to block it all out. It was a horrible cycle.

With all that in my mind, here I was returning to the Stoop for the first time, for the Quins v Grenoble semi-final. The Gyspygate affair had taken its toll, massively. I'd had a week off after the Six Nations but it wasn't just a physical break I needed. Mentally, I felt done in.

Returning to Quins after a stint away on international duty normally feels great. A place I know so well, surrounded by our wonderful, loyal supporters, I'm always happy to arrive back at the Stoop. It's like going home. But this time I had a horrible feeling in my gut and a tightness around my heart. I was really struggling, so much so that I wished I could turn the car around. *What's the point? It's just a game. Why am I putting myself and my family through all this shit?*

I pushed myself to get changed, do the warm-up. All the time telling myself I could do it. I had to do it. I wasn't winning the psychological battle I was having with myself. When I finally walked out of the tunnel to face Grenoble I was in a very negative place, my head full of dark and gloomy thoughts. *This is pointless. I don't want to be here. I'm done with this game. What am I doing here?*

The taunts from the French players started up even before the whistle. Some of them were vile – unprintable – but I sucked it up. It was no surprise they were calling me out like that. It's what rugby players do, to get under your skin and try to throw you off your game. It's what I'd tried to do to Samson Lee.

About halfway through the first half I felt a hand on the back of my neck. I was trying to pick myself up off the field but this sticky mitt was holding me down. I was not happy. When I finally got to my feet and moved off I saw Grenoble's hooker Arnaud Héguy on the ground in front of me. I flicked out my leg as I jogged past him, giving him a little kick in the head.

It was another mistake. Another disciplinary hearing to attend. No doubt another ban to add to the list. The media were having a field day because 'bad boy Marler' was living up to his reputation. Out of control, unable to deal with the red mist. That's what they were all saying.

'What happened?' Daisy asked, exasperated but keeping calm, like she does. 'What were you thinking?'

'Honestly, I don't know, Dais. It's what happens on a rugby field. They were winding me up and I just lost it. I'm sorry. Red mist, occupational hazard. You know that.'

Richard Smith QC was representing me at the disciplinary hearing. They had the kick on video so his advice was to say sorry and take the medicine.

'How are you feeling?' he asked as we waited to go in.

All I wanted to do was crawl under a rock and hide from everything, but I didn't tell him that. 'Fine,' I said as boldly as I could muster. 'Bring it on. Let's just get it over with as quickly as possible.'

I walked into the hearing, my mood dragging on the floor beside me. There were three people sitting on the panel and I looked at them in turn. Then I took a very deep breath and made a decision that came from nowhere.

Despite how I'd tried to present myself to Richard Smith, I wasn't feeling bold at all. Far from it. *I'm not just going to apologise and keep my mouth shut,* I thought. *I want this to be real. I'm going to be straight with them.*

When it was my turn to speak I immediately started to tell the panel how I'd fallen out of love with rugby, that I'd been under a huge amount of pressure because of Gypsygate and that I couldn't get my head around the media.

'I was getting a lot of flak from the Grenoble players about my previous ban, which I fully expected,' I said. 'That's what I would have done, to try to get an edge on the opposition. But it wasn't just that they wound me up. There is more to it than that.' I took a drink of water. You could hear a pin drop. 'I'm struggling, you see. I don't like the sport at the moment and I feel in a dark place.'

The members of the panel looked taken aback. This was clearly not what they expected of 'bad boy Marler', a player they no doubt had down as your archetypal meathead thug.

We adjourned for half an hour, and when I was called back in the head of the panel acknowledged my honesty and the fact that I'd clearly been struggling. I was told I was being given a four-week ban reduced to two because of what I'd shared, and the panel recommended I seek help to get to grips with my red-mist moments.

I appreciated that they'd listened to me. The reduced ban was a result, of sorts, but I wasn't exactly cheering. I felt flat. Numb. Disinterested, even. Like before, there was a part of me that wanted an even bigger ban so I could be away from the game for longer.

I took the panel's advice and saw a sports psychologist, briefly. He focused on teaching me coping mechanisms to stop me losing my temper and lashing out on the pitch. The trouble was, the Héguy head-kick was not the red-mist moment everyone assumed it to be. It was a despondent, lacklustre flick of my foot. More of a red-flag moment than a red-mist one.

I was unravelling, mentally. Losing the plot in a much bigger way. I don't blame the panel or the sports psychologist for not realising that, because I didn't really get it myself. *Angry, you say? Aggressive? Snappy and sappy? I'm a prop forward! It's my job to lock horns with the biggest rugby rhinos in the world. What do you expect me to behave like?*

I was in denial, hiding behind the red mist. And because the red mist is such an intrinsic part of the game, that's an incredibly easy thing for a rugby player to do.

Sweet and innocent.
Before I was tall enough to
reach the sweet cupboard.

My first day at school, age
5, with my dad's blue Ford
Granada in the background.

13 years old. Little did I know then that the girl beside me in braces would become my wife and that we'd go on to have an amazing life together.

Although I was slightly bigger than most of my schoolmates, I was never afraid to live up to a larger than life expectation (yes, before you ask, I am wearing an Ireland Rugby jersey).

Skiving school to go to the 2003 parade for England's World Cup win.

Sporting "Beckham curtains" and sitting in mid-front row of the season's undefeated U14s Eastbourne Sharks team. Look closely and you'll see my head is strapped — but not my ears. From the start I never took things seriously.

The first letter I ever received from Quins, at age 14, inviting me to join ranks with Collin Osborne and the team.

Playing against Haywards Heath RFC. You can just about make out PHYSCO on the back of my shirt — a nickname and a reputation I had to live up to.

NEC HARLEQUINS
ENGLAND RUGBY ACADEMY

Mr Joe Marler
12 Holly Close
Heathfield
TN21 8AP

20th December 2004

Dear Joe,

I am delighted to inform you that you have been nominated by Sussex to be a member of the NEC Harlequins Elite Player Development Group (EPDG). The EPDG selects the most talented players from the Under 15 squads from both Surrey and Sussex and it is from this group that nominations for the full regional academy are usually made.

To introduce players and parents to the EPDG there will be a parents and players meeting at our training base at Aldershot on Monday 10th January 2005 at 7.15pm and I hope that you and your parents will be able to attend.

Travelling directions are attached and I hope to meet you on the Monday evening. Please confirm by telephone or e-mail whether or not you are able to attend.

Yours sincerely

Collin Osborne

At a community event before the 2019 World Cup where the fans' anticipation and enthusiasm was our first realisation of just how much love and support we had. It was really happening. We were going to Japan. (George Kruis lobbed my hat into the crowd which is why I look like this. I never tracked the hat down.)

My first ever red card in professional rugby for fisticuffs with Marcos Ayerza. The start of a long love affair between me and refs. Also the start of crazy haircuts. (© David Rogers – Getty Images)

Me and my old mucker "Hazza". This was just after the Super Saturday 2015 Six Nations game and I couldn't wait to crack open my Red Stripe but felt obliged to take this photo, him being royalty and all.

The CUCC boys after winning the 2016 Grand Slam. (© David Rogers – The RFU Collection via Getty Images)

The Barbarians' front row, taken just before I came out of international retirement. I owe a huge amount to them for helping me fall in love with rugby again. I blame my roomie John Afoa and chief and partner in crime Richard Hibbard for a complete lack of sleep and incredible fun in the best week of my career.

"Gypsygate" when I got a 2-week ban for the tussle with Samson Lee. Little did I know that this would be the start of grappling with demons and discovering the other side of rugby – the high profile media shit storms which I didn't understand at the time. (© Ben Stansall/AFP via Getty Images)

9 June 2012 at the famous Kings Park Stadium in Durban. My first taste of international rugby on the world stage, age 21. Also in the match was 'The Beast' Tendai Mtawarira who would be the master of our demise in Japan in 2019. (© David Rogers – Getty Images)

L-R: Chris Robshaw, Jason Robinson, Jason Leonard, Me. Growing up the legendary Jason Leonard aka "Fun Bus" was a hero. I still pinch myself when in his company, it's surreal. (© Amanda Heathcote)

Paul Gastard, Nick Evans and I on the pitch, realising we're getting old and bald very quickly.

Winning the 2012 Premiership Final against Leicester Tigers and celebrating with Welsh International and good mate Olly Kohn.
(© Ben Hoskins – Getty Images)

I managed to get on *The Jonathan Ross Show* in my best "Saturday-night gear", alongside Manu Tuilagi, Tom Curry and Ben Youngs. They forced me to sing Adele with out-of-sync music, which broke my heart as I would have smashed it acapella.
(© Brian J Ritchie/Hotsauce/Shutterstock)

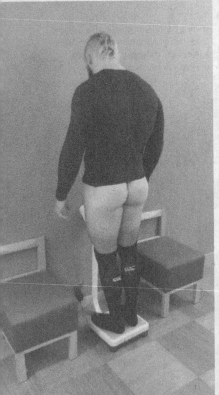

Left: At a Japanese onsen (traditional hot spring) where the etiquette is to bathe naked. Tattoos have an association with gangs, so I'm covering them up so as to not offend. And yet I look more offensive — and it did nothing for my hydration levels.

Mark Lambert, Will Collier, Me, Rob Buchanan. One of many fancy dress socials that Quins led. This was a *Sons of Anarchy* look.

At Will Skinner's wedding with some of my closest mates from Quins.

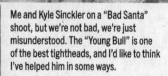

Me and Kyle Sinckler on a "Bad Santa" shoot, but we're not bad, we're just misunderstood. The "Young Bull" is one of the best tightheads, and I'd like to think I've helped him in some ways.

Another Quins social, famous for how seriously we took the fancy dress themes!

4 November 2015. Our wedding day featuring an 18-month old Jasper. Daisy and I were helped out by four lovely ladies in the local area who agreed to be our witnesses for the ceremony. We've always wanted to say thanks for that day but not been able to track them down since!

Left: My Mugwump.

The nearest and dearest in my life. My people.

Celebrating a wedding with a *Peaky Blinders* theme.

Jasper already showing me how it's done on the rugby field.

The Three Bells. Matt and Sean, my two best mates.

Jasper and Maggie posing with 1-week old Felix, their little brother. My world.

Thanking the fans after losing the 2019 World Cup Final. Obviously I was gutted, but some of the best experiences in life don't always end with a gold medal. Although we'd fallen, I'm incredibly grateful to the England fans, the Japanese people for welcoming us so warmly, and the unforgettable moments we made as a team which will live with me always.

(© Dan Mullan – Getty Images)

Playing for the British & Irish Lions was a dream come true and I loved every minute of it. This from the 2017 match against New Zealand Provincial Barbarians.

(© David Rogers – Getty Images)

Post-match in Biarritz during the Heineken Cup in 2013. This was the game where I pissed my pants to save myself freezing to death on the rugby pitch… which might explain the expression.

Eddie taking the front row boys out for sushi in Japan before the start of the 2019 tournament. Eddie told us that we would be responsible for winning the World Cup, because our scrum would be so important and vital to our success. And it was – up until the Final where we were dismantled.

I often hosted the boys in my room, and always had contraband for tough days. My specialty was extra thick chocolate biscuits – dealed under darkness and out of sight of the team nutritionist.

The CUCC boys again.

March 2020. Winning the Triple Crown Trophy after beating Wales. This would end up being another furore after "Fondlegate". (© David Rogers – The RFU Collection via Getty Images)

Winning the Calcutta Cup in 2014 against Scotland.

The 2019 Rugby World Cup England squad. I'm the one not looking at the camera (I must have missed the memo).

Roll call for the captains of the 2015/16 season at Harlequins F.C. It was a privilege and honour to rep the world-famous club I'd looked up to since boyhood.
(© David Rogers/Getty Images for Aviva)

8

BARE TRUTHS

Five days to go until we play New Zealand in the World Cup semi-final and it's time for our routine dope-testing. In Japan you provide samples through blood, hair and urine. Filling a little pot with wee is a very simple way of sharing your bodily matter. Or so you might think.

The Japanese drug-testers come early doors on the Tuesday, but not early enough for me. I've already been for my morning wee but I reassure them I'll go again. We have to produce our wee sample in front of dope-testers so they can be sure there's no funny business going on like switched urine or fake penises. Blokes have been caught filling sample cups with someone else's wee pissed out of a plastic dick. The drug-testers take no chances, none whatsoever.

I'm used to the process by now. I'll need to fill the sample cup with urine while he watches me, and I have to be the one who transfers the urine from the cup into two separate pots that cannot leave my sight until they are sealed.

I go into the bathroom dressed in shorts and a T-shirt with the serious-looking Mr Sugiyama Masayuki following me, clipboard clutched to his chest. He crouches down right next to me as I pull my pants down, and then he trains his eyes on my crotch. As I take hold of my cock and prepare to wee he moves in closer. And closer. And then even closer. *What the fuck is going on?*

His face is an inch away from my knob. An inch. No exaggeration. It is an utterly discombobulating experience. Or should I say discom*knob*ulating?

Unsurprisingly, I can't squeeze out a single drop of wee. Mr Sugiyama speaks broken English and my Japanese is sadly wanting. I can't even make a joke to try to make this situation any less embarrassing.

We agree to take a break. We leave the bathroom together, do the bloods and then I try again, once more with Mr Sugiyama's face right next to my knob, making sure it really is my own member I'm using. It's no use. We go through the same routine again and again, going back and forth to the toilet. It's impossible.

After an hour of this charade I realise I need a poo. Mr Sugiyama doesn't understand me or my inadequate hand signals, and I realise I'm going to have to get the translator to break it to him. We go back to the testing room and I just have to come out with it: 'Please can you tell Mr Sugiyama that I need a poo?'

When the message gets through, Mr Sugiyama goes bright red, but he stays calm and professional. I feel for him. Why would anyone sign up to do this job?

We go into the toilet again. He's watching my every move, eyes on stalks, sample bottles at the ready. We're both assuming I'll pass water once I've pooed, like you do. I sit down. Mr Sugiyama's face is between my knees this time. *Poor man,* I think. He's probably thinking, *Thank God this will all be over soon.* I know I am.

What Mr Sugiyama doesn't know is that I've been for a Mexican meal with the team the night before. The food was hot, hearty and absolutely huge. You can see where this is going.

I sit down and *explode*. It's like an angry volcano erupting, and there's noise and fumes and … you get the picture. This is honour beyond the call of duty, but Mr Sugiyama is as conscientious as they come. Unblinking, he stays with his head between my knees, eyes glued to my willy as I finally pee into the sample bottle. I know he has to see the urine coming out, but really?

'There you go,' I say, not sure whether to look apologetic or triumphant. 'There's your sample.'

I'd been in a similar situation to this once before. Keith Jarrett was the unlucky tester on that occasion during the World Cup in 2015. He turned up at my house at 6am with no warning, as testers do. I was naked when I went to answer the door. 'Fucking hell, mate, what you doing here so early? I'll have to go and put some clothes on.'

'That's quite alright, Sir, but I'll have to mark that down.'

I laughed. 'I'm going to put on a dressing gown, not a fake dick filled with horse piss!'

Keith Jarrett didn't laugh. And there then followed an awkward hour and a half during which we went through a similar 'will he/won't he' charade, punctuated by cups of tea and awkward small talk, before I finally cracked and told him he'd need to get my sample while I had my morning poo.

'That's quite alright, Sir. It's happened many times.'

Keith Jarrett accompanied me into my downstairs loo and watched me open my dressing gown, crouch down and sit on the toilet. There's not much room in there and he was right in front of me, eyeballing my meat and two veg with a look of deep concentration on his face.

There was an instant *plop, plop, splash!*, which Keith Jarrett was kind enough not to react to. A gentleman to the end, he didn't even hold his nose when the fumes started to percolate around the room. The sample bottle was filled up and Keith Jarrett put it on the side where he could see it, with his back turned to me so I could finish off my business and preserve my last shred of dignity.

I wait for Mr Sugiyama to do the same. And I wait. Nope. It's not going to happen. Super-diligent Mr Sugiyama doesn't turn his gaze to the bottle and he certainly doesn't turn his back to me. He continues observing me for the rest of the poo and then watches me tidy up. Every last wipe. That's the worst part of all.

*

'Hey, Fatso. What you doin' round the corner?'

'Er, nothin'. Just getting dressed.' I blushed bright red as I grappled with my too-small towel, trying and failing to cover up as much of my wobbly flesh as I could.

I loved PE at school. Football, rugby, athletics, cricket, netball, I loved them all. They'd put me in goal in footy because I nearly filled it, and I played netball as a way of getting in with the girls, though sadly it didn't lead to love. Even the one girl in the class who had similar weight issues to me wasn't interested. *Fucking hell,* I thought. *We should be helping each other out here.* She wasn't having it.

Still, nothing put me off PE. Even the torturous, humiliating ordeal of showering and changing in front of the other boys.

'Hey, look at Marler, he looks like a fridge!' one of the cool kids said one day. I'd revealed more of my big, white body than I intended to. 'And he can empty one in record time! Ha-ha! Let's call him Fridge!'

Fuck's sake. The nickname stuck for a while and I was absolutely mortified. I was also appalled at the lack of imagination displayed by my classmates. I mean, they could have at least called me Smeg.

I chuckle when I think of my awkward adolescent self because I don't give a monkey's about being seen naked nowadays. It's not just because rugby is a game for all shapes and sizes. There's more to it than that. I've been stripped of my inhibitions because the whole culture of rugby normalises and positively encourages nudity.

'Take off your clothes!' Rugby says. 'Peel off your shorts and expose those bare buttocks! Reveal your willy with wild abandon!'

'But why?' you cry. 'What's nudity got to do with rugby?'

'Ah-ha!' Rugby says. 'Your nakedness is a powerful tool. It binds teammates together and helps you win the game!'

There is no statistical evidence to back up this bold claim, but there's definitely some truth in the bonding power of nudity. In the amateur era the whole team would pile naked into a giant bubble bath after a game, crack open the beers and relax together. The ritual has almost died out now, mostly for health and safety reasons, although the French still cling on to it. I love going to the Stade de France because they have this wonderful state-of-the-art hot tub where, win or lose, we can wallow like hippos and have a good drink together after the game.

We're in this together. We hold no secrets. We trust each other. That's how the communal bath makes you feel. If you can feel comfortable with your teammates when you're stark bollock naked, how much more at ease will you feel when you run out on the field together, all spruced up and turned out in matching kits? It certainly works for me.

The other thing is, if you're used to naked male bodies day in and day out, the intimate physicality demanded of you on the pitch is less intimidating Teammate's crotch in your face when you lift him for a line-out or a sweaty opponent grabbing your arse to wind you up in a ruck? No problem. Seen it all before. Smelled it all before.

*

I'm 17, just starting out in the Quins academy, and it's time for me to shower up after doing a session at the old training ground at Roehampton. There are separate changing areas for the front row, second row, 9s and 10s and the backs – most of them windowless and the size of a cupboard – and from there you have to go down a long corridor to reach the communal showers.

I'm the last to leave the pitch and when I get to the front row changing room it's empty. Result. I'd rather have the privacy, thanks very much. Also, you don't really want to bump into any of the first-team players when you're the new young pup, especially not when you're on your own. The seniors don't speak to the youngsters at the best of times, so imagine how awkward it would be if you found yourself squashed in a cupboard with one of the big dogs, both of you starkers and surrounded by nothing but silence?

I strip off and prepare to walk naked down the corridor to the communal shower area. As I get close I hear water running. *Fuck. Someone's there.*

I'm starting to tone up a bit now that rugby is my job, but I'm still overweight and I'm self-conscious about my body. Nobody expects the forwards to be as ripped and shredded as the agile backs, but I'm not even slightly torn.

Come on, Joe. You don't look like a fridge anymore. OK, maybe just an upright model, rather than a big-boy American fridge freezer ... I suck my belly in and put my shoulders back as I reach the end of the corridor. *Don't worry about it. Just do it.*

I stop in my tracks as I reach the open-plan showers. I'd expected it to be one of the other academy boys in there, but it's not. It's a senior player, and not just any senior player. It's England international Andy Gomarsall, one of the biggest names at Quins.

'Oh, hiya!' I stutter, doing a double-take. Not only am I feeling anxious at the thought of sharing a naked shower with a man who was in the World Cup squad of 2003, but there's something else weirding me out. Andy Gomarsall is covered from head to toe in soap suds, and I mean completely covered. Somehow, he's managed to cover every part of his body except for a Zorro mask around his eyes. Not only that, there's a dog beside him, also coated from head to toe in foamy lather.

'Hello!' he replies, sounding very posh and very confident. He cracks on with his shower. He doesn't look twice at me. Doesn't acknowledge that he's taking a shower with his family pet and they're wearing matching soap-sud suits.

What the hell had I been worried about? There's no time or place for coyness in the changing rooms, and the quicker you learn to leave your modesty at the door, the better.

I let it all hang out now. No coyness at all. In fact, I positively strut my stuff and don't care what anyone thinks. Life's too short for all that nonsense.

★

When we were in Japan for the World Cup, Coley was desperate to try out the onsens – the traditional hot-spring baths and saunas. The etiquette is that you go in naked, men and women in separate areas. The Japanese consider it offensive to wear clothes in them; it's seen as dirty and disrespectful.

'Will you come with me?' Coley asked.

'No, mate. I don't fancy it. I don't mind getting naked with you but I don't like heat.'

He wasn't giving up. 'But it's an experience. Something you can't do anywhere else in the world.'

'Look, I've been in spas before. It's just a sauna with a Japanese name. It'll be too hot for me.'

We had a private onsen in our hotel but Coley wanted to go to the public one for the full traditional experience. 'It's good for recovery,' he went on. 'Go on, come with me?'

'No, I'm not interested. I'm going to bed. That's my recovery.'

He tried again the next day. 'We can't not do it. Please come with me, mate?'

I sighed. 'What about the tattoos? How can I go in with all this ink on display?' Tattoos have an association with criminal gangs in Japan and showing them off is as disrespectful as wearing clothes in the onsen. Maybe more so. I was looking for my next excuse. 'Apart from anything else, the press would have a field day.'

I'd found out that some members of the media team staying in our hotel had gone into the private onsen in their swimming trunks. When they tried to ask serious rugby questions at the next press conference I called them out for violating Japanese bathing protocol.

'Apparently you lot have offended the Japanese culture,' I said accusingly. 'Swanning about in swimming shorts. It's ridiculous!' I went on so much that they ran out of time for all the serious questions they'd prepared, which was my aim all along.

The press pack were well used to me by now, and I don't think any of the journalists in Japan were surprised when I insisted on talking about their onsen attire instead of the World Cup. It's what they've come to expect and I'd like to think they'd be disappointed if I didn't give them a little bit of banter to alleviate the dullness of the media machine.

'You can cover up your tattoos,' Coley said, rolling his eyes. 'That's allowed. You know that.'

I caved, if only to shut him up, and the next day we headed off to a public onsen together. I didn't really mind. I just like to make Coley sweat and beg, to be honest.

When we arrived in the changing rooms I started preparing myself, working out how best to cover the tattoos. I'd seen some people use flesh-coloured tube grips as sleeves but I didn't have any of those. I just had to do my best with what I had.

I had a lot of tattoos to cover up. J for Jasper on my left calf. Rolling Stones lips on my right calf, to remind me of seeing them at Glastonbury. M for Maggie on my right pec. That one had the most potential for offence. 'Why does it look like a cock and balls?' was the first thing Daisy said when she saw it. She had a point. I'd gone for 'circus' font but somehow it hadn't quite worked out. Never mind, you can't win 'em all. Then there was my left-arm sleeve with flowers and Japanese koi fish – the latest but not the last, as I was now planning to mark my body in honour of baby Felix.

'OK, mate, I'm ready.' I still had my back turned to Coley and I was glancing over my shoulder as I spoke because I wanted to see his reaction. I could tell he was trying to keep a straight face as he looked me up and down.

'Is that the best you can do?' he asked, deadpan.

'Yes, mate. Got a problem, have you?'

'No. All fine. No problem. Let's go.'

I turned to face Coley. I could see the corners of his mouth turn up but he was still trying not to laugh.

'What, mate?' I said. 'I'm being respectful here. The least you could do is not take the piss when I've gone to all this trouble. I didn't even want to come here in the first place ...'

Coley couldn't stop himself now. He was pissing himself at the sight of me in my onsen outfit. Admittedly, it was quite substantial as far as nude sauna attire goes – a black, long-sleeved under-skin top and thick black compression socks up to my knees. The only bits of me on display were my bum and, of course, my cock and thighs.

'What's funny?' I asked him. Now it was my turn to try to keep a straight face. 'This follows the bathing etiquette to the letter, mate.'

I knew full well that I looked anything but respectful, and it was a double whammy once we were in the onsen. I'd like to say I was sweating my balls off, but they were the only part of me not overheating in the 80-degree heat.

★

Even the team meeting room offers no sanctuary from nudity. I learned that right at the start of my career at Quins, when I was sitting cross-legged on the floor and waiting for the main team meeting of the week to start. A couple of the other academy boys were beside me, and watched quietly from our lowly place as the rows of chairs started to fill up with the first-team players.

It was all very new to me still, and I didn't want to be the butt of any jokes or piss-takes again. I'd already learned that you must never accept the offer of a seat from a senior player. Tani Fuga, the Samoan hooker, had already got me with that one. I looked up to Tani. If he'd said, 'Jump,' I'd have said, 'How high?' So like a dickhead I'd sat in the chair he offered me for all of two minutes before Ceri Jones had come in and shouted at me, 'Get back on the fucking floor!'

Fucking hell. Don't let anything happen to me today. The first-team players were also known for balancing jugs of water above the door to prank the coaches when they came in. It might have been a dozen or so years since rugby had become a professional sport, but Quins were still upholding some of the old amateur-era traditions. That made me nervous.

The big boys started to file in and take their seats. Tani and Ceri, followed by Nick Easter, Ugo Monye and Mike Brown. The coaches were up front, watching them all settle in, and when I looked up I saw Dean Richards glancing through the window as he walked along the corridor.

Mark Lambert, who'd been at the club for about four years, came in next and I watched as he manoeuvred his huge body into a seat a couple of rows from the back. As soon as his arse hit the chair the room erupted. It was as if the seat had been booby-trapped and set off an explosion.

'Go on! Fucking get him!' Four or five players dived on top of him and started ripping his kit off while I sat there looking at the other academy boys wondering, *What the fuck is going on?*

I clocked Dean Richards again, having a little look in the window. What the fuck was going to happen now?

The players tore at Lambert's kit like a pack of hyenas while they shouted, 'Get it all off!' His entire kit was ripped off his body and torn to shreds. Even his underpants were pulled apart and thrown in tatters to the floor. He was left sitting there totally naked, taking it all in remarkably good spirits and covering himself up as best he could with his hands.

Lambert's mistake had been to randomly select the chair that had been chosen by the most senior players as the one that would trigger their little game that day. Once their job was done all the boys sat down quietly, waiting for the meeting to start, as if what had just happened was the most normal thing in the world. It was obviously a regular occurrence because the coaches didn't turn a hair and didn't say a word.

It was a review meeting, with the focus on breaking down the penalties from the previous game and looking at how to improve discipline. *Is this how you improve discipline?* I thought. *This is totally nuts.*

Dean Richards came in to talk to us at the end and I was intrigued to see how he would react. He could hardly fail to notice what had happened. So what did Dean Richards do? He cracked on with the meeting as if it was the most natural thing in the world to have a six-foot-three, twenty-stone player bare-arsed in his chair, ruined kit at his feet and hands strategically placed over his dick.

(Ugo Monye felt guilty and bought Mark Lambert a new pair of Calvin Klein classics the next day, a fact I only learned when I reminded Lammy of this story recently.)

*

Even the pitch offers no immunity from random nakedness. Just ask Jonny May. The two of us were playing against Australia in the 2010 Junior World Championship in Argentina when Jonny got the ball 20 metres out. I was struggling to keep up with him, and when I looked up I clocked one of the Australian boys grabbing the back of Jonny's shorts. *No fucking way!*

Jonny kept going at full pelt and the Australian held on. There was only going to be one outcome. The elastic had reached full stretch on the waistband of Jonny's shorts and they were pulled clean off his backside, revealing his bare buttocks to the world.

I was pissing myself laughing but Jonny was as focused as ever, still going strong. Surely he was going to have to stop and sort this out? I mean, it wasn't just a bit of a bum crack or half a cheek peeping out. This was a full moon.

Jonny kept going. He was so determined to make the try that he dragged the guy the full 20 metres down the pitch with him, still clinging to the waistband of his shorts like a dog on a lead, before touching the ball down.

Christian Wade finished off the show by giving Jonny a slap on his bare arse before pulling his shorts up for him. It was brilliant. Jonny didn't give a hoot, and on his next birthday he got a lovely big cake from his family, topped with a sugar-icing model of him and his bare bum.

*

Initiation ceremonies and drunken nights out provide the biggest platforms for nudity, exhibitionism and all manner of embarrassing body experiences. I was on loan at Worthing in 2008, playing men's rugby for the first time, when I was introduced to the dreaded initiation ceremony. There were a couple of other newbies too.

'What d'you think they'll make us do?' one said, looking a bit pale. We knew we were in for some kind of humiliation but we didn't know what. There's usually a veil of secrecy around initiation ceremonies, to maximise the impact on the night.

'There's always nakedness involved,' one of the other boys declared, trying to sound less out of his depth than he was. 'I bet it's naked karaoke.'

We all joked that we'd put our clean underwear on for the occasion. Bless us. We were lambs to the slaughter, all of us secretly shitting ourselves but not wanting to admit it.

'Marler! Over here, you're first!' It was one of the most senior guys at the club, who on that occasion we had to refer to as 'Judge'.

'Yes, Judge.'

'Get your shorts down.'

Fuck me.

'And your underpants.'

'Yes, Judge.'

'That's it. Now bend over this stool.'

What the fuck? I had to go with it, didn't I? I was only 18. I didn't see what else I could do when there were dozens of men standing around laughing, the same men I had to play rugby with for my job. It was horrible, but bomb out of this and I'd lose all credibility. I couldn't have that. I wanted to be one of the big boys, a team player who could roll with the punches off the pitch as well as on it.

Judge picked up a big metal spatula, the sort with holes in it, and started whipping my arse as hard as he could. He carried on until I had an imprint on my bum cheek that looked like one of those *Tom and Jerry*-cartoon cheese slices. And my initiation still wasn't over. After that they made me drink snakebite out of my brand-new Nike trainers.

'It's all fun and games,' I said, laughing along with everyone else.

It wasn't fun and games at all though really, was it? My arse was stinging, my new trainers were ruined and I'd basically been ritually humiliated. I have no lasting beef with what happened to me. It was a different era and no real damage was done. The marks on my bum soon faded and I would get a new pair of trainers. I'd also passed the 'test' of the initiation, so my humiliation was not for nothing.

But you can't go round whacking people like that. I didn't exactly give my consent to be whipped on the bare arse, did I? I'm all for tradition and having a laugh, but there are much better ways of doing it than that.

Naked bowling is an initiation I don't mind, as long as the human bowling ball is fully on board. That was the challenge at the next initiation ceremony I went to, also at Worthing. This time it was for a little scrum-half. I watched in fascination as the dance floor of the clubhouse was greased up and chairs and bins were strategically placed at one end of the room, to act as the pins.

When the stage was set and the scrum-half was in position – suspended by his arms and legs by four other players – everyone was cheering and whooping. The little player was relishing his initiation, stark bollock naked and laughing his head off as the four burly players swung him back and forth to build up momentum. They then fired him on his back down the makeshift bowling alley.

He glided beautifully, enjoying the fun of it and not giving a monkey's about his bollocks bouncing all over the show. We all joined in, willingly, after a few pints. Of course we did. Rugby players relish a bit of rough and tumble, naked or otherwise. I loved it. There were a few bumps and bruises but nobody got hurt and nothing was damaged. Best of all, it gave us a great story to talk about in training, which is what it's all about. It's fabulous for team spirit when you're that comfortable in your own skin with one another.

*

Confession time. Sometimes you can go too far with your immodesty. I've fallen into that trap. But there were mitigating circumstances, I swear.

Quins were playing Biarritz away in the Heineken Cup, back in January 2013. The rain was coming down so hard that the pitch was filling up with huge puddles. My teeth were chattering inside my gum shield and the rain was spiking my skin like icy needles. I hate cold more than pain, and this was baltic and brutal.

I'm gonna suffocate. You have this thought at the best of times in a scrum because it feels like your body is being squeezed by a giant vice. This felt ten times worse because the freezing-cold air was so hard to inhale. The more I gasped, the more the icy breaths burned my lungs. And it wasn't even as if I wanted to inhale – the smell in the scrum was absolutely horrific.

As soon as I stuck my head in it hit me. It's the same every time. Every player has been in the same kit since before the warm-up and the stink is brewing up nicely right from the whistle. When you get to the eightieth minute, you do well not to throw up. It's an unmistakeable stench of body odour mixed with whiffs of undercarriage and the distinctive smell of shitty, wet mud. Ass and grass. Deep Heat and smelly feet. Dried blood and Vicks VapoRub. It was all in the mix on this occasion. And, as is not unusual in France, we had an extra ingredient added to the potent cocktail: wafts of garlic-ponging breath.

However, the smell was the least of my worries on that winter's night. We went into a ruck and I thought I was going to end up face-down in the water and never come up again. Either that or

I'd die of the cold. The same two thoughts kept swirling round my head. *Oh, my God, I can't breathe! I don't want to drown in a field in Biarritz in a pair of muddy rugby shorts. Don't let me freeze to death in a cloud of garlic breath and BO.*

There was a pause in the game, for a 22-metre drop-out. Standing there waiting, I'd never felt so bitterly cold on a rugby pitch in my life before. The rain was torrential, chilling me to my bones. A desperate idea came to me. Nobody would ever know. The rain would cover my tracks. *Shall I? I'll have to. Nobody will notice and I'll perish on the pitch if I don't.*

The tiny splash of warmth was such a welcome relief. My life was saved. What a genius move! I looked round and saw my team-mate Olly Kohn giving me a funny look.

'What are you doing?' he asked, eyes fixed on mine.

I gave a little shrug. 'Nothing, mate.'

'You're not … I know what you're doing!'

Kohnan had sussed me out. 'Yeah, I am.'

He held my gaze. 'So am I, now.'

'Are you?'

I burst out laughing. There we were, pissing our pants in unison in an effort to save ourselves from freezing to death on a French rugby pitch. Afterwards, Kohnan and I were united in our vow: 'This is never to be spoken of again.'

Until now, of course. Sorry, mate.

★

When John Kingston was director of rugby at Quins he had a habit of starting the Monday morning team meeting with 'any other business' instead of saving it for the end. Usually this meant talking about any good work the boys had done in the community, or the latest charity initiative the club was involved in. The idea was to kick things off with a positive, to set the tone for the week ahead.

One day he came in with a very stern face and said 'any other business' was a very serious matter on this occasion. We all looked at each other. *What the fuck's happened?*

John launched into a monologue about the club's loyal and long-serving maintenance guy Bim, saying how hard he worked and how much effort he put into keeping the facilities running smoothly. We had no idea where this was going and we started to worry about Bim. What had happened to him?

John finally got to the point. The toilets, it seemed, had been getting blocked. But instead of getting the problem sorted out, we had continued to use them. It seemed like a bit of a storm in a toilet pan, but John was not finished on the subject yet.

'I just don't get it,' he went on, his voice raised. He was very animated now. 'Why would you do that? Why?' He paused for breath and then delivered the best line I've ever heard in a team meeting. 'You wouldn't shit on a shit at home so why the hell would you do it here?'

It said it all, really. When you're a rugby player, even your 'any other business' is not your own. You don't just leave your modesty at the door, you say goodbye to a large dollop of dignity too.

Looking back at Japan now, I don't know why I even blushed when Mr Sugiyama Masayuki watched me do a shit and wipe my arse. I should probably have just been grateful that John Kingston wasn't there too, making sure I flushed properly afterwards.

9

IMAGE

This is absolutely great! I thought, looking at the huge glossy images displayed inside the Stoop. Quins had really gone to town with the new branding and posters. I was so impressed as I walked along the corridor. All the club's key players were there, captured in fantastic shiny action shots and mounted magnificently on the walls.

There were Kyle Sinckler and Chris Robshaw. Danny Care, king of sharp, looking great as always. James Chisholm, Mike Brown. Brilliant life-size shots of all the boys, running with the ball, scoring a try, celebrating a win, making a big tackle. Everyone looking their best and at the top of their game. Just the message you want to send out.

I carried on down the corridor. I felt proud to be a senior player at the club, to still be one of the boys who got to pull on the famous quarters at the Stoop after all these years. I had had my wobbles sometimes. Days when I thought, *Haven't I done this for long enough? Shouldn't I do something less punishing? More meaningful?* But this wasn't one of them. I was loving it.

There was no sign of my picture yet, but I wasn't surprised. It'd be tucked a bit further down the corridor. Forwards don't expect to be centre stage and we don't want to be. We're always happy to leave that to the prettier backs. The boys who like to preen and are happy to stand in the spotlight.

Danny Care's stag do tells you all you need to know on that score. There we are, a full crew of lads posing for a photo in the sunshine at the Ocean Beach Club in Ibiza, the positions we occupy on the pitch reversed: the boys posing proudly on the front row are the shredded and ripped backs, tops off and killer abs on display. Luther Burrell, Nick Evans, Ugo Monye, Chris Ashton and Danny himself. Meanwhile, I'm on the back row, along with my fellow forwards Mark Lambert, Olly Kohn and Nick Easter, plus Danny's school friends. No bare chests on display for us. I've got my T-shirt covering my wobbly bits, looking like a fat dad on holiday.

I don't worry about comparisons. Props can't compete on looks – we wouldn't be in the job if we weren't built like bull-dozers, would we? At least my body is fit for purpose, and I take pride in that.

I continued down the corridor. I was nearly at the tunnel. You veer off to the right for the away changing room and go left for ours. I looked to the right and stopped in my tracks. There, opposite the door of the away changing room, was a five-foot-high picture of me. Not just any picture, but the worst picture ever.

I'd been at the club 12 years. If you'd trawled the complete photo archive of my time at Quins you wouldn't have found a worse shot of me. I looked 23 stone and bloated and my shorts were tucked up to my tits. There was a cut on my face and a bit of blood, but I didn't look intimidating at all. Somehow, I looked more like a giant cuddly teddy bear than a professional rugby player.

I stood and stared at the photo, wondering what to do. This was the first image the opposition would see when they came out of their changing room, ready to go out onto the pitch. I was seriously not happy. My opponents would think I was an absolute joke. An out-of-condition pushover. A bulldozer destined for the scrapheap.

I wanted it taken down but there was a voice in my head saying, *What's happened to you, mate? You take the piss out of the divas – you can't be one!*

I was thinking about my game, how I needed to feel when I go out on the field and the image I needed to send out to the opposition and my own teammates. This was a step too far. It was compromising my performance on the pitch and I couldn't stand for it, could I?

I thought about Gavin Henson, rugby's pioneer of personal branding. One of the highlights of his career was when he was playing for Wales against England in the dramatic opener to the 2005 Six Nations. What happened before kick-off is written in rugby folklore.

The Welsh captain Gareth Thomas, aka Alfie, wanted all the boys to huddle together for a final pep talk before running out on the field. Henson was holding things up because he was in the toilets, checking his hair in the mirror. When Alfie told him to get a move on, Henson's reply was epic: 'Alf, your mother and father have come to watch you play today, but there's 72,000 out there who have come to watch me!'

Henson famously went on to kick the winning penalty from 44 metres to secure a nail-biting 11–9 victory in that memorable game, and it paved the way for Wales to win the Grand Slam. He wasn't even their regular goal-kicker. 'We gave it to him because he was so confident and we kind of knew he wouldn't miss,' his teammate Martyn Williams said. 'And we knew he was confident because of what happened just before kick-off, in the dressing room.'

That was it. I was taking a leaf out of Gavin Henson's book. I was going to take pride in my image and ask for that picture to be replaced with a better one. Leaving that cuddly teddy bear there on the wall was more than my job was worth. It was a total own goal. The boys would take the piss out of me if they found out I kicked off about it, but they didn't need to know, did they? I'd sort it out quietly behind the scenes.

I was just about to head off to Japan for the World Cup. I had no time to speak to anyone at the club before I left, but that wasn't a problem. There was plenty of time to put this right. As long as it was replaced before I played for Quins again I'd be happy.

A week or so later I was in Japan and a message arrived on my phone. 'Missing you here, mate, but at least we have this to remind us of you. Good luck this week.' There was a photo of Phil Swainston and Chris Robshaw, posing in front of my giant picture and pissing themselves laughing.

More photos and messages arrived. 'Good luck for the game this week! Looking good back here.' They were ribbing me about my unflattering shorts, pointing at my bulging midriff, commenting on the state of my face, my hair, you name it. There was not one flattering thing you could say about that photo, and the lads really tore me to shreds.

Fuck it, I thought. *I'm gonna call the club right now and ask to have it taken down. I never want to see that picture again. And I don't want anyone else to see it either.*

I called Paul Gustard, Quins' head of rugby and a good mate of mine. 'Guzzy, listen, I won't be coming back to the club post-World Cup.'

'What? Don't tell me you're retiring again?'

'Nah, mate. It's that fucking picture in the changing-room corridor.' I explained how I felt about it and questioned why Graeme Bowerbank, Quins' team manager, had let this happen. 'Is he taking the piss?'

Once I'd finished getting it all off my chest, Guzzy said, 'I'll sort it, mate.'

'Good. Because I mean it. I'm not comin' back to work if that doesn't get removed. If the opposition see it I'm finished. And I don't want any more piss-taking from the lads either.'

The messages from the boys dried up and I forgot all about it while I focused on the World Cup. Months went by and I didn't give it another thought. Even when I was on my way back to Quins for the first time, post-Japan, it didn't enter my head. After all, Guzzy had agreed to sort it out and I trusted him. It was all dealt with, ages ago.

Besides, I had other things on my mind. I was returning to Quins having played in the World Cup final. The fucking World

Cup final! I was still processing it. I'd arrived at this club as a lardy teenager and had gone all the way to that dizzying final in Japan. Ask my 17-year-old self if he ever thought that would be possible and he'd never have believed it. You dream about *going* to the World Cup, never mind making it to the final. It's every professional rugby player's dream. And I'd actually made it a reality.

I'm not normally one for revelling in my success. I prefer to quietly soak it up or just not address it at all. Crack on. You're only as good as your last game and all that. But that day, I have to confess, I felt like a returning hero. OK, we hadn't won the World Cup. What would I have given for that? It was a major disappointment, but I wasn't focusing on that right now. I was focusing on my career and what I'd achieved. Allowing myself a little bask in the glory of Japan, letting my pride bubble away. I could vividly remember being one of pups who would say, 'Look, there's Nick Easter – he played in that fantastic England team of 2003 and here he is playing for Quins!' This was my moment to be on the other side of the fence and I was quietly enjoying the feeling while it lasted.

I wandered down the corridor, minding my own business on my way to the changing rooms, when I suddenly remembered about my new picture. *I wonder what they've gone for?* I was on my way to making 200 appearances for the club, so there were plenty to choose from. Would I be lifting the Premiership trophy? Making a huge tackle? I was sure they'd picked something really impressive this time after all my fuss about it.

I stopped in my tracks and my blood instantly rose. *What the fuck is going on here?* The same horrendous picture of me was still here, in all its hideous glory. I'd just come back from playing in a World Cup final and here I was, looking like I couldn't even get a place in the Old Rubberduckians.

Why's that not gone? I thought. *He promised me he'd sort it.* I went to confront Guzzy. 'I'm really not happy, mate. You promised.'

'Are you really serious?' he giggled. 'This isn't like you. Turned into a bit of a diva in Japan, have you? Been to the World Cup final and think you can come back and boss it?'

'It's not a joke! That picture needs to go and you said you'd sort it.'

He was still laughing. 'But that's how you look, mate. Maybe you should work harder to get in better nick?'

I was trying hard not to completely lose it. 'Look, I just want a different picture. No professional rugby player in the world would want to look that bad, especially when the picture is the first thing the opposition see when they head to the tunnel.'

It was only when I threatened once again not to come back to work if the picture stayed up that Guzzy took me seriously. Even so, it took a further two weeks of nagging and threats from me before he finally sorted it out.

'All done,' he told me, in a tone that made clear how ridiculous he thought this all was. 'Everyone will forget it was ever there. Hope you're happy now.'

'Thank you,' I said. I was desperate to check out which picture they'd gone for to replace it but we were training in Guildford that day. I'd have to wait for the weekend for the great unveiling.

When Saturday came and I arrived at the Stoop I walked down the corridor to have a look. *Thank God this is finally sorted,* I thought. *It's gone on long enough.*

I couldn't believe my eyes. *What the fuck?* Instead of a shiny new picture of me looking heroic and at the top of my game like all my teammates, there was nothing but a gaping hole in the wall. It wasn't a plain old hole either. It looked like someone had wrenched my poster off with a crowbar, leaving a nasty great mess and crumbling bits of plasterboard on display. It stood out like a sore thumb in the otherwise pristine wall of images.

Inevitably, the hole in the wall attracted another load of unwelcome attention. 'Where's that picture of you gone?' the boys asked, raising their eyebrows. Of course they started ripping the piss out of me all over again. 'You've changed, mate.'

I was on a hiding to nothing. The hole is still in the wall today, and I'm not saying another word about it. Gavin Henson would not have stood for it, but I know when I'm beat.

*

Image matters to a rugby player. We all need to feel confident in our own skin and the hardest men of rugby are known for being supremely self-possessed. Not only do they look physically invincible, they play as if they have no fear of pain or injury. Their reputation alone is enough to set the opponents' teeth on edge.

Look at Julian White, my all-time hard-man hero. One of the biggest and most powerful props the game has ever seen, he never once flinched in the face of conflict and was notorious for his formidable punches. His right-handers were so jaw-dropping that videos of them were posted on YouTube. I watched them in awe when I was a teenager, imagining what it would be like to come up against the great man. I loved it when White was playing for

Leicester and Sale's Andrew Sheridan boldly threw the first punch against him back in 2009. White swiftly retaliated, knocking Sheridan flat on his arse with one clean blow. His physical presence was incredible, the power of his punch unbelievable.

How good would it be to be knocked out by Julian White? I always thought. *I'd love to be in one of those video clips!* Of course, I never thought I'd get the chance. It was a teenage pipe dream, a little fantasy I allowed myself as I tucked into my bacon butties on a Saturday morning, laptop balanced on my knee.

When Quins were playing Leicester in a 2011 'A League' final we were expecting them to put out their youngsters like me, as it was a reserve team league, designed to help the development of young players. However, they clearly wanted to win the final and decided to field several senior players. When I looked at the team sheet I did a double-take. There was Julian White's name, in black and white.

The hairs on the back of my neck stood up. I couldn't believe I was going to get the chance to play against one of my all-time heroes. I was 20 years old and this was terrifying but incredibly exciting, all at the same time. *This is it,* I told myself. *My big chance to become the next victim of the legendary Julian White. Bring it on!*

I knew what I was going to do. My bold plan was to antagonise him as much as possible so that he snapped and knocked me out with the biggest punch of his life. One that would be the Julian White punch of all punches, the most viewed YouTube video of them all.

We went into a ruck early in the first half and I saw my chance. Steeling myself, I got hold of his hair and gave it a pull. Not enough to rip it out, just enough for that 'ooh, you bastard' response. I was bracing myself, waiting for his reaction, but he didn't even seem to notice me. My blood was up now. I wanted him to react so badly and I did it again and again, getting bolder each time. Still I got no response at all and I was getting impatient.

In the second half I decided to up the ante. The next time we were in a ruck I gave him a shove when he wasn't looking. Still no response. What the fuck?

I was looking at the clock. Only about ten minutes to go. I had to up my game even more if I was going to stand any chance at all of muscling into the Julian White YouTube hall of fame. I knew he was nearing the end of his rugby career and his sights were set on devoting more of his time to his sheep farm. I knew I might not have another crack at this.

We went into a maul and I saw my opportunity, grabbing him by the collar. He half-cocked, preparing for a punch, and my pulse raced. This was it. My moment had come. I was going to be punched by the hardest man in rugby.

Julian White looked me straight in the eye. I looked back at him, bracing myself once more and goading him to do it. My eyes were on his legendary fist, willing it to fly at my face, just like he'd done with Andrew Sheridan and so many others. But it didn't. White started to slowly take his hand down. I was still staring into his eyes, trying to read what he was thinking. He looked back at me, his hard man expression telling me, *Don't, mate. I don't wanna do it. You're a kid. I'm fed up of all you youngsters trying to provoke me. I can't be bothered with you.*

He turned his back and that was it. I got no jab, not even a bit of a slap. I was bitterly disappointed, and you can't often say that about not getting punched in the face.

★

A hard-man reputation for a player adds to the fear factor. It can intimidate the life out of you. And this kind of image is the reason I quickly learned to embrace my nickname Psycho as a kid when I was playing for Eastbourne Sharks. I could see what a difference it made on the pitch. Not just to how I played, but also how the boys on the other team looked at me.

The nickname hid a multitude of sins. My opponents had no idea that I was a novice who didn't have a clue what he was doing. A kid who was lacking in self-esteem because he was fat and couldn't run as fast as the more athletic boys. A child who never for one second thought he would shine on the pitch and would have been happy just to have some fun on a Sunday morning then go home and watch the telly.

Hearing me called Psycho made my opponents think I was a crazy, violent player. It scared them and I loved that reaction. What young rugby player wouldn't?

One day our coach Will Stadler said he was getting us all shirts printed up, with our names on the back.

'Really? That's a fantastic idea,' I said. 'So mine will say ...'

'Psycho, of course. That's your name.'

'Great. Just checking.' I was really looking forward to having my nickname emblazoned on my back. I always loved it before a match, when the opposition heard me being called Psycho on the sidelines and I could see the fear sparking up in their eyes before we even kicked off. I had the psychological advantage before the whistle blew, and having a shirt with my name on would really ram my reputation home. It would announce me as the Julian White of Eastbourne Sharks.

I was buzzing with excitement when the shirts arrived and the coach began to dish them out. I couldn't wait to tear mine out of the packet and put it on. 'Here's yours, Psycho.'

I took it eagerly and ripped the wrapper off. Then I did a double-take. My heart sank. '*Physco*? What's that all about?'

'What do you mean?' Will said. 'It says Psycho.'

'No, it doesn't. You've spelled out P-H-Y-S-C-O.'

'Is that not how you spell Psycho?'

I was staring open-mouthed at our coach. He was a man I looked up to, but in that moment I felt bitterly let down. How could he fail to correctly spell a simple word like Psycho?

There was the fear factor gone, just like that. I refused to wear the shirt, but reputational damage had already been done. I wasn't going to be the next Julian White, but even at that age I understood the value of at least attempting to create the illusion of being the hardest player on the pitch.

★

The gym is where today's rugby players carve out their image and reputation. Kyle Sinckler is a monster, a freak of nature. He has tiny calves. They're non-existent. Yet he headed our squats leaderboard at Quins, pushing 230 kilos. Everyone stopped and clapped and cheered him on, like we do when anyone goes for their personal best. The atmosphere was giddy, and the strength and conditioning coach had to intervene and tell us to get back to work.

Sink works his tits off in the gym to be the best he can and he's also the most fanatical player I know when it comes to recovery. It's no wonder he's one of the best in the world in his position. His house is a shrine to recuperation: infrared sauna and lights, hot tub in the garden, pressurised recovery pumps that you squeeze round your legs, a single-man hyperbaric chamber. He's got something so specialised I don't even know what it's called. It's a weird kind of tent that you stand up in to help your muscles recover.

He'd come into training and complain about being a bit knackered, but I'm not surprised. It's probably because he's spent six hours doing recovery when he could have been sitting in front of the TV doing nothing.

The backs always compete for the best-looking abs rather than the heaviest weight-lifts, and some forwards are just as vain. Our gym mirrors at Quins were taken out because the Flash Harrys were always checking out their physiques and posing. Danny Care, flicking his hair. Chris Robshaw, pulling a comb out of his back pocket like he's Kenickie in *Grease*. Ugo Monye, smoothing down his eyebrows. Mind you, I've even seen him do that going into a huddle on the pitch.

Cheers for that, lads. I need the mirrors to check on technique. I want to see if the lines are correct when I'm squatting and bench-pressing. You have to get it right when you're bench-pressing 200 kilos or deadlifting 300 kilos. But now I can't because the pretty boys abused the privilege of the mirrors.

It's rough on forwards like me. We don't want to prance and preen; we just want to get the work done. Bulk comes before beauty, especially for the front rowers. Which is just as well, I guess. One time I was lying down, bench-pressing, when a 50-kilo dumbbell slipped out of my hand and landed square on my nose. The croissant was crushed. It hurt like hell and I saw stars, but it wasn't a huge deal, aesthetically speaking. I break my nose every year, just not normally with a 50-kilo weight I've dropped on my own face.

*

After Japan, Jonathan Ross invited me, Tom Curry, Ben Youngs and Manu Tuilagi onto his show. I was tickled pink. Daisy and I are huge fans and have watched it for years. 'Great, bring it on. Anything I need to know? What do I wear?'

'Smart Saturday-night attire. No logos, stripes or checks.'

Perfect. That's easy.

Tom and Ben were already there when I arrived at the TV studios. I was feeling excited. I might enjoy being in the shadows on the pitch, but it doesn't mean I don't like to pop into the spotlight from time to time. I was loving the chance to do something different, as well as texting my mates to tell them I was going to meet Nicole Scherzinger, who was also on the show, because I like to piss them off and make them jealous.

Tom had been out shopping with his agent and was looking sharp in brand new trousers, blazer and a Vivienne Westwood shirt. All very befitting of a suave and athletic flanker. Ben was on point too, rocking a smart shirt and blue tailored jacket. And then there was me.

The production assistant looked me up and down. 'Do you need anything pressed?'

'What d'you mean?'

She nodded towards the suit bag I was holding. 'Do your clothes for the show need pressing?'

'Oh. Are you saying you want me to wear a tuxedo?'

'I'm sorry?'

'That's what's in the suit bag. I wasn't planning to wear it on the show. I've brought that for a charity do I'm going to afterwards.'

'Oh, I see. But what about your clothes for the show? What are you wearing?'

I patted my chest. 'What I've got on. I thought I'd come ready, make it easy.'

She looked me up and down again. I was dressed in a pair of dark shorts, a white T-shirt and a pair of brown Doc Martens. Exactly what I'd wear on a Saturday evening at my local, although to meet the 'smart' requirement in the brief I'd ironed the T-shirt and chucked on a black gilet. I like a gilet. I get too hot in long-sleeved jackets and why not show off my tattoos?

'So you don't have an alternative?'

I could see her mind was racing. Would they have anything in wardrobe they could change me into? She cast her eyes over my bulky frame and I could see panic rising because rugby players are the most difficult buggers in the world to kit out. Will Carling once said he couldn't cross his legs because his thighs were too muscly. I can identify. Trousers have to be bought specially. He could only wear Armani, apparently. I go to High and Mighty and buy Jacamo trousers if I have to, but it's much easier to stick with shorts.

It's not just the bottom half that's a struggle. 'Why are you wearing your wife's top?' people say when I'm trying to get away with a new T-shirt that doesn't come in any bigger sizes. 'Did that shrink in the wash, mate?'

Even the England cap doesn't fit the average rugby player, which is quite some design flaw. Every time a player is capped it's the same old joke. He puts the cap on his head because that's what's expected of him during the presentation, and everyone laughs because it's too small so he snatches it off as quickly as he can. Isn't that hilarious? No! Stop laughing and just make 'em bigger!

The production assistant told me that nobody had been on the show in shorts before. Not unless you counted Sandra Bullock or Pixie Lott, who both had the legs to pull it off. She disappeared in a bit of a flap, saying she needed to talk to her boss.

Meanwhile, Manu arrived. I greeted him with a big smile. He was wearing a traditional flowery Samoan shirt, flip-flops and a necklace of red flowers, all in honour of his heritage.

'Mate, you look amazing,' I told him. Privately, I was giggling to myself and thinking, *Sweet. She's gonna forget all about me and my boring black shorts when she clocks Manu.*

I didn't say anything to him about the conversation I'd just had. Manu's characteristic death stare tells you he'd snap your neck in half if you said the wrong thing to him, and I didn't want to invoke that. Who would take any chances with pissing Manu off? Besides, he really did look amazing. I just wasn't sure *The Jonathan Ross*

Show would agree, as it wasn't exactly your standard smart-casual Saturday-night look, was it?

The production assistant reappeared.

I saw her look Manu up and down, the question *Is that what you're wearing?* resting unsaid on her lips. There was a momentary pause and I wondered how she was going to tackle this. 'Are you all ready too?' she said with a smile. 'Oh, you look *brilliant!*'

My shorts and T-shirt were in the clear now, obviously. Funnily enough, Manu wasn't even planning on wearing the flip-flops or the floral shirt on the show. He'd brought a cool white shirt and white trainers to change into. But I reckon they'd have let him on naked, covering his manhood with just a rugby ball, if that's what he said he wanted to do.

★

Being mistaken for a thug or a mad man is an occupational hazard of the professional rugby player. It's always going to happen when you pick up black eyes, cuts, bruises and swollen lips every time you go to work. Monday mornings are the biggest flash point. You look your worst after a weekend game, and people cross the street to avoid you. I hate to see it. I want to tell them I'm a big softie really, but you have to let it go.

'You a professional fighter?' I've been asked many times by a doorman, on a night out. 'You UFC, mate? Just so I know to avoid you, if it goes tits up.' I suck it up and crack on. What else can you do? As long as I'm not actually frightening someone, I go with the flow.

Some players make a big effort to spruce up their image. Chris Robshaw's one of the biggest advocates of male grooming you could come across. He works tirelessly to hide his battle scars and present a civilised face to the world. He's got it down to such a fine art that GQ magazine even made him one of their Grooming Awards judges a couple of years ago.

'So, England Playahhh, what's all this?' I say, nosing through his shelf in the changing room as I replace my solitary can of deodorant. Sun cream, moisturiser, hair products galore. Oh, there's the Kenickie comb …'

'Oh, Joe. It's important to look one's best. Little things make all the difference, you know.'

Danny Care, always on point, is exactly the same. 'What's that?' I said to him one time, when we were sharing a room.

'Veet. Great for hair removal, mate,' he replied enthusiastically.

'Hair *removal*? Where from?'

I'm not knocking the boys for taking grooming to the next level. If that's what makes you tick, all well and good. Some boys love the attention, and apart from anything else there are sponsorship deals and your post-retirement career to think about nowadays. Just ask James Haskell. Nobody was surprised when the man who'd once posed semi-naked with a load of French rugby players for a book called *Dieux du Stade* – Gods of the Stadium – ended up on *I'm a Celebrity*. The jungle shower had had his name on it for years.

By contrast, my name was on a McDonald's chip. They asked me to do a Free Fries Friday advert, based on the premise that I was 'hard and crispy on the outside and soft and fluffy on the inside' – just like McDonald's fries. The nutritionist at Quins wasn't happy with me. 'Listen,' I said. 'I'm not endorsing a junk-food diet.

We're all allowed the odd packet of chips, as long as it's in moderation. What else am I gonna do? I'm not exactly the next Diet Coke man or the new Calvin Klein underwear model, am I?'

Daisy questioned me too, but you've got to provide for the family while you can because who knows how long this is going to last? As Jason Leonard said to me all those years ago, 'You're a long time retired.' Besides, I'd quite like more people to know that I really am soft and fluffy on the inside because it isn't exactly apparent, is it?

Before our disastrous World Cup performance in 2015, the *Daily Telegraph* ran an article entitled TEN BEAUTY TIPS FROM THE ENGLAND RUGBY TEAM. It started with the ominous line: 'While we don't want to damage the 2015 squad's rugby field credentials, we have it on good authority that England's World Cup contenders are also a grooming force to be reckoned with …'

The paper had dug up all kinds of clean, from all the usual suspects. Robbo talking about moisturising, Danny Care championing Bio-Oil for scars. James Haskell popping his head above the dressing table to confess to using an ex-girlfriend's 'moisturiser', only to wake up on the day of an England game with an orange tan. Even Ben Youngs was mentioned, rating Palmer's Cocoa Butter for soft skin.

Fucking hell, boys – we're fighting a World Cup here! What kind of image are you trying to give out? Do you think Martin Johnson put Cocoa Butter on his arse in 2003? No, he didn't – and he didn't get booted out in the pool stages either. We're not male models, we're rugby players, and you've got to send out the right message to the opposition.

Some boys get sucked into it by their wives or girlfriends. I sympathise with that because we all want to please our partners, don't we? We once had a Northern Irish tighthead prop at Quins called John Andress. When he showed up for training one day something was different, but we couldn't work out what. 'What have you done, mate? New trim? What is it?'

He wouldn't say. And then someone finally got it. 'Your eyebrows! You've dyed your eyebrows!'

He was getting married and he explained that his bride-to-be wanted his near-invisible eyebrows to be dark for the wedding and photos. The trouble was, they were jet black on his pale Irish skin, and once you'd seen them you couldn't stop looking. They stood out like a couple of angry slugs.

Still, he stepped up to the plate better than I did on my wedding day.

'What are you doing?' Daisy asked.

'Ironing a shirt.'

'Why? You hate wearing shirts.'

'I know, but it's our wedding day. I thought I'd put a shirt on.'

She looked at her watch. 'We're gonna be late. Just put whatever's ready on. Let's go.'

I did as I was told and got in the car. This was a big day. I was already nervous and I didn't want anything to go wrong.

The registry office was a converted old people's home in a small town not far from our home in Heathfield. When we arrived we realised two things. Firstly, the insulation was wonderful if you were 90 and struggling with the cold. Secondly, we needed a couple of witnesses, as we had no guests apart from Jasper, who was 18 months old. 'I'll go and find someone,' I volunteered.

Even though it was November I was sweating my tits off, on account of my jangling nerves as well as the incredible insulation system. I peeled my jacket off as I headed outside and asked a couple of friendly-looking passers-by if they wouldn't mind doing the honours and witnessing our marriage.

They declined, straight away.

'But I'm about to get married and we need two witnesses. Would you not be willing to help us out?'

'Sorry, we're very busy today.'

I was surprised. Daisy and I had thought this would be easy. If someone had come up to us in the street outside a registry office we'd have said, 'Brilliant! Of course.' But it wasn't like that at all.

I approached every single person walking down the road. 'Sorry, mate. Love to help but can't stop.' 'Sorry, got to dash.' 'Really sorry, but no, we can't, not today.'

Why was everyone so unwilling to help a man on his wedding day? The clock was ticking now. I didn't know the town and started running haphazardly around the streets and into shops, asking anyone and everyone.

The shoppers in Waitrose backed away. Same in Morrisons. That's when I started to think about how I looked. Not only was I sweating like a pig, I'd been training at Quins the day before and had a couple of cuts and bruises. Nothing out of the ordinary, but to the average man or woman in the street I looked like I'd been in a bar brawl. I'm normally much more aware of this, but clearly I had other things on my mind that day.

I darted into a working men's club. *Great! There's a bloke at the bar.* When I got closer I realised he wasn't sitting at the bar. He was slumped on it.

Fucking hell, it's only 11am! We were desperate, but not that desperate.

Finally, I stumbled on a community centre, where I could see four ladies sitting down together, chatting and drinking tea. I didn't want to scare them off so I ran and got Daisy. 'This could be our last chance,' I said. 'You ask them. Hopefully they'll look at your bump and go, "Poor girl."'

Not an ideal scenario, hoping strangers will look at your pregnant bride-to-be with pity on her wedding day, but that's how it was. It worked, thankfully. The four lovely ladies walked with us back up the road to the registry office and sat with Jasper during the ceremony.

It was wonderful. Simple and quiet, exactly as we wanted it to be. I even shed a few tears. Daisy was my wife at long last, and I loved her so much. She didn't judge me on my looks. She had supported me so loyally and was the loveliest person in the world. I was a very lucky man.

We had just one photograph taken that day. When I looked at it I cringed at first and then did a double-take. An embarrassing truth dawned on me. The fact that I looked like I'd been in a bar brawl was not the only reason I'd struggled to find witnesses in the street.

The T-shirt I'd chosen in haste was a hideous shade of phlegm-green. No other way to describe it. Snotty green. Who would believe I was getting married to the love of my life when I looked like that? I had to be a crazy con artist pretending he needed a witness for his wedding. Obviously, I was going to bludgeon some poor sucker over the head and steal his wallet, wasn't I? You really couldn't blame anyone for backing away from me that day.

At least I learned a lesson from that experience. Image matters. However you are built and whatever looks you have been given, there are times in your life when you need to put yourself in somebody else's shoes and see yourself as they do.

Which takes me back to the cuddly teddy bear poster on the wall at Quins. Daisy might not judge me on my looks, bless her, but the opposition would, every time, and that's why I kicked up such a fuss. I'm not a diva, just a guy who knows very well how a rugby player's mind works and how much difference it can make if you look like a psychotic hard man, even if really you're all soft and fluffy on the inside.

10

RITUALS

It's a tradition that you sing a song to the other boys in the England squad when you get your first cap. Usually this happens after the game on the team bus, so you can use the microphone, and something cheesy and fairly easy to sing, like 'Build Me Up Buttercup' by the Foundations, is usually the way to go. I'd heard the stories. Without exception you're met with a tirade of abuse – called a wanker and a prick and told to sit down. You just have to take it. Every player goes through it. It's a rite of passage and a ritual that provides a bit of entertainment for the team. The boys lap it up, united in their relief that they have gone through this charade already and someone else is getting it in the neck this time round.

I was going to make my England debut against South Africa in 2012, when I was 21. It's hard being the youngster in the squad. You're at the front of the bus, everything to prove. I was determined to make my mark and hold my head high.

In the two weeks running up to the match I was thinking about the song I'd sing on the team bus more than my scrummaging.

I'd decided I didn't just want to muddle through a cheesy number. I wanted to take the boys by surprise, deliver a quality performance. One they might remember and that would hopefully make them think, *Ooh, we underestimated this one. Who'd have thought he had it in him?*

I chose one of my all-time favourite songs, and ten days before my debut I started practising it in front of the mirror in my bedroom. It wasn't the easiest song to sing and I wanted it to be pitch perfect.

'Nervous about your England debut, mate?' friends would ask.

'Not particularly, but I'm shitting myself about singing in front of my teammates.'

I don't think anyone believed me when I said I wasn't nervous about my debut, but it was true. 'Believe in yourself, son,' Jason Leonard had told me all those years earlier. 'Never forget, you're 'ere because you're good enough.' It was excellent advice – something I now pass on to the youngsters I mentor – and I'd clutched it to my chest.

I still had niggling worries about my ability, of course I did. What if I had an absolute stinker on the day and never got selected again? That would be horrendous, but I couldn't think like that. I'd set myself a target. I wanted to earn 23 caps because that would be one more than Tim Payne, who'd previously played in my position for England.

In moments when self-doubt crept in I made myself focus on the positive, the successes I'd had. I'd secured my place as a regular starter for Quins and was really making a name for myself. We'd won the European Challenge Cup and the Premiership, and I was being talked about because I was mobile for a prop, which was unusual then. It's changing now, as more demands are put on players, but I was raising the bar, and with it a few eyebrows. Who'd have thought it? Me, mobile? But at that young age I was as fit and lithe as I'd ever been, ever would be again. I sweated like a pig in the gym, pushing myself to my limits, and my body was working and moving exactly as I wanted it to. I wasn't just a fat lad who was good at pushing. I was putting my hand up to carry the ball and make a tackle. I was proving my worth, attracting attention from the press not just for my crazy haircuts but because I was getting in people's faces, playing abrasive and aggressive rugby, upsetting the apple cart each week.

I could do rugby. I knew that. I had proof of it. But singing? I like a bit of karaoke but I had no experience of performing on my own like this. It was a big deal, and that was why I'd been serenading myself in the privacy of my bedroom for ten long days. I could always hold a tune, but I knew I had to practise like mad if I was to have any chance at all of pulling this off the way I wanted to.

I was making my debut at the famous Kings Park Stadium in Durban on 9 June 2012. Being on the world stage was exhilarating and terrifying, all at once. Daisy was in the crowd, along with several members of the family. I wanted to make everyone proud.

My memories of the experience now involve the feelings and sounds more than the details of the day itself. When I walked out on the pitch my heart was thumping in my chest. There were 50,000 fans in the stadium and the sound was so deafening it coursed through every nerve in my body. *What the fuck is this?* I was overwhelmed, not quite able to grasp that this was actually happening to me, the fat kid at school. The troublemaker with the mohawk.

In the build-up to the match I'd been thinking about my old Sharks coach Will Stadler, and how fantastic it was that I was playing this match at the home of the actual Sharks. As my first ever coach he'd been so influential in my career and it seemed so fitting that I was making my debut in his native South Africa.

When I started to sing 'God Save the Queen' I was trying hard not to cry. Being here, dressed in an England jersey, felt like a dream. A surreal fantasy. *How the fuck was I here?* The question was screaming round my head.

★

I hadn't arrived in the England team via the conventional route, that's for sure. I'd never even set out to be a rugby player, let alone play for my country. Some kids sacrifice their childhood to rugby, hoping they might be able to make a career of it, but it wasn't like that for me. More a series of happy accidents and fortunate turns of fate.

Even once I was playing rugby every week for Eastbourne Sharks and loving it, I never thought further ahead than the next match. Why would I? As if a lardy, lazy lad like me could be a sportsman for his actual job? It never entered my head.

From Sharks I moved up to Haywards Heath RFC Under-16s and started going to county trials with my mates, who were all much more into rugby and far more committed than I was. I didn't want to miss out, though, and that was the main reason I went along. I loved the game and if I could play at a higher level, along with my mates, why not try?

At one county trial, when I was 14, I was spotted by a scout from Quins called Collin Osborne. He invited me along to some training sessions with the club. I agreed, flattered to be asked by such a prestigious club, though at the same time I was thinking, *Fuck, what about the security guard who threw me out? What if he finds out it's me?*

Happily, the training would take place at the old Quins training ground at Aldershot Barracks, so there was no danger of me being identified as the foul-mouthed kid who tried to jump the barriers and nick the grass off the pitch.

I still had zero expectations of where rugby might take me, which was probably just as well because when I walked into the first training session I felt instantly out of place. I was the odd one out. I didn't belong or fit in. I felt that very acutely.

The other boys who'd been scouted had been playing the game since they were small boys, and most of them went to private schools that had first-rate rugby teams. Meanwhile, what had I done? Played football at school and fallen into rugby by chance. In the end I came to think of it as a bus trip to Aldershot Barracks, a good training session every month or so and a bit of kudos from being able to say I'd been scouted by Quins. That's all it was to me. No more, no less.

The sessions petered out after a while, which I wasn't too bothered about. Quins scouted boys all the time, most much more suited to the club than I was. It had been made very clear to me from the start that I shouldn't get my hopes up, as only a tiny percentage of players broke through. And when it ended I thought no more of it.

It wasn't until I dropped out of sixth-form college, on account of the fact I never got further than the common room every day, that I started to seriously think about my future. I was mowing grass for my uncle's turfing firm. Sixteen years old and going nowhere, except up and down a field on a solitary lawnmower. I had all the time in the world to think, and rugby was where my mind kept going. What else was I going to do? What did I have to lose?

Five months into my lawn-mowing career, I plucked up the courage to write to Collin Osborne. *Dear Mr Osborne, I'm not at college anymore. I've started turfing for my uncle and I wonder if you could recommend any teams that are a good level and I could play for in Sussex …*

I was fishing, wasn't I? It was my way of saying, 'Please, Sir, remember me?' Mr Osborne's response was gold dust. He explained that Quins were starting a new apprenticeship programme in partnership with Richmond College. It was for 16- and 17-year-olds who were half good at rugby but not quite there yet. They would go to college two days a week to do a BTEC or a vocational qualification, and on the other three days they'd train at the Quins academy. This was Mr Osborne's brainchild. He was an ex-teacher and had always been very clear that boys had to have an education to fall back on, whether they made it as a professional rugby player or not. 'Would you be interested?'

Interested? It sounded fucking incredible! 'Yes, Mr Osborne, I definitely would be interested. But it would be quite a trek from Heathfield to Twickenham every day …'

'No, you silly sod, you'd have to live up here. We'd get you some digs near the ground.' The whirlwind had begun.

I never got the BTEC, I'm sorry to say. A few months in and Mr Osborne had to reluctantly concede that further education didn't agree with me. This time I rarely got as far as the common room, let alone the classroom. I stayed in bed on college days, hiding under the duvet, counting the hours until I could play rugby again. That's when Mr Osborne very generously agreed to let me become a full-time academy player, and I signed my first professional rugby contract. Seventeen years old and I was on my way.

*

Now here I was, four years later, about to make my England debut. *How unbelievable is this?*

Remembering the match is like trying to relive a dream. It's a muddled blur in my head, a crazy, heady mixture of players and fans, noise and sweat and raging adrenaline. The Springboks played an incredibly intense, physical game. They always do. It's in their DNA. It was carnage, that's how it felt. We were pumped. I was sweating my head off. We lost the game 22–17.

Despite the result, it had been an absolutely brilliant battle. I'd held my own, which was a massive result. It had been an incredible experience, one huge adrenaline buzz that I desperately wanted to repeat if I was lucky enough to get the chance. But whatever happened next, I'd earned my first cap and nobody could ever take that away from me.

Now that the game was over, my next challenge awaited. It was time for me to step out of my comfort zone like never before and sing the song I'd been rehearsing like mad.

When my big moment came when we were driving along a South African highway, and I could feel my hands shaking when I took hold of the mic. Just as I'd expected, this was infinitely more nerve-wracking than running out in an England jersey to the sound of 50,000 fervent rugby fans. *Fucking hell, I'd rather be pumped in a scrum. I'd rather break my nose and have my ears pulled off by a giant South African.*

'What you singin', mate?'

I looked down the coach at the boys. All eyes were on me and I could see by their faces what most of them were thinking, *Let's see what this gobby little shit's gonna come up with. He likes giving it the big 'un on the pitch – let's see what he's really made of!*

As the new boy in the squad I respected where I was in the pecking order on this tour, which meant trying not to 'give it the big 'un' when I was off the pitch. All through the training camp and the tour I'd followed protocol, taking the lead from the seniors and keeping my gob shut more than I naturally would.

'Wait and see,' I said meekly, my voice croaking.

I scanned the players. Rugby bus etiquette is just the same as it's been on the school bus for years: young pups at the front, cool kids and leaders of the pack at the back. I could see Jonny May at the front grinning at me, loving the drama and egging me on. Jonny had flown out late to replace the injured George Lowe and was yet to make his first cap. As the two newbies we'd been sitting together, or more like clinging together, because we didn't really know anyone else.

I cleared my throat and tested the mic. Then, after a little dramatic pause, I took a deep breath and started up.

Total silence fell on the bus. *What's going on? Why's this young prop singing a ballad? What the fuck?*

I carried on unperturbed.

It's Adele. Why the fuck is this little wanker singing Adele?

Though I say so myself, all my painstaking rehearsals were paying off and I was delivering Adele's 'Someone Like You' well. I was doing what I set out to – taking the boys by surprise. Maybe even impress them.

'Sit down, you prick! Shut up, you little wanker!'

I wasn't allowing them to get to me. It was the opposite. I was letting rip now, really giving it all I had. Eyes closed, feeling every note.

'Sit the fuck down! This is shit! Why you singin' Adele, you prick?'

Even though I was delivering the song well I wasn't surprised in the slightest by the tirade of criticism. I knew the drill, and I wasn't going to let the abuse put me off. I carried on without missing a beat, letting the insults and empty plastic water bottles fly over my head. I'd practised the whole song and the whole song was what the boys were going to get. I gave it everything I had until I hit the very last note.

I took a breath and looked around. *Smashed it!* I thought. I'd delivered the song exactly how I wanted to and I hadn't let the boys put me off. I thanked my unruly audience and sat down feeling very relieved. *Thank God that's over,* I thought. So what if they thought it was weird for a young rugby player to croon his way through Adele? I'd have been disappointed if I hadn't got that reaction.

Tom Waldrom had to provide the music next. He'd been dreading it and I felt for him. This is the same guy who's so shy that, when his son Troy came to him complaining that his tennis teacher kept calling him Steve instead of Troy, Tom's response was: 'Look, I know your name's Troy, son, and that's all that matters.' He preferred to let it go rather than have to speak to the tennis teacher. To his credit, Waldrom got up and did a very decent rendition of 'Yellow Submarine', which was no mean feat. The poor guy got the same abuse as I had during his performance, and he couldn't wait to get to the last line and sit back down as quickly as possible. It must have been one hell of an ordeal for him.

There was still half an hour to go on the bus when all the singing was done. It had been a long journey and now things had gone a bit flat. We had no more entertainment lined up and there wasn't much of a vibe going on. I started looking around and thinking, *What now?*

Then I had an idea. I knew Jonny was brilliant at doing 'Ice Ice Baby' by Vanilla Ice. He knew all the words off by heart. I'd heard him do it a few times and had been really impressed. I nudged him. 'Mate, why don't you get up and sing?'

'What, me?'

'Yeah. We could do with some more entertainment. Everyone's bored now.'

'No, I can't do that. I haven't been capped yet, have I?'

'Don't worry about that. They'd love it if you did your "Ice Ice Baby". You're brilliant at it.'

'Really? Nah!'

'Yeah, they'll love it.'

'No. I can't. You can only sing if you've been capped.'

'Nobody cares about that, mate. You get up there. It's entertaining the crowd. You know it word for word and it'll be fantastic. They'll go mad for it.' I wouldn't let it drop. I nagged him for a good ten minutes before he finally relented.

Jonny didn't make an announcement or tell the boys what he was doing. He simply took the mic and the next thing you knew, there he was, beat-boxing out the track.

Murmurs of 'what the fuck?' started drifting down the bus. The senior players were not happy. This was not on the programme because Jonny May had not yet been capped.

Jonny was three lines in when it became clear that nobody on that bus was prepared to collaborate or listen. All hell broke loose. Plastic cups and bottles rained down on him, chucked from every corner of the bus, far worse than before.

'What the fuck? Who is this kid? We don't know your name! You haven't got a cap!' The abuse was brutal and sustained. 'Fuck off! Who do you think you are? Go and get your cap first! You're not welcome here, you prick!'

Jonny tried to carry on, but he knew when he was beat and he gave up before reaching the end. He came and sat back down next to me, looking at me like I was the biggest traitor in the world.

'You fucker!'

I was trying not to laugh – and failing miserably. 'It's not my fault, mate!' I said, but I knew it was.

'Are you joking? It's all your fault! Why did you make me get up?'

'Make you? You make your own choices, Jonny.'

'Fucking hell! You're the biggest fucking wind-up ever.'

I couldn't believe Jonny had let me talk him into this. I knew how it would go down. How could he not have seen it coming?

He was shaking his head. 'This is going to scar me for ever!'

*

In Japan we spent hours on the England team coach, including the famously slow bus trip to the final, which took longer than it should have because the police escort was too polite to ask traffic to move. I don't think arriving late made any difference to our performance. Eddie didn't either. We were all pumped up to the max anyway. It was just annoying and for me a tad embarrassing.

On that journey I was sitting on the back row, to the right, which is always my place nowadays. I was never one of the cool kids at school, so as soon as I earned the right to sit at the back of the bus, 60 caps into my England career, I embraced it. I don't think you ever get over being a bit of an outcast as a kid and I feel like I've arrived when I sit there with Faz next to me, in the middle, and Courtney next to him. I've finally made it. *Look at me now! Sitting on the back of the bus!*

Dan Cole, who had more caps than any of us and was the second oldest in the squad, was always a couple of seats in front, going against the grain.

'Avoiding me, are ya?' I'd ask.

'No. Just happy here, mate.' That's Coley. Doesn't want to be on the front row of life or the back row of a bus.

In front of Dan were Ben Youngs and Mako Vunipola. Like the rest of the squad, always in the same seat, every single time. I like the ritual of it all. It saves you having to think or make decisions every time you climb aboard. You just get on the bus and go to your seat, like a well-trained homing pigeon.

For a pup, it's tough. You're stuck at the front, realising you have a hell of a long way to travel to get to the back seat, never knowing if you will ever even get that far.

I feel for the youngsters now, doing their first cap song, because I can still remember, very acutely, the anxiety I was suffering back there in South Africa. It's fucking scary. The worse rite of passage imaginable. Of course, that doesn't stop me hurling abuse their way when their time comes. It's tradition, after all.

★

Another tradition when you make your first cap is that you have to have a drink with every other capped player in the squad. They choose your poison and they have to drink exactly the same thing, so if they want to stitch you up with a double absinthe they have to drink it themselves. That's little comfort. With 23 players in a match-day squad you're going to have to take up to 22 drinks.

My turn came after the third game of the South Africa tour, when we still had two matches to play. I was dreading it and looking forward to it at the same time. I love a drink and it was another step on the England ladder, but I didn't want to fuck it up. I wanted to still be standing come the end of the night, and not the subject of a piss-taking story the next day.

When I walked into the bar one of the first players I saw was Geoff Parling. *Fucking hell, what's he gonna go for?* I thought. Seven years my senior, Geoff is a player with a reputation for upholding the old-school drinking values, a stickler for tradition. He is also a man who would happily down a double absinthe in order to make this already dicey ritual as challenging as possible for a youngster like me.

I had a flashback to the last time he'd bought me a drink. It was luminous blue and glowed ominously in the dark, looking more like something you'd pour down the shower to unblock it than tip down your throat. 'Cheers,' I'd said gamely.

I was brand new in the squad then, at a training camp, and there was no way in hell I was going to refuse. It was Geoff Parling's private initiation, wasn't it? I hoped it was just WKD as I drank it, but it wasn't. Of course it wasn't. It tasted toxic and the room started spinning as soon as it hit my stomach. That's where the flashback ends, because I couldn't tell you what happened next.

This time I decided to swerve him, for now. I'd see him later. I went over to James Haskell, who gave me a glass of red. I was enjoying the Malbec and then I had several more glasses, plus a Jack Daniel's or two, with Dan Cole, Ugo Monye, Ben Youngs and Chris Robshaw. I was feeling great, loving celebrating my first cap with this elite group of players and taking part in the decadent rite of passage.

I was so well lubricated that when Geoff finally approached me and handed me a glass of something unrecognisable I accepted my fate unquestioningly.

'Cheers, mate!' I smiled and quickly downed the poison he gave. Like the time before, I couldn't tell you what it was. It was colourful and tasted like mouthwash, that's all I can recall. We were well into the night and I'd had at least a dozen drinks already. I'd been holding it together, just. But as soon as I knocked back Geoff's potion I was done for. Pissed as a fart, inhibitions gone and a lamb to the slaughter, which is exactly the effect Geoff was after.

The commentator Stuart Barnes was across the other side of the bar. Geoff nodded over to him. 'Come and meet him,' he said. Most rugby players don't tend to have great relationships with commentators and I knew Barnes had a reputation for possessing a sharp tongue.

'What? You're joking, aren't you? I'm pissed.'

Geoff had a glint in his eye. One that told me he was looking to have some fun. 'Don't worry about that. It's your first-cap night. Listen, I'm gonna give you a dare.'

'What?'

'Come over and meet Stuart Barnes. And when you've said hello and nice to meet you, I dare you to call him a helmet.'

'What the fuck? No way!'

Geoff was insistent. 'It's a dare. You have to accept it.'

There wasn't any logic in his argument. Nowhere in the rules of rugby tradition was it written that you were obliged to accept dares from senior players when under the influence. However, logic had been lost in the bottom of at least 13 glasses.

I allowed Geoff to steer me over to meet Stuart Barnes. 'Stuart, this is Joe Marler.'

'Hello, pleased to meet you,' said Barnes.

I stood there grinning like an idiot.

'Can I help you?'

'I just wanted to say it's nice to meet you and also ...' Geoff was willing me to go on and the Dutch courage had kicked in. 'I also just wanted to call you a helmet.'

A flabbergasted expression flashed onto Barnes's face and I immediately turned on my heel, not wanting to hang around for his response.

Geoff was loving this and I was finding it much funnier than I ought to. 'Fucking hell!' I giggled. 'Did I just call Stuart Barnes a helmet?'

Geoff didn't reply. He was scanning the bar to find my next victim. 'Steve Walsh!' he declared. 'Now you have to do the same thing to Steve Walsh.'

'He's a ref. I can't do that,' I said unconvincingly. I'd got a taste for this now. I was laughing and feeling like a naughty kid, going back into the kitchen to grab another biscuit when I knew I shouldn't. *Fuck it,* I thought. *What have I got to lose?* Even at that young age my reputation wasn't great among the refereeing community.

I staggered over and cut straight to the chase this time. 'Hello. Good to see you. Can I just say, I think you're a helmet.'

'Pardon?'

'Sorry, gotta go. All the best. Bye!' Again, I scooted off before hearing the reaction. However, the following year Steve Walsh was the ref in our Six Nations Grand Slam shambles against Wales. Oh dear. I was on the wrong side of him from the first minute of the match, giving away penalties as Adam Jones bent me in two. I guess it serves me right. It was such a fucking catastrophe of a game for me. Maybe I'd made my own misfortune. Who knows?

I look back now and cringe at how I behaved with Geoff. It was so childish, and we were the ones being helmets, not anybody else. Having said that, the drinking tradition had served its purpose well, because really the first-cap rituals are all about bonding and team-building. Geoff and I laughed about it for years afterwards. Just as Jonny and I can look back and laugh about his performance of 'Ice Ice Baby'.

Well, at least I can …

★

Some players are seriously superstitious, indulging in no end of pre-match rituals that they feel will improve their performance on the day, while others prefer a minimum of fuss. Everyone has a different way of getting prepped for a game.

I've tried a few rituals in my time. Going out last was one. I gave up on that, as it had no positive influence on my performance whatsoever. Always taking a drop goal at the end of the warm-up was another. That stopped when I hit an unsuspecting spectator in the face while she was trying to eat a pie on a cold Friday night away at Sale Sharks. Now I just put my socks on the wrong feet and crack on.

Some boys chill to music, others play games on their phone or do every stretch under the sun as their routine preparation. I thought I'd seen it all until I was in the changing room at Twickenham, getting ready for an autumn international against South Africa in 2014. I bent down to put my boots on and when I looked up

I clocked Dave Attwood – the 6 foot 7 and 19-stone second-row man mountain – sitting in his pants, one leg crossed over the other as he filed his fingernails. Each to their own, I guess, but how can you prepare to go up against the most physical team in world rugby by giving yourself a manicure?

There was a Quins player who always refused to wipe his bum when he went to the toilet before a game. I was absolutely horrified. Not least because I've endured a few smelly arse moments in my time, holding players at crotch-height in line-outs or encountering a stinky backside in a maul and wondering – out loud – when the offending player had last had a shower.

'That's horrible!' I said to my teammate, wrinkling my nose in disgust. 'What the fuck would you do that for?'

'Ring sting,' he said very seriously. 'I don't want to get ring sting.' He refused to change because he was convinced it would be bad luck to stop his dirty habit.

In New Zealand, the night before the first Lions Test, the Welsh players went in search of fish and chips, which I thought was odd. 'You mean proper greasy fish and chips?' I asked.

'Yes, the nearest we can find to what we can get at home.'

'Why on earth would you eat fish and chips before a game?'

The night before a match most players – myself included – go for a bit of carb-loading. Chicken wraps, spag bol – it's the carbs that are important, as they are what will fuel you the next day. No professional rugby player eats a load of fatty, greasy food on the eve of a big game. At least I didn't think they did. I asked Justin Tipuric to explain it to me.

'Well,' he said in his lovely Welsh lilt. 'About six years ago we beat South Africa by three or four points, and the night before we'd gone out and eaten fish and chips.'

'So?'

'Well, it's what we do now. It's become a thing. The entire Welsh team always have fish and chips before a game. It would be bad luck not to.'

'Hang on a minute,' I said. 'Are you saying you've won every game in the last six years?'

'Oh no, of course not.'

I was scratching my head. 'So why the fuck do you still do it?'

To be fair, we England boys have a guilty food secret too. Long before I arrived, the squad began a tradition of having secret-recipe chocolate biscuits whenever they were at Pennyhill Park. The hotel is famous for its desserts and the biscuits are fabulous, small molehills of wonder. Once the tradition had started the boys tried to replicate it on tour, always ordering in a batch of specially commissioned chocolate biscuits from each hotel. However, they were never as good as the Pennyhill Park ones and the disappointment was palpable every time we went for afternoon tea and biscuits.

When we went on a six-game losing streak in 2018 we blamed the replica biscuits, which always seemed to taste healthier and therefore not as good as the originals. There was only one solution. We asked Pennyhill Park to make us up a batch of 80 biscuits to take away with us so every player in the 25-man squad could have three each as a snack the day before our next game. We won, and the tradition has stuck. People think winning Test matches is all about how hard you prepare physically, tactically and emotionally.

They think it's about coping with the smouldering pressure on the world stage. I say that's bollocks. We take the Pennyhill Park biscuits with us everywhere we go now, to give us the best chance of success. We've learned our lesson and it's the one ritual we all adhere to. Don't fuck with the biscuits.

★

Going into the 2014 season, team manager Conor O'Shea was under pressure to make changes at Quins. We'd won the Premiership in 2012 but had stagnated a bit since then, and Conor wanted to ring a few changes. 'Joe, how would you like to be captain?'

'What? Are you serious? No, thank you.'

'Why not?'

I knew that, if Conor asked 100 players if they thought it was a good idea, 97 would have said it was ridiculous and the other 3 would only have said it was a good idea to see me fail.

'It's just not me,' I said. 'I'm flattered to be asked. It's a huge honour, but I can't see myself as captain.' I didn't want to admit it, but I figured I wouldn't be able to muck about and have a laugh if I was captain, and I wasn't having that. Why would I want more responsibility in return for less fun?

'Think about it,' Conor said.

I did, and it was actually quite enlightening to really sit down and think about how I behaved as a player and what worked for me as a member of the team. This is what I recognised, all of it still true today.

I play my best rugby when I'm chilled and having fun, but I also have the ability to flick a switch and refocus on my job, either melting someone in a tackle, going after someone in a scrum or giving some advice to a teammate after a mistake has been made. Switching between clown and hitman is when I'm most enjoying myself, but you need to get the balance right, which isn't easy. I'm usually too far one way or the other, too much pissing about, trying too hard to be a tough guy, or at least to look like one. Coping with being captain and still being true to myself did not seem possible and I told Conor no, I couldn't do it.

He didn't give up. In fact, he used a bit of emotional blackmail. 'Chris Robshaw will benefit if you do. It will take a lot of pressure off him.' Robbo was going to captain England that season. I'd always go the extra mile for Robbo. But it wasn't all selfless on my part. Conor's second choice for captain would not have been my choice at all, so rather me than him was how I saw it, and that was how I reluctantly came to take up the mantle.

We had a pre-season team-building day and the bosses were setting out the goals and values for the season ahead. The other players didn't yet know that Robbo was standing down and I wondered when the announcement would be made.

We were about five hours into the session when Conor stood up to speak. I'd been losing focus, but this woke me up. 'Chris, you've been a fabulous leader and you've got a big year ahead of you as captain of England ...' Conor started, and he proceeded to break the news.

I glanced around and saw the anticipation on the other players' faces. Who was going to take over? Who would have the honour of captaining this esteemed and highly respected rugby club?

Conor put up a picture of me on the screen. I felt really awkward and wanted the ground to swallow me up. 'This,' Conor said with a flourish, 'is your new captain. Congratulations, Joe!'

I stifled a laugh and watched all the boys looking around anxiously, wondering where Ant and Dec were with their cameras.

'Joe, do you want to say a few words?'

Fuck's sake. 'Yeah. Cheers for the opportunity. Let's have some fun!'

I don't like to run myself down, but how could a player with a reputation as a bit of a dickhead – I have to be honest with myself – stand in the immaculate shoes of Chris Robshaw and captain a club that had a proud history spanning almost 150 years and was one of the founding members of the RFU? I didn't back myself at all. I had it in my head that I'd have to emulate Robbo's professionalism in order to pull off being captain. That was unattainable for me. I knew that.

The only way to make this work would be to stop thinking I had to change who I was and how I behaved. I needed to do things my way and, if it didn't work, at least I'd tried.

I decided to introduce a new Monday-morning tradition, my aim being to inject a bit of fun and drama into proceedings, get the lads going before we started the regular team meeting.

'What the fuck is that?' the boys said.

'Let me introduce you to our new fines system.' For years the fines system we'd had at Quins was the same as at most clubs. A player had to chuck £20 in the kitty if he showed up with the wrong kit or missed the start of a meeting, and at the end of the season all the boys would go on the piss with the money.

This was changing under my captaincy. I'd asked my mate to build a huge 'wheel of misfortune', the idea being that an offending player would have to spin the wheel to find out what his penalty was. Ten foot tall and with each section brightly painted, the wheel was spectacular. A plastic cock pointed to the forfeit the wheel landed on.

The forfeits included fines up to £100, washing the other players' cars, having a spray tan, being the 'office wanker' for a week (which meant you had to wear a suit and tie and carry a briefcase to and from training) and doing a 60-second dance to no music. This last one evoked the most fear.

Every Monday morning I brought the wheel out to kick things off before the regular rugby meeting. The coaches were a bit pissed off with it. I could see them thinking, *What the hell have we done here?*

Danny Care was one of the early victims, though landing on the spray-tan forfeit was hardly a hardship for him. He'd just go for his usual at his favourite salon. On James Chisholm's spin of the wheel he landed on 'office wanker'. *This is more like it,* we thought. But it turned out that James was heavily into am-dram and he embraced his challenge too, wearing a beautifully pressed suit, having his hair neatly cut and even carrying a smart leather briefcase. 'Good morning co-workers!' he'd declare. 'What's in my in-tray today?'

We finally got what we wanted when Kyle Sinckler hit the jackpot: the 60-second dance to no music. Sink was no mover on the dancefloor, even after a few drinks and with the best dance music you could imagine. What would he be like in a team room, silent but for the baying cries of a load of piss-taking rugby players?

I'll never forget the sight of Sink self-consciously shaking his body, brow creased with sweat and humiliation as the boys roared with laughter. His physicality seemed to diminish with every embarrassing jiggle of the hips. It was impossible to imagine that this was the same 19-stone juggernaut who terrified opponents and dominated the most skilful players in the game.

The wheel of misfortune would become my most memorable legacy as Quins captain. In fact, it was my only legacy. After four or five months I put my hand up and said, 'Look, being captain isn't for me.'

All my initial misgivings had come true. I couldn't be myself – interchanging between joker and hard man on the pitch – as well as carrying off the responsibility of captain. For one thing, the referees didn't take me seriously. I'd go to speak to them at the start of the game and I could see them thinking, *Is this for real? This guy, captain?* I always enjoyed that, actually. Wayne Barnes and Romain Poite thinking, *Hang on, I've yellow-carded this clown. How am I supposed to rely on him to speak seriously to his teammates?*

I thanked Conor for the opportunity and told him straight that I didn't enjoy doing it. 'I think I can have a better influence on the team as a lieutenant rather than a captain'. He didn't argue, and I packed up my wheel of misfortune and handed the reins to Danny Care, who took over for the next two seasons. Danny was a fantastic choice and made a much better job of it than I ever could.

The wheel of misfortune ended up gathering dust in my garage. Still, rugby has enough traditions to be going on with. Newly capped players continue to sing songs and drink 22 drinks and the England team will carry on singing the national anthem and eating Pennyhill Park biscuits.

The wheel keeps turning, as they say. Just not the wheel of misfortune.

11

FANS

Rugby fans are amazing. Look at Shaun Pollard, the New Zealand supporter who got a tattoo celebrating the All Blacks as 2019 World Cup winners – before they went and lost to us in the semi-final. 'If you're a loyal fan, you believe they're gonna win,' he said before the game.

I can identify with Shaun's optimism, because following that match I was convinced the World Cup had our name on it. How far we'd come seemed unbelievable and very believable, all at the same time. We were actually in the World Cup final. It was absolutely fucking brilliant.

'We can do this, boys,' we were all saying. 'We've beaten the best team in the world. Get in! If we can beat the All Blacks we can win the World Cup.'

In the changing room after that win Steve Hansen, the New Zealand coach, came over to let us know he was glad we'd embraced the challenge of the Haka. He told us, 'You blokes were brilliant tonight. No qualms. You beat us fair and square.' Afterwards it felt like the whole world was echoing his words, praising us for dominating the All Blacks in an incredible game. That was all fantastic for our confidence too, though nobody was complacent.

We really thought we could do it. We were pumped up, riding high. Not only were we in the final, but we'd earned ourselves another week in the camp and another week of fun together in Japan. We had an extra day off to recover because it had been a big old game. After playing some cricket together, it was back to intensive training.

The chat was all: 'We go again, we've got another life.' The trophy was in touching distance and we were determined. Sure, we arrived late to the game after getting stuck in traffic, but so what? Nothing as trivial as that was going to knock us off course. *This was our year,* that's what we thought. The vibe in the camp was so good and had been throughout our campaign. Everything was going our way.

Of course, it wasn't our day when we faced South Africa in the final, and the way we lost still eats away at me now, if I let it. The closer we got to kick-off, the more pressure started to show. During the warm-up I could sense an edgy, nervous energy in the boys. It wasn't a good energy, and I didn't have a great feeling. I regret not saying something, but then again, what difference would it have made?

When things started to fall apart so quickly – Sink knocked out in the opening minutes the way he was – I felt like I was unravelling. It wasn't our time after all. We weren't going to get the chance to taste success the way the England boys of 2003 did, and that was incredibly hard to take. What ifs would remain what ifs.

I've never watched the game back because I remember every moment. South Africa were doing an incredible job of beating us thoroughly in the scrum – which didn't get sorted out until the second half, but by that point the trickling effect of a first-half scrum that conceded penalty after penalty meant the boys at the back were losing confidence.

Even though the scoreboard read 12–6 at half-time – still in with a chance – I knew in my gut that we were not going to turn this around. They were dominating us massively and they were on it, mentally. By the time I was subbed on and their little winger Cheslin Kolbe found me on the outside on my own with Faz – me looking like I was running in quicksand and Kolbe zooming past me like a roadrunner – it was too late. We'd already lost.

Afterwards, all the boys were looking at each other and quickly looking away. Registering the disappointment but not wanting to speak about it, not yet. Then it would really be over. A line drawn.

There are two things that ease the pain of the loss: the knowledge that we could not have done any more in terms of being prepared, and the fantastic memories we made as a group of men. They will live with me, always. I look back at Japan as one of the best experiences of my life. Not just in terms of rugby, but my whole life. The way we pulled together – the boys and all the staff too – was phenomenal. Yes, we came short of our final goal and winning it would have topped it off spectacularly, and no doubt changed our lives. But not all experiences in life can be measured by success, can they?

The world keeps turning and you have to accept that sometimes the ball doesn't bounce your way. It's something I tell myself often, a little mantra I coined and have taken to heart: *When the ball is up in the air and it's a perfect kick, it doesn't matter how great it looks, cos there's no telling which way it's going to bounce when it hits the floor.*

That's true of life in general, not just rugby. You think it's going great one minute and it all looks wonderful, but you never know which way life's going to take you.

I'll still always be grateful for the opportunity and deliriously proud that we got that far. How many players can say they made it to a World Cup final? Nobody can take that away from us. And the fact that I can accept the hand fate dealt us that day doesn't mean I don't care enough. You can't get stuck thinking about what might have been, or you'll forget what is happening in the here and now.

The only way you can move on is to suck it up and stay positive. Which is exactly what superfan Shaun did when he was landed with a tattoo that was not only inaccurate, but thanks to the Internet and social media had been seen by millions all over the globe. 'I'll never modify it, no matter what,' he said, explaining that it was a symbol of hope and his devotion to the men in black. Good for him, I say.

I understand the fan mentality, having been one myself as a kid, idolising Jason Leonard, Jonah Lomu and the England players who brought home the 2003 World Cup. Even so, it's taken me years to get my head around the lengths some fans will go to. I enjoyed watching rugby before it became my job, and I supported Quins above other clubs, but I was never obsessive. I would never have travelled to every game, to stand in the freezing cold and get pissing-wet through. Even now I look at fans standing in the rain at the Stoop and think, *If I wasn't playing, I wouldn't be here. Hats off to you.*

I was astonished by the efforts fans made to get to the World Cup. The Wales fans who decided to spend money saved for a house deposit on a two-month journey to Japan by trains, buses and boats. A couple of England fans who spent just 22 hours in Japan for the final, after holding out until the last minute to buy their match and plane tickets.

Their devotion is inspiring. And when I have those days when I ask myself why I'm playing rugby for a living, I think of the fans. I might be running around a field with a load of sweaty men chucking a ball around, but at least the game means something. There's a reason to go and train in deepest winter, sideways rain stinging your body, aches and pains making you want to lie in a hot bath. There's a purpose to sacrificing precious family time to go away on tour for a month and play just two or three Tests.

The fan who brings this home to me more than any other is a 12-year-old boy called Ewan Laws. He blows my mind. Ewan has cerebral palsy and is quadriplegic, yet his attitude to life is just brilliant. We have a great laugh together – he's got a fantastic sense of humour – and he has a lovely family around him who bring him to every Quins game. I understand that rugby gives him another reason to attack life the way he does. He's mad for it. And our relationship works both ways. I love seeing Ewan at the game. He helps me put things in perspective and he is a massive inspiration to me.

I love the fans who paint their faces and wear crazy costumes in sweltering heat or freezing cold, rigged up in wigs and hats or all-in-one England body suits. They spur me on and never fail to lift my spirits.

In Japan I saw some hilarious creations. A French fan sat astride a giant blow-up chicken. Burly Welsh supporters with huge daffodil hats framing their cheerful faces. Australians in wallaby and koala masks. A whole group of French fans dressed as characters from *Asterix the Gaul*. The die-hard fan at the South Africa v Canada game who had a two-foot-tall replica of the Webb Ellis Cup balanced boldly on his head. I could never be bothered with that – imagine what a pain it would be – but I love the effort and commitment to the cause.

The Japanese fans were absolutely fabulous. Once Japan were knocked out of the World Cup they were mad for us, supporting England all the way. We did an open training session in the week of the semi-final and a big group of Japanese mums with babies in papooses came to watch.

'Photo?' one of them said afterwards, thrusting her sleeping baby at me. I hesitated. She obviously wanted me to hold her precious baby while she took a photo of us, but should I? There were media people all around. 'What's that idiot up to?' they'd be saying. 'Is he chucking Japanese babies around now or what?'

Sod it, I thought. I took the baby carefully in my arms and the mum was ecstatic, grinning from ear to ear. She pulled out her camera and took her photo. I could see the other mums were getting ready to hand me their babies too.

I felt quite emotional, standing there cuddling that tiny bundle. I didn't want to let him go. My youngest, Felix, was just weeks old when I had to leave him behind in England for the World Cup. *What I wouldn't give to cuddle Felix right now,* I thought. *Have a big hug from Jasper and Maggie. Have them jump all over me, swing from my ears.* Anything, just to have them close.

I spent the next half hour in this fantastic huddle, cuddling every single baby in turn and having my picture taken with each of the mums. It was a reminder about what matters in life. How lucky was I to have three gorgeous, healthy kids? They'd be there when I got home. That was what was important.

Before we all said goodbye I got a great picture of us all together, making the peace sign to the camera, the babies strapped in their papooses. It's one of my favourite memories of the World Cup, second only to beating the All Blacks. I'm sure the Japanese mums would be surprised by that, but it's absolutely true.

*

As great as so many of the fans are, there are some oddballs out there. Some surprise you enough to take your breath away.

One incredibly loyal Quins supporter once sent in a watch that had belonged to a relative who had passed away, wanting her favourite player to have it.

'That's touching. Was the person who died a Quins fan?'

'No. But the woman who sent it in is.' That's devotion for you, if ever I saw it.

Then there was the England fan who wrote to say how much he loved rugby and that his favourite players were Manu Tuilagi and Jonny May. I happened to be in the office that day, talking to the communications staff, and they gave me the letter to read. It was in a plastic envelope and had a funny-looking stamp on it.

'What's the significance of the plastic?' I asked, holding it up to have a closer inspection.

'Oh, that guy's in prison, serving life for murder,' came the reply.

Then, of course, there are a handful of fans who make life a bit more difficult or awkward for you. Sometimes you get people pretending they are fans, asking you for autographs and then selling them on eBay for a couple of quid, or you get parents pushing their kids out to ask you to sign a shirt or a ball. 'Who is he, Dad?' the child says. Why make things so awkward for everyone concerned? I try not to let it get to me. Better to save my energy for the real people. But then on some occasions ...

After our horrible defeat to Wales in the 2013 Six Nations we had to travel by two coaches from our hotel to the Hilton in Cardiff, where the post-match dinner was being held. Trying to get through the streets of Cardiff was an absolute nightmare. We were moving at a snail's pace through the rammed city and there were jubilant, pissed Welsh fans everywhere.

This is torture, I thought. I felt responsible for England's hefty defeat and this was too much to bear. I understood how the Welsh fans were feeling. They'd won the championship on their home turf and beaten the English into the bargain. It was one of the best results they'd ever had and the fans were loving it, but whose idea was it to have us drive through the middle of them like that? Absolute madness.

Inevitably, some of them started banging on the sides of the buses, giving us the finger. That was all we needed. We were trapped in the bus, inches away from them, like sitting ducks. *Keep your temper,* I told myself. *They've got the bragging rights. Just let them have their fun.* Now was not the time for the red mist to descend.

Then I spotted a couple of young fans, lads in their twenties, who were really going to town with the hand gestures. These two weren't just giving us the finger, they were giving us the wanker sign and shouting and swearing. I did a double-take, realising that they had England shirts on under their Barbour jackets.

Something snapped. 'Oi, you two, wanna come up here?'

The bus was crawling so slowly that I was able to open the side door and invite them on. They didn't realise how angry and upset I was, and they were so drunk they accepted the invitation in spite of the fact that they must have known I'd seen them flashing the Vs at us and hurling abuse.

When the coach door closed behind them I let them have it. 'You're wearing England shirts. What are you giving us abuse for, calling us wankers? We didn't mean to lose by 27 points. We tried our hardest. We didn't go out to lose. We never go out to lose. It's just that we got pumped on the day and that's it!'

'We didn't mean anything,' one of them said. 'We just got a bit carried away, that's all.'

I'd said my piece and I told them both to leave, opening the door. The other one got a bit arsey and refused to budge, so I got one of the other players to help me eject the pair of them from the bus. The arsey one dropped his glasses in the process, which I chucked out after him.

It wasn't a good scene, and in the cold light of day later, when my adrenaline had settled, I wasn't proud of myself. I shouldn't have risen to their taunts and I regretted bringing them on the bus only to give them a piece of my mind and chuck them off again. But unfortunately these things happen when everyone's blood is up.

I put it out of my mind. No real harm was done and I thought no more of it – until the next England campaign when we were due to play Wales again.

'Something very strange happened after our last trip to Cardiff,' Chris Robshaw said casually to me one day. 'A fan sent in a complaint about me.'

This struck me as very odd, seeing as Robbo is as courteous as they come and never puts a foot wrong. 'What, a Welsh fan?'

'No, an English fan. Remember those buses we took from the hotel? This guy said I threw him off the bus and his glasses got broken. Isn't that bizarre? I mean, why would a fan even be on the bus?'

Oops. The complaint had gone in to the RFU and had been passed to our team manager, who had been just as perplexed by the accusation as Robbo was. I had to come clean, didn't I?

I told Robbo the whole story and waited for him to tear a strip off me for being such an idiot. But that wasn't how he reacted at all. He was horrified that the fan's complaint had been dismissed out of hand as it had, of course. But far, far worse in his eyes was the fact that a ripped flanker who treats his body like a temple as he does had been mistaken for a lump of a loosehead like me. He was absolutely mortified.

★

Of course, we can't always give the fans the kind of attention they'd like. On the Lions tour in 2017, Coley and I had been put in charge of sourcing the props for the end of tour 'court' session – the traditional mock kangaroo court where daft penalties are meted out, usually involving dressing up, performing dares or drinking weird concoctions. Coley was carrying our shopping as we headed back to the hotel.

'Shall we get a taxi?' I suggested.

'Nah, mate. Let's just walk.'

Minutes later, just as we reached the pedestrian crossing, we were spotted by a load of Lions fans who came over to say hello. The light was on red so we had no choice but to stand and make small talk as we waited for it to turn to green. It seemed to be taking forever, and Coley was looking very hot under the collar.

'Daddy, what's all that stuff?' a little lad suddenly asked. The child was exactly the right height to be able to peer into the top of Coley's carrier bag. With that the Colar Bear lost his cool completely and shot across the road as fast as his legs would carry him, ignoring the red light and dodging traffic as he went.

'I'm really sorry about that,' I said to the fans. 'He's desperate for the loo.'

When I caught up with Coley I ribbed him mercilessly. 'That'll teach you for being so tight and not getting a cab!'

'Yeah, well. It's usually me apologising on your behalf. And what else was I supposed to do? What if that kid's dad had looked in the bag?'

He did have a point. The carrier bag was from the sex shop we'd been in and the 'stuff' the young lad had tried to make out was all the props we'd bought, including dildos, nipple tassels, lube and butt plugs.

*

The Quins fans are incredibly loyal and devoted. I was 18, on the brink of making my first-team debut, when Quins played Leinster in the Heineken Cup quarter-final of April 2009. A game that has become notorious thanks to Bloodgate.

Infamously, winger Tom Williams had been persuaded to bite on a fake blood capsule so a subbed player could come back on. It was a disgrace I could not imagine the club moving past.

It was common knowledge within rugby that most of the big clubs used dodgy tricks to get subs on in those days. The old razor blade in the towel was a well-known classic: the physio would put the towel over the player's head and nick his scalp so he'd be able to come off bleeding. I'd heard the stories and didn't think much of it, mostly because I couldn't imagine ever being involved. I was routinely blood-splattered coming off the pitch – why would you need to use fake blood?

Still, I was stunned when all the details emerged. A joke-shop blood capsule? It was so embarrassing, so amateurish. Quins' reputation was in absolute tatters. I'd always been so proud of being a Quin and this had tarnished each and every one of us, even if we had nothing to do with it.

I was shit-scared of what would happen to the club. Selfishly, I was focused on myself and my career. What would I do for a job now? Would I have to go back home, pick up at my uncle's turfing firm? I really thought that was possible, and all before I'd even got to make my first-team debut. The club was finished, surely?

In the aftermath I remember lots of conversations in corridors between the first-team players, the staff and the coaches. And those of us further down the food chain were all whispering among ourselves, asking what would happen now.

The eventual fallout was huge. Dean Richards left the club and was banned from rugby for three years. The man who could have sacked me the year before for having a scrap at a nightclub. How the fuck was this possible? I was gutted to see him go like that. Steph Brennan, the team physio, was struck off by the Health Professions Council (he won a High Court appeal almost two years after the incident), and Charles Jillings, the club's co-owner, resigned as chairman.

Williams himself was banned for twelve months, reduced to four on appeal, after he decided to tell the full truth about what went on that day, including how the team doctor made a real cut in his mouth when he came off the pitch in a bid to 'prove' he had been injured.

There was huge division in the club, some players saying Williams should have fallen on his sword, kept shtum, while others backed him for coming clean and salvaging his career. Such a tough decision. Nobody asked my opinion – why would they? – and I've no idea what I would have done in his position, though I'd like to think I'd stay loyal to the club and take the longer ban.

Who knows? I was just a pup and not party to all the nitty-gritty behind the scenes, but I do remember one thing very clearly, and that's the reaction of the fans. They stayed loyal. Despite all the shame and uncertainty, our regular supporters continued to come to the Stoop, and that was a huge tonic for all the players, me included. I'd look at the fans and think, *Yes, we still have a club. This is going to carry on*. The lovely fans who bake cakes and give them to the players at the gate were there, same as ever. The crowd looking as lively as they always did on match day, fans decked out in suits the colours of the quarters, waving flags with harlequins on and wearing club scarves over their Barbour jackets. They really are an incredible bunch, and Bloodgate brought out the very best in them.

They also came into their own after England bombed out of the World Cup in 2015. At our first game back at the Stoop the fans began applauding me, Chris Robshaw and Danny Care when we started to warm up. The World Cup was still going on – just around the corner at Twickenham Stadium – and we were all absolutely devastated.

The applause of the supporters told us, 'We still love you! We're all in this together, boys!' That was a really positive turning point for me. I'd been finding it really tough after that defeat. I couldn't get my head round how it had gone so badly wrong in a home World Cup. I'd been feeling like shit, every single day since we bombed out.

I hadn't wanted to go to the Stoop that day. I'd wanted to barricade myself in at home, avoid contact with anyone who might shout, 'What went wrong, mate?' But the Quins fans didn't do that. It was the opposite. They made me see that England was only part of my job. I had a responsibility to my club, and I wanted to fulfil it and give the fans the best I could.

*

The royals love a bit of rugby. How can they not, with Mike Tindall in the family? The first member of the royal family I ever met was his mother-in-law, Princess Anne, many years ago, before an England game in Scotland. There I was, sweating my tits off, not knowing what to say or how to behave when I got to the front of the line and Her Royal Highness shook my hand and said, 'Good luck.'

I overheard Princess Anne say something about my beard. I didn't quite catch it, but the look on her face was quite disapproving. I'm sure I heard the word 'scruffy' and then she said, 'It seems to be the in thing at the moment.'

What was all that about? I thought. *Aren't the royals meant to give us a bit of a morale boost?* To be honest, I didn't understand what all the fuss was about royalty.

All that changed a few years later when Prince Harry – a massive England fan and Patron of the RFU – came to Twickenham to watch a team run the day before an England game. I knew he liked to pop along and see a big game and chat to the players, and at the end I spotted him mucking about with Hask as all the players came off the pitch.

Wow – Prince Harry! I thought. He clearly got on well with Hask – they had met many times, it turned out – and I watched as he started doing the rounds, chatting with all the players gathered on the side of the pitch and gradually getting closer to me. Next thing I knew, he was just a few feet away from me and it was going to be my turn to meet him any minute.

I started to feel nervous. All the other boys appeared very calm and collected, smiling and exchanging pleasantries, looking as if they chatted to royalty all the time. Meanwhile, I felt completely out of place. I had a mohawk and tattoos and I didn't speak as nicely as a lot of the boys. It took me back to when I first arrived at Quins and met all the private-school toffs. I felt outclassed, lacking in education, about to be judged or make a show of myself. What would I say to fucking Prince Harry? Nobody had coached me about etiquette and I was terrified of putting my foot in it.

I'd heard various things over the years, like you need to wait for a member of the royal family to speak to you first in this kind of situation and you must avoid eye contact. Was it true? I had no idea and it was too late now. Prince Harry was on his way over, and my anxiety was going through the roof.

Daisy's a big royalist and she would have loved to have been in my shoes at this moment and I had to conduct myself well. I didn't want to let her down.

Prince Harry was standing right in front of me, smiling and holding out his hand. I shook it, and at the same time I bowed my head and gave a little bob. I knew it was all wrong, and when I looked back up Harry was studying me, with a quizzical look on his face. 'What *are* you doing?' he said.

I could see he was quite amused and so I responded with a half-smile and an awkward shrug that meant: 'Is this not how it goes? Should I not have bowed?'

Harry giggled it off and moved on to the next player while I stood there going, *Fucking hell. What did you do that for? You've completely embarrassed yourself. You can't tell Daisy this!*

The next time I saw Prince Harry I was determined to put this right. He came to one of the Six Nations games and popped into the changing rooms after the match. This time, as Prince Harry put out his hand and said, 'Hello,' I shook it politely. So far so good. I didn't bow my head like last time. No, I wasn't doing that again. This time I had a much better idea.

'Hello,' I said in my poshest voice, dropping a little curtsy. Harry looked amused and tried to catch my eye, but I looked away quickly, making a deliberate point of avoiding eye contact. When I glanced back he was smiling as he moved on to the next player. *Nailed it!* I thought. *He got what I was trying to do.*

After that, contriving some kind of awkwardness became my go-to move whenever Prince Harry popped up to say hello. It always put a smile on his face and I was satisfied I'd improved my image in his eyes. I wasn't a thick rugby player who didn't understand royal etiquette, was I? No. I liked to think I'd proven myself to be a far more sophisticated beast than that.

On one occasion I was ready to try a low bow and no-eye-contact combination, but this time Harry didn't hold out his hand to me. Instead he just stopped and stared, putting me off my stride. 'What *do* you look like?' he said.

I gasped. I wasn't expecting this at all. Normally he didn't speak. He just let me do my thing and gave me a smile in return, acknowledging my latest move with a twinkle in his eye. 'Pardon?' I stuttered. 'Sorry, Sir?' He was staring at my beard, I realised. Were there bits of toast left over from breakfast? Some chicken fallen out of my pre-match wrap?

'What *have* you come as?' Harry went on, a cheeky smirk stretching across his face.

'Pardon?' I said. I hadn't anticipated this level of conversation, though perhaps I should have, thinking back to how Princess Anne had remarked on my beard all those years ago.

'That beard,' he said, shaking his head. 'You look like a hobo with that beard!'

That really threw me. Had Prince Harry really just said I looked like a hobo? I had to come back with something, fast, or the moment would be gone. 'A hobo?' I blurted. 'Hang on a minute – you look like the most dishevelled royal there's ever been with your beard!'

He looked surprised but took it on the chin, so to speak, before moving along with a bit of a grin on his face.

Shit, I thought, immediately wishing I could take the words back. Daisy was not impressed when I told her. 'If you ever get the chance to meet him again,' she said, 'you'd better be on your best behaviour.'

It was Super Saturday in the 2015 Six Nations and, for the first time in the competition's history, three other teams as well as us could potentially win it, so everything was up for grabs. We were against France and we were on fire, playing a much wider game than we normally did. *This is how the game should be played,* I thought at half-time. *There's no fear, we're being ambitious. This is wonderful.*

With 17 minutes to go we were winning 48–30. I was substituted and watched the rest of the game with blood on my cheek and my arms draped over an advertising hoarding. Physically I was spent, but my mind was running at a hundred miles an hour. 'Come on, lads!' I was slamming the board, lapping up the atmosphere, loving every second.

We won 55–35, a massive tally that's unheard of in the Six Nations, and we finished second overall in the competition. It had been an absolute blast – one of the best games of my life.

I'd just come back through the tunnel and couldn't wait to crack open a beer with the boys, but I was asked to do a dope test first so I went to the testing room. I pulled on the blue surgical gloves they give you, to stop you getting piss on your hands, and gave my sample as quickly as possible before heading back to the changing room.

'Can you put these socks on please, Joe?' It was World Down Syndrome Day, I was told, and the multi-coloured stripy socks were to show support. Loads of the lads were wearing them, as the daughter of one of the England physios had Down syndrome.

'No problem,' I said.

'Great. We'll need a photo of you in them. There'll be a photographer along soon.'

I put the socks on before I'd even taken the surgical gloves off and then I grabbed a can of Red Stripe lager, sat down and took a swig. I was absolutely jiggered. I'd go and join the boys in a minute, once I'd caught my breath. I dropped my head forward, feeling exhausted.

'Joe? Are you OK if we do that photo now?'

'Yeah, yeah …' I looked up expecting to see the photographer and maybe a press officer, but instead standing in front of me, dressed in a suit and stripy socks, was Prince Harry. He smiled politely and I smiled back, wiping my mouth with the back of my hand, just in case I had any drops of beer on my lips – or, worse, my beard.

'Hi!' I said gamely, though I wanted the ground to swallow me up. Why had nobody prepared me for this? I must have looked like a rabbit caught in the headlights.

'Fantastic game,' he said. 'Congratulations. May I?' He indicated to the space on the bench next to me.

'Of course,' I said. 'Take a seat.' I would have given anything to at least have had a shower first.

'If you could both look this way,' said the photographer. 'Thanks. One more! That's perfect. Thank you both.' With that, Prince Harry was on his feet and saying his goodbyes. It had all happened so fast that I had to sit there for a minute or two wondering if I'd imagined the surreal encounter.

When I showed Daisy the picture her face dropped. 'How disrespectful have you been?' she said. 'You're wearing a pair of surgical gloves, drinking a can of lager and pulling a silly face. What were you thinking?' I thought she would at least have liked the fact that we were wearing matching stripy socks.

I'm not one for having rugby pictures all over the house but I've made an exception with that one, and it's hanging in the downstairs toilet, just to wind Daisy up.

*

The royal family aren't the only famous rugby fans, and you tend to find out which celebrities are rugby mad during big tours and competitions. On the night of the World Cup final in Japan we had a private party back at our hotel, family and friends included. A celebration of losing the World Cup final – just what none of us wanted.

I didn't have any family with me and Eddie had given me a special bottle of whisky that I tucked into – not realising until Coley enlightened me later that it was worth about £400. As the night wore on I was wandering around, looking for someone to chat to. I ended up talking to our security guys, Bill and Fergus, who were guarding the doors and checking guests in.

All of a sudden I saw people whispering and looking over at a ginger-haired man who was standing in another area, outside of our party and with a few friends around him.

'Fucking hell, boys!' I blurted out when the penny dropped. 'That's Ed Sheeran! What is happening? Why isn't he in our party?' I knew Ed was a massive rugby fan and surely this was no coincidence. 'I'm sure he'd love to come and meet all the boys.'

Bill and Fergus shook their heads. 'He's not on the list. He can't come in.'

'What? This is nuts! It's fucking Ed Sheeran. Please go and invite him in. I want to meet him. Come on, boys, what are you thinking? Aren't you as excited as I am?'

They clearly weren't starstruck at all, having guarded royalty and A-list stars for years throughout their careers. And they were absolutely adamant that Ed Sheeran was not on the list and was not coming in.

'This is a big fuck-up!' I complained. 'Do you realise what a fuck-up this is?' I had to give up eventually, and later on I decided to wander outside for a fag, thinking that, if I hung around for long enough, maybe I'd catch Ed as he left the hotel.

My heart leaped when – *fuck me* – not long afterwards the man himself stepped out of the lift and walked out onto the street, just a few metres from where I was standing. I was so stunned and star-struck that I didn't have the bottle to say or do anything. I just stared at him silently, eyes on stalks. Then I watched as Ed disappeared into the night. An opportunity missed. It still eats away at me now.

Ronan Keating reluctantly serenaded us on the Lions tour in 2017, though disappointingly sang a song I'd never heard before instead of my favourite Boyzone banger, 'Life Is A Roller Coaster'. Michel Roux Jr. is a massive Quins fan and I've met his mate Gregg Wallace a few times, who's a lovely bloke. Though when I introduced him to Daisy at a game, I'd no sooner said, 'This is Daisy,' than he'd put his hand out and said, 'Hi, I'm Gregg Wallace from *Masterchef*.' OK … And, also on the Lions tour in 2017, Nick Knowles, from *DIY SOS* got chatting to us in a bar. Rory Best, who'd clearly never seen the show, was having some trouble with his builders and ended up asking the king of DIY sob stories to pitch up and finish off his building work. Er, maybe not, Besty?

When we lost to Wales in the 2015 World Cup pool stages Samuel L. Jackson tweeted Chris Robshaw:

'Tough but epic game @CRobshaw. Still all to play for against Oz. Hope Wales can get backline together for Fiji! #ENGvWAL #One4theboys'

It was a boost, and exactly what players need from fans when the chips are down. That Wales match had been catastrophic. To this day I've never watched it back, but unfortunately I remember it all. We'd been losing 28–25 with minutes to go and then we got a penalty near the Wales post.

Robbo, Faz and Geoff Parling had a conversation about whether to go for the three points and settle for the draw or go for a line-out and a win. We went for the win and it backfired. It was a horrible moment. A stab in the heart, a kick in the guts. *That's it. We've lost to Wales at home and we've lost the World Cup now. Second game in and we're fucking done.*

I remember looking at Robbo and he was just devastated. He blamed himself for making that call and he was subsequently hammered in the press and pilloried on social media. Someone even made a meme parodying *Who Wants to be a Millionaire?* that mocked Robbo mercilessly for his decision.

The reality, however, was that we hadn't lost the World Cup, not yet. Samuel L. Jackson was right when he said 'still all to play for against Oz'. His tweet was very welcome and well intentioned, but of course things didn't pan out for us. We went on to lose to Australia, and our win against Fiji wasn't enough to get us out of the pool stages and keep us in the competition. We were out after three pathetic games.

It was one of the lowest points of my career. I was mortified, broken. It was one of those moments when you know life is never going to be the same again. I was as gutted for the fans as I was for myself and the whole squad. We'd let everyone down and I was terrified of what people would say. *What will I tell Jasper when he's old enough to understand?* was a thought that haunted me. I was sure I'd get abused in the street and I just wanted to lock myself away to lick my wounds.

There was never any need, thank God, because the fans were amazingly supportive. There was no 'What the fuck was that pile of shit?' The vast majority said, 'Bad luck, mate. It wasn't your year. Hope you get to play in 2019.' Their comments brought me back to reality. Nobody had died. Life would carry on. It was rugby, not the real world. You might get another crack at it. People cared, but this wasn't life-changing, not in the big scheme of things. It was like the Quins supporters who really got me back in the saddle, spurring me on and welcoming me and the boys back to the Stoop. I'll never forget that.

Because, you see, rugby fans make this game of ours. We'd have no show without the die-hards who ink their bodies, travel the globe and turn up in outlandish fancy dress. There'd be no sport without the loyal supporters at the Stoop and clubs all over the country. No international competition without Japanese mums and babies in papooses. Rugby fans really are amazing.

12

MENTAL HEALTH

'You tried to run over that squirrel! What are you doing?' Daisy shouted.

'No, I didn't!' I'd stayed straight and kept driving, like you're supposed to. 'It's more dangerous to swerve or stop in case there's a car up your arse. It's not like it's a deer or something. It's just a squirrel.'

Big mistake. Daisy is a vegetarian, a huge animal lover and has a heart of gold. She loves everything that walks this earth.

We rarely argue, but it all kicks off. 'That's a load of bollocks – you tried to run over a squirrel!'

It's a Friday night in May 2019. Daisy is seven months pregnant and we've just dropped Jasper and Maggie at her mum's because we're going to a mate's thirtieth birthday party. We drive home to finish getting ready but the bickering carries on. Escalates.

By the time we walk through our front door Daisy is screaming at me. 'It feels like you're never here! And even when you are, you're not present. You're not engaging with us. You're either on your phone or it's like talking to a brick wall. What's the point?'

'That's such a load of bollocks! I've been trying my hardest. I'm doing the best I can!' Being branded a squirrel-killer is bad enough. Calling me out as a crap dad and absent husband is on another level. Something in me turns. I'm shouting and screaming at Daisy now, and she's storming up the stairs. I tell her we need to sort this out, discuss what's been said, but she's not listening. She hates confrontation.

'That's it!' I shout. 'Run away as usual.' I'm so frustrated and furious. How can she say those things then refuse to talk to me? 'We need to talk about this, Dais! Fuck's sake!'

I'm in the hallway, standing in front of the cupboard under the stairs. There's nothing but silence coming from upstairs. 'Dais! What the fuck? Come on, we need to talk.'

I can't take the silence and suddenly I snap. My fist goes through the cupboard door. It's not a decision I've made. I'm not in charge of myself, and now my feet are kicking the fuck out of the door. I've lost the plot.

This has never happened to me before, not like this. Red-mist moments on the rugby pitch are one thing, but this? I've never felt this way with Daisy, never reacted this explosively. I charge into the kitchen and cave in the fridge door. Now I'm wrecking more of the kitchen, turning over furniture and punching walls. *What the fuck? How can she treat me like this? She hasn't got a fucking clue how hard it's been. How fucking hard it is. Fuck this!*

Eventually I burn myself out. I walk slowly up the stairs to Daisy. I find her sitting on the bedroom floor, crying her eyes out. 'Are we going to sort this out?' I say – but it's more of a demand really.

She's not responding, not even acknowledging I'm there.

'Dais, are we going to sort this out?'

She's still not answering, not engaging with me at all.

'Dais?'

Still no response. I might as well be invisible.

'Fuck it! I'm leaving. *I'm done!*'

I storm back downstairs, grab my keys and drive off in my truck, leaving the battered kitchen in my wake. I don't know where I'm going or what I'll do next. I just keep driving and driving, my head spinning with questions. *What the fuck is going on? What are you doing? Who even are you? She's heavily pregnant. Fuck's sake, what's happened?*

I don't have any answers. I've hit my lowest point, that's all I know.

★

I've known Daisy since we were kids in school together. She plaited my blonde curtains at our Year 8 camp, when were both 13, and that was the start of a whirlwind of love.

I fell for her in a big way. I knew a lot of her friends were saying, 'Daisy, what are you doing with the fat kid with the high-lighted curtains? Are you the only one who can't see he looks like Cartman from *South Park*?' But neither of us gave a fuck.

We spent break times eating each other's face off and we held hands when I took her to see *Scary Movie 4*. Yeah, *I'm the boy now*, I thought. *Fuck all you lot who called me fat and laughed cos nobody fancied me. I've managed to bag a worldie!*

On Valentine's Day I bought her R. Kelly's album and a banana. It had all been going so well until then. The next day I got a message on MSN: 'I'm sorry, Joe, but I don't want to go out with you anymore.'

I'll never forget the moment I read it. My heart shrivelled. I'd been dumped, on MSN Messenger. It felt like the end of the world. I loved Daisy and I'd gone to such a lot of trouble, even personalising the banana by drawing a smiley face on it. OK, in hindsight the album wasn't the best present I could have chosen, but nobody knew then what the future held for R. Kelly, did they?

There was nothing I could do. Daisy had made up her mind. She had better offers on the table – of course she did – and the boyfriend she picked up next was the popular, good-looking leader of the cool gang at school. He was also not fat.

I didn't hold anything against Daisy. We'd had three wonderful months of teenage love and we remained friends throughout school. Even when I joined Quins and moved to Kingston, we still kept in touch. I'd see Daisy whenever I went back to Heathfield.

Then, out of the blue, she started to send me very different messages to the MSN bombshell. 'Miss you,' she said. Admittedly, it was usually when she was on a drunken night out, but I didn't let that put me off.

I started grafting. I wanted her back. And eventually, it worked. We were 19 when we moved in together in Heathfield. Yes, I loved Daisy so much I was prepared to commute two hours each way (and the rest on some days) from East Sussex to Surrey every day. Now that's commitment.

*

A decade on, and here we were, married with two kids and with another baby on the way. And what was I doing? Sitting in my truck on my own, having run out on the love of my life. What the fuck was I thinking? Leaving her crying when she was heavily pregnant. Damaging the house we'd built up together, worked so hard to turn into a happy family home.

Shame started to sting me as I thought about what I'd done. I had to get back and sort things out with Daisy, make sure she was OK. But the shame I was feeling almost stopped me. *What the fuck?* But I took a deep breath and squashed it down. I turned the truck around, my heart racing. I had one overriding thought in my mind: *I hate myself for what I've done.*

I was shaking as I drove home. By the time I parked up and prepared to walk back inside the house only about 20 minutes had passed since I ran out – but it felt like a lifetime. I'd finally come back to earth.

I found Daisy still on the bedroom floor, outside our bathroom, where her clothes and dressing table are. She was sobbing her heart out, just as she was when I left her. 'I'm so sorry, Dais. I don't know what happened. I'm so sorry.'

She didn't say anything, didn't respond in any way. I looked at her and realised why. There was fear in her eyes. *She's scared,* I was thinking. *Part of her is scared of me.*

Somehow we made it to the birthday meal. I said I'd phone and cancel – I thought we had no choice – but Daisy was adamant that we had to go. We were taking the cake and other bits and bobs and she didn't want to let our friends down. That's Daisy for you. We drove to the restaurant in deathly silence and sat at opposite ends of the table, hoping nobody would notice that things weren't right between us.

The next day she still wanted nothing to do with me. I had a game and left fairly early. We were playing Saracens at the Olympic Stadium. I hated Saracens because they were so much better than us. The players were phenomenal and the club were always producing so many fantastic England players. They still do.

Long before it all came out in the wash there was a deeply held suspicion that Saracens were cheating by busting the salary cap. When everything came out we discovered that their cheating had had a bigger and wider impact on the game than anyone had suspected. It really pissed me off to think, *What if?* about past games and results. I didn't want to go there. Shit like that drives you mad, and I'd always detested them anyway.

We were meeting in a hotel before the game. On the drive there I was cursing having to play this fixture, today of all days. It was the last thing I needed. I wanted to hide away, fix my problems in private, not battle fucking Saracens with TV cameras pointed at me and thousands of fans looking on.

I'd really hurt my hand. I hadn't realised how badly until now. It was killing me. As soon as I arrived at the hotel I went to see the club doctor, John Berry. 'Look, doc, I've hurt my hand,' I said matter-of-factly. 'Can you take a look?'

'What happened there? Did you do it in training?'

'Nah. I was moving some weights at home last night. Dropped one on my hand. I think it's broken.'

There was a pause. The doc gave me a look. One that said, *I don't believe you for one minute, Joe.* He fixed his eyes on mine and said, 'Are Daisy and the kids OK?'

My breath caught in my throat and I could feel shame burning through my chest.

The doc said something about this being a 'classic boxer's knuckle', or words to that effect. 'You don't do that dropping a weight on it, Joe.'

That's when I started to break down. 'What's going on with me, doc? I don't know what's going on with me. Can you help me, please?' I was blubbing like a baby. 'My world is falling apart.'

He sat me down, talked through stuff and said he was going to arrange for me to get professional help.

I play the game with my broken hand strapped up. The boys can tell something's up and most of them steer clear of me, giving me the space they think I need. We lose.

Afterwards, I'm standing under a towel in the changing room, bawling my eyes out. I've no idea what the boys are making of me and I'm too upset to pull myself together. My tears are falling uncontrollably. I can't look at the lads. I can't let them look at me.

Guzzy talks to me afterwards. I'm grateful my boss is also a good mate, because I need to talk. 'What's going on, Joe? Can we help?'

'I don't know. I'm not a good person. Mate, I'm a bad person.' I tell him what's happened. The row. Me turning the house over. Daisy being scared. 'It was all over a fucking squirrel,' I cry. 'A fucking squirrel.'

'A squirrel?'

'Yes. A fucking squirrel.'

★

I knew it was not all over a fucking squirrel, but I didn't understand what it was really about, not in the way that I do now. Daisy was even more in the dark. She had absolutely no idea what I'd been going through, no idea that I'd been struggling with my mental health for a long time. How could she when I told her nothing and was trying to swerve the conversation even with myself?

I was a rugby player, for fuck's sake. A 20-stone prop. A loose-head who played for his country, carrying the weight of the best rugby players in the world on his shoulders in a scrum. How could I not be as strong as an ox, mentally as well as physically?

Weird things had started to happen to me as far back as 2016. Quins were playing Worcester away in a Premiership game right at the start of January. For some reason we never seem to play a good game against Worcester and I've never enjoyed going up there.

On the way up I was staring out of the window, not engaging with the boys on the bus. *What's the point?* I was thinking. *I hate rugby. What am I doing here? Why do we have to play fucking Worcester, in fucking Worcester? How am I supposed to walk out on the pitch and give the fans what they want when I feel like shit?*

I tried to talk myself around. Daisy and I had finally got married, just a couple of months before. Maggie was due in a few weeks' time and Jasper was two and wonderful. I was playing for Quins and being regularly called up for England. Why was I so fucking miserable and disenchanted?

I played terribly, overpowered and outwitted in the scrum time and time again. It doesn't take much to get it wrong. One small loss of concentration and you might get your foot in the wrong position, your bind too short or your angle wrong. That's all it takes, and the next thing you know you've got the reverse lights on and your arse is getting kicked.

I'm sure my mood had an impact on my performance. How could it not? It doesn't matter how much iron you pump in the gym and how physically dominant you appear on the pitch, you also need to be mentally strong and alert to play your best game of rugby.

It's not just the glory boys who have to think about killer skills and tactical moves. We may look like wallowing hippos, but props use our grey matter just as much. Every second you're playing your brain is whirring, thinking about tactics, where to put yourself next, how to outwit your opponent and avoid getting suffocated in the scrum. You need to be sharp, not have a head full of black clouds. Same as in most jobs, I would imagine. When you feel good you perform better. It's not rocket science.

That day my main thought was: *How do I get through this?* Don't get me wrong. I was doing my best. I didn't give up. It's just that a huge proportion of my effort was going into keeping focused and making my body work the way I needed it to. The rest of it – clever scrummaging, sneaky little digs, an extra lift or clever shift in angle going into a line-out or maul – had to come second to nailing the bare bones of the job. I wasn't going to sing Adele in the scrum to throw my opponents off their game. No chance of that kind of effort when I was putting so much energy into trying to silence questions in my head about what the fuck I was even doing there.

By some miracle we ended up winning by four points. We'd just about done the job we went up there to do but I was very unhappy with my performance. I'd been outplayed and looked like a push-over in the scrum.

As I came off the field I was thinking, *That was shit. You were shit. I fucking hate coming to Worcester. Why did I bother?* Heading down the tunnel, I had the crowd on either side of me. The Worcester supporters were giving us a load of abuse even though they'd lost, which was really winding me up.

I just wanted to disappear. I was walking as quickly as I could down the tunnel when I suddenly looked up and saw a face smirk-ing at me. It was Dean Ryan, Worcester Warriors' director of rugby. *What's he smirking at?*

I didn't know him. He'd been a forward for clubs like Saracens and Wasps and had a reputation for being a hard man of rugby. I knew that much, but I'd never had anything to do with him. *Why's he fucking smirking at me?*

He was properly grinning at me now. *What the fuck have you got to smile about?* I thought. *Worcester have been mediocre for years and they've just lost, again!*

Then it came to me. *He must be smiling because they did so well in the scrum.* He was taking the piss out of my shit performance, wasn't he? *Fucking hell. Be the bigger man. Don't rise to this.*

I marched on, wanting to turn the other cheek, but then he spoke to me. 'Well played, Joe,' he said, that smug smile still on his face.

That was it. He'd started something here. 'Oh, fuck off!' I snapped.

I carried on walking past – still trying to be the bigger man, despite having already failed – and from behind my back I heard him say, 'Oh, that's mature, isn't it? That's really mature.'

Bad move. Dean Ryan had hit the red-mist button. I turned round and confronted him. 'Mature? You want fucking mature, do you?' I said. I could see him wondering what on earth was going on here but he had no time to react before I made my move.

What did I do? I slapped him square in the cock. It was your classic schoolboy move, taking me right back to Heathfield Community College. 'What's the capital of Thailand?' the boys would say. 'Bang*kok*!' But the whack I gave Dean Ryan was a bit more than your average schoolboy little hit. I gave him a full-on cock-slap, a good belt in the family jewels.

He looked at me in disbelief and then lashed out, as any man would in that situation. You instinctively go to defend yourself, don't you? And his gut response was to kick me in the shin. I took it and walked off.

The Quins subs were coming up the tunnel behind us. They'd seen what had happened and I could see them looking at me, wide-eyed. I carried on walking back to the changing room, not giving Dean Ryan a second look.

I sat down on a bench, head in hands. *Did I really just give Dean Ryan a cock-slap?*

'What the fuck was going on there, mate?' one of the subs asked.

'Nothing, don't worry about it.' I didn't have an answer. I was asking myself the same question. I could hear some of the subs whispering in the corner as they started telling a few of the other lads what they'd seen. I kept my head down, got myself showered and said nothing.

On the bus journey back the slap was the main topic of conversation. The boys were now taking it in turns to crease up as the story was retold and passed around. 'Come on, Joe, what happened there? There's got to be more to this. What the fuck?'

'I dunno, lads. I just took exception to Dean Ryan's smirking. I didn't want to get into a full-blown punch-up. Assaulting him in the penis seemed like the fairest way of dealing with the situation.'

Cue more laughter. I was glad they were laughing because it was a distraction, but I wasn't finding this funny because I had no answer to the real question of what on earth was going on in my head.

There was no comeback from Dean Ryan and I pushed the incident out of my mind, wishing it had never happened and trying to forget it ever did, because what did it say about my state of mind? I didn't want to go there.

★

The following week we beat Saracens at home, winning 23–20. It was their first defeat of the season. It was a brilliant result for us and I played well. I'd managed to move on from the Dean Ryan incident, I thought. It was a weird blip, that was all. I was fine now. Well, I didn't feel completely fine. I was still questioning what I was doing with my life. Getting up at 5am every morning to drive to training, leaving Daisy, heavily pregnant, still sleeping or changing Jasper's nappy. Breakfast at the club before starting training at 8.30am. Eggs, porridge, piles of fresh fruit. What's not to like? Then on to doing drills, practising throwing and catching and lifting weights, all the way through until 1pm. *So I liked PE at school? Doesn't mean I want a five-hour intensive PE session four mornings a week, does it?*

We train every weekday except Thursday, for all but five weeks of the year. Sometimes more, depending on international duty. In the gym I typically bench-press with 140 kilos. Five lots of five. Then chin-ups, four sets of twelve. Plus single-arm dumbbell rows with 50-kilo weights. Four lots of eight or twelve. Biceps too – curls for the girls. And they're always trying to make me do power jumps or some sort of explosive exercise. That's not my bag, so I just ignore them.

It doesn't matter that your body is still aching like a bastard from the previous game. Shoulders, knees, hips all creaking, shot through with varying amounts of pain. You crack on, keep pushing through.

There's another wonderful spread laid on for lunch. Barbecued lamb. Fillet of beef wraps. Salads with grains and carbs. Our current Quins chef, Omar Meziane, has cooked for the England football, cricket and rowing teams. He's into all the science, like all the best sports chefs, working out exactly what you need to eat to be the right weight and have the correct body fat percentage to run around as efficiently as possible for 80 minutes.

Fuck this, I'm not a runner, am I? That's what I'd be thinking sometimes, when my mood was low. *Why is everything in my life so fucking controlled?*

I had nothing to complain about, not really. Fantastic, healthy food served up twice a day. Protein shakes. Supplements. Multivitamins. A drip-feed of painkillers, if needed. Physios, nutritionists and medics on hand. Everything worked out to support your body to play rugby in the very best way possible because your body is the tool of your trade. It *is* your job.

The rest of your diet you sort out yourself. After a match it's always the same for me. I have a McDonald's as a reward, to put the carbs back in. Always the same order, picked up at the nearest motorway services: a couple of cheeseburgers, a Big Mac, two packets of fries, nine chicken nuggets and a milkshake. Not what every sportsman would do, but that's one of my ways of finding balance and normality. A way of not feeling like a battery hen, stuffed with all the right food for one sole purpose, to be a good prop.

I realise I've digressed, but there's a good reason for that. The pressure of professionalism and the effect it has on mental health is something rugby players have been opening up about more and more in recent years. It's a huge problem in the sport, one that should have been brought into the spotlight long before it was.

Look at Jonny Wilkinson. He explained how he used to live for the 'beautiful moments of being in the zone' during games. He told himself those moments were the result of the ridiculous suffering he went through and the sacrifices he made. 'So I told myself I had to suffer more, because that was the way I was going to get back into the zone.'

Unfortunately, when Jonny won the World Cup in 2003 the anticipated reward never came for him. The joy had gone, the beautiful moments nowhere to be found. Jonny had always suffered with anxiety, which grew and grew until the worry and pressure he put himself under left precious little space for enjoyment of the game, even when he was lifting the World Cup.

I can identify. I've looked at kids in the crowd during big games, at the excitement on their face, a look that says, *I want to do what you do. That's my dream.*

Meanwhile, what am I thinking? Honestly, sometimes I'm wondering if I can feign an injury to get off the pitch early. Do something stupid to get myself a ban for a few weeks. Because I'm so fucking knackered and fed up of the same routine, the same physical punishment, of putting my body into a human vice made up of 300 stone of knuckle and muscle. I'm thinking, *Fuck this*.

The former Wasps lock Kearnan Myall – a six-foot-seven Yorkshireman I played alongside for England on our 2013 tour of Argentina – says intolerable pressure and scrutiny took him to the brink of suicide. He was in Dubai, standing on the wrong side of his hotel balcony, 15 storeys up, when one of his Wasps team-mates grabbed him and dragged him back. When reflecting on it, he said the 'horrific' training he did at the England Under-18s national academy camps was a contributory factor to his mental state. The camps made him not want to play rugby anymore, and his negative reaction to the camps made others perceive him as being mentally weak for not wanting to be there.

There's a theory that we're seeing such a tsunami of mental-health issues in my generation of players because we were coached by men who came from the amateur era. I think it holds some water. Their old-school attitude was 'you need to be tough and macho, show no weakness, no chink in your armour' – arguably much easier for them than it is for us. Training was a part-time release from their 'real' job, not their whole life, although many of them played in the professional era too.

How are players now supposed to stay unwaveringly tough and strong as standards continue to rise and training gets more challenging and intense? As players get bigger, faster, better and stronger while injuries increase exponentially? Be mentally unflappable when you're thousands of miles from home, missing your family for months on end and playing 30 or more games a year? Stay robotically strong and committed to the cause when you have a bad day at the office and the keyboard trolls call you out for being a fat wanker, a useless piece of shit?

Of course, amateur-era players weren't immune from mental-health problems. Taboo and stigma conspired to keep them underground, and the old boys played along and put on a brave face. A couple of years ago a Rugby Players' Association survey of retired players showed that more than six out of ten had experienced some sort of mental-health problem in their career. Nearly half of those had played for their country and more than three-quarters had played a hundred matches at club or international level. Thankfully, awareness is growing very rapidly now, with more players speaking out and clubs from grassroots level right to the top addressing mental-health issues and offering support and advice.

Unfortunately, there was much less awareness when things started to unravel for me. I didn't even realise I had any mental-health issues, let alone that I should be discussing them.

*

Back to our win against Saracens at the Stoop in January 2016, the week after my bizarre altercation with Dean Ryan in the Worcester tunnel. As soon as the final whistle blew and my teammates started celebrating the victory, I began to lose the plot. I don't know where it came from but I started effing and blinding and calling anyone in my path every name under the sun. It didn't matter who it was

– our players, their players, our management, their management. 'Fuck off! Fucking pricks! Absolute wankers!'

I stormed off the pitch and grabbed my keys. It was pissing it down but the Quins fans didn't care about the rain. They were absolutely buzzing, waving flags, singing and laughing as they revelled in beating our bitter rivals. I stomped through the cheering crowds to the exit gates still dressed in full kit and with my boots on.

It's unheard of for a player to walk straight out of the ground after the final whistle like that. Normally I'd stay and walk round the pitch, chat to fans, maybe do an interview or pose for a few photos with supporters. It's what's expected and I normally enjoy it, especially when we've had a win like that.

This time I was having none of it. I wanted out of there, as quickly as possible. 'Fucking hell!' I was ranting as I headed to the exit gates. 'Fuck this!' I didn't care if the fans saw me like this. The crowd merged into one noisy blur of magenta and brown and blue and grey as I pushed my way to the gates and click-clacked across the car park in my boots. Eyes blazing, I was too angry to focus on anything but getting in my truck and closing the door on the world.

I started the engine and drove out of the car park as fast as I could. I was bawling my eyes out. *What the fuck?* I had no idea why. What had taken hold of me? I cried the whole way home, sobbing uncontrollably.

Nothing made sense. We'd just beaten Saracens, at home. Why was I reacting like this? I couldn't think straight. I was telling myself that it was the stress and pressure. I wanted to believe that. It was a bizarre blip, just like the Dean Ryan incident. These things happen. I wasn't going crazy, was I?

When I got home I put on the bravest face I could. Daisy was due to give birth in the next couple of weeks and I didn't want to stress her out. She had enough on her plate already. It wasn't fair.

I hid it very well.

★

In May 2016 I was at an England training camp in Brighton. I'd been on a rollercoaster all year and now I had the stress and pressure of a new campaign to face. It felt relentless and I was anxious about how I'd cope.

We'd won the Six Nations Grand Slam just a few months earlier, Eddie Jones's first gig as our new boss and the team's chance to put the mortification of the World Cup behind us. Fresh blood, new ideas and we smashed it. My first Grand Slam and I was so unbelievably proud to be part of the winning squad.

Maggie had been born in the middle of it all. Our perfect little girl, a beautiful little sister for Jasper. We were a family of four now and I was so proud of Daisy and what we'd achieved together. Home was a haven. I loved being there. But the big, bad world outside? I didn't want to know.

As well as the Dean Ryan incident and my funny turn after the Saracens win, I'd also had Gypsygate to contend with, followed hot on its heels by my appearance in front of a disciplinary panel after kicking Arnaud Héguy, when I came clean and confessed I'd fallen out of love with the game. I'd had a lot going on, to put it mildly.

I'd sought help with my red-mist moments, as they'd advised me to do. But I still wasn't right. Far from it. England had a tour coming up, a three-Test series against the Wallabies. I should have been on a high, chasing the next big victory after the Grand Slam. But I wasn't. I was dreading it.

It was a 25-minute drive from my house to the camp in Brighton. All the way there I wanted to turn my truck around. *I don't care. I've got zero interest. What's happening to me?*

Putting on the England training kit and seeing the boys again did nothing to lift my mood. It was the same when the training session started. I felt no excitement, no blood-rush, nothing. I was ducking out of the drills, just standing on the side, not getting involved, trying to hide from everything. Nobody said a thing and I don't blame them. I was giving off the vibes that I didn't want to talk, and if anyone looked at me I gave them 'fuck you' eyes.

I had a one-on-one session with a physio, as I needed a bit of rehab on my shoulder. Or so I said. Really, I just wanted an excuse to stop training.

'There's nothing wrong with it, mate,' he said, after checking me over. 'Are you OK?'

'I'm not fucking doing it anymore.'

The physio was looking at me and frowning. 'What's going on?'

The physio took me to the coffee shop at the gym and we sat looking out to sea. It took me a few minutes to start talking because I hadn't planned this and I didn't know how to explain what was happening. My anxiety and negativity came out as anger. 'I just don't want to be here. I hate it here. I hate it at Quins too. I hate playing rugby.'

I let it all out, explaining my guilt at being an absent father and husband. 'I don't want to go on the Australia tour,' I said. 'I don't want to do it. Why the fuck would I want to fly to the other side of the world to play a few games of rugby? I'll be away from home for more than a month. What is the point in missing out on all that precious time of seeing my kids growing up?'

The physio listened patiently before saying, 'OK. And how do you think that's going to go down with Eddie and the team?'

'I don't care. Fuck it.' I'd made up my mind. I was going to do what I wanted to do. I wasn't going to worry about the consequences of saying 'fuck you' to the tour.

I was well aware of what an honour and a privilege it was to play for England and I knew I might not get the chance again, but my emotions were ruling my head. Enough was enough. I had to take myself out of this situation. I didn't feel I had any choice. I texted Eddie: 'Can I meet you for a coffee?'

I didn't know him very well at that stage and had absolutely no idea how he was going to react. But I had to speak up because going on that tour would have destroyed me. It was not an option.

I met Eddie in the bar of the hotel we were staying at, down at Brighton marina. He was looking intently at me across the table.

'I'm not enjoying myself. I can't do it anymore. I'm sorry, I don't know what's going on,' I started. 'I can't come to Australia. I don't want to do it anymore. I don't love the game anymore and I don't want to be that guy who is just there to pick up the pay cheque. It's not fair on the team.'

There was a pause while Eddie registered what I'd said. Then he gave a little nod of his head. 'Yes, mate. I can see it in your eyes. Your eyes don't lie.'

I felt instant relief that I'd been listened to. There was no 'Come on, mate, pull yourself together. You can do it!' Just quiet understanding.

Eddie asked if there was anything he could do to change my mind or help in any way. 'We could give you this week off?' he suggested. 'Put you in touch with someone to speak to? You might feel differently about it.'

I told him no, my mind was made up and that was that.

'OK. You do what you've got to do.'

When I explained the situation to my mates in the squad – Dan Cole, Ben Youngs, George Ford – I don't think any of them were that surprised. They'd all read the signs in training and could tell that something was coming. I wished them all the best for Australia and said goodbye, but I had no clue if I would ever see them again, at least not as an England player. I felt very emotional walking away, but I was also flooded with relief. The thought of being away from it all, watching the series on TV, was so liberating. I'd miss the boys but wouldn't miss being out there, not one bit.

I immediately packed my bags, got in my truck and drove away from the hotel. *Brilliant. I'm going home. I've got the whole summer off.* With every mile I travelled I felt like more weight was being lifted from my shoulders. I was leaving behind all that pressure, all that stress. My life was going to be my own again. All the shit I'd been dealing with was going to stop.

★

I papered over the cracks with Daisy.

'Are you sure you've done the right thing?' she said.

'Yes, totally sure. It feels like exactly the right thing to do. Don't worry. It's just been a tough year so far. I'll be fine once I've had a break. Let's start planning our summer!'

One of the problems with being a rugby player is that you miss out on a lot of special occasions. Weddings, parties, weekends away. Daisy had been on her own to so many events. I'd made sacrifices for years. It's what you have to do to get to the top, whatever your sport. Spending hours in the gym or honing your skills on the pitch instead of going out with your mates. I'd done it all, but I was bored of it. Fed up to the back teeth.

The fact that I'd dropped out of my England duties meant I got to do a lot of 'normal' stuff for a change, and I couldn't wait. One of my best mates, Shaun, was getting married, and not only did I manage to go to his stag do in Edinburgh, I also made it to the wedding, which was amazing. I have to be honest, going to Shaun's wedding had been on my mind when I told Eddie I was quitting. I desperately wanted to be there. I was 25 years old and it felt like rugby was stealing my life, stopping me from sharing good times and making memories with the people I love. What was life for if you couldn't do that?

I think this is something the RFU and World Rugby need to consider. We're young men in the prime of our lives. No wonder we suffer mental-health problems when our lives become all about rugby and 'normal' life takes second place, crammed into five measly weeks of the year.

New Zealand have a good model. They allow their players to take sabbaticals to play rugby in another country if they want to, or just take a few months off to travel the world. The break keeps their players fresh, happy and extends their playing years. I'd have taken that option, no question, if it had been on the table.

After Shaun's wedding Daisy and I took the kids to a Greek island. The holiday was just what I needed. My own self-imposed mini-sabbatical. Chilling out and enjoying precious time with my family, I felt like a member of the human race instead of a rugby team. *This is what I want to do. I want to be a dad. I want to contribute to being a parent.*

We were sitting at a café, overlooking the beach and feeling properly relaxed. Maggie was asleep in my arms and Jasper was sitting happily in his pushchair, babbling about sandcastles and seashells. A text arrived from Eddie Jones.

'How's things?' His texts are often short and straight to the point. I told him I was doing OK, loving spending time with Daisy and the kids. 'Good, mate. Get yourself to the beach. Sea air is good for you.'

I wasn't thinking beyond this holiday. I had no idea if I would play for England again. It was too early to tell how I would feel after my time away and who's to say Eddie would even ask me back into the squad. Let's face it, I'd bombed out after England's biggest success for years. The Six Nations Grand Slam was a huge triumph for Eddie, and now the boys were beating Australia in Australia.

They'd won the first game in the three-Test series 39–28, on the day of Shaun's wedding, funnily enough, so I missed it all. They won the next game 23–7, when it became obvious just how big an opportunity I'd given up. Mako Vunipola was playing phenomenally well, making the number-one shirt his own.

I've had my time, I'd thought, sipping a beer as I watched some of that second game in a bar. *There've been ups and downs but I've had a good five years playing for England. I'll set goals for myself at Quins now, try to rediscover my love for the game.*

Eddie could have been forgiven for thinking, *Good riddance to Marler. We're doing pretty well without him.* They *were* doing pretty well without me. But Eddie hadn't forgotten me, and I really appreciated his text.

The third game was being played during our flight home. As I boarded the plane with Daisy and the kids I felt like an excited fan, wishing I could watch the game on TV. It would be over by the time we landed, so I'd just have to wait until we got to Gatwick to find out the result.

Halfway through the flight, a member of the cabin crew came up to me. 'The pilot has sent this for you.' She handed me a piece of paper and explained that the pilot was a big rugby fan and had recognised me when I boarded. He'd written me a note with the score on and a bit of detail about the game.

I opened it up, desperately hoping the boys had done well. *Get in!* We'd outplayed Australia. Demolished them. The final score was 44–40. We'd done a proper job on them in front of a record crowd, with Faz as man of the match. Fantastically, it was the first whitewash by a touring side since South Africa did it in 1971. We'd made history or, should I say, the boys had made history.

'What's that?' Daisy said, seeing me devouring the note.

'Oh, nothing, Dais. Just the score. Boys won. All good.' This was family time and I didn't want Daisy to be bothered with it, but for the rest of the flight my mind was working overtime. I couldn't have been more pleased for the boys, but for the first time I felt disappointed not to have been part of it. Very disappointed. I'd missed out on one of the best moments in an England shirt.

I looked out of the window at the clouds beneath us and began to acknowledge something that I'd lost sight of. *I actually like playing rugby. I love it. I don't want to miss out like this again. I want to be one of the boys again.*

'Are you sorry you weren't there?' Daisy asked casually.

'No, because I'd have missed this holiday and it's been brilliant, the best ever.' That was true. I'd loved every minute and I'd needed the break to help me see clearly again.

I'd have to make more sacrifices if I pulled on the England jersey again. I knew that. But I couldn't get the idea out of my head. I wanted to play again.

I didn't share how I was feeling with Daisy, not right there and then. It didn't seem fair and it would have been hard to explain how I'd made such a rapid emotional turnaround. She'd accepted my decision to quit England without argument. No 'What about the money?' or 'Can't you just do another season and see?' None of that, and I hadn't even been totally honest with her about how depressed and despondent I'd felt at that camp in Brighton. How could I land this U-turn on her now, so soon after quitting?

My emotions were up and down like a rugby ball, I could see that. One minute I was slammed into the turf, covered in mud.

Now here I was, hurtling towards the crossbar, dancing in the sunlight. I was fizzing at the thought of getting back in there and grabbing another piece of the action.

★

In late September 2018 we were away to Bristol Bears. I wasn't in a good frame of mind. My head felt clouded. I was due to meet up with the England team the following day in preparation for the upcoming autumn internationals, and the dread of going away had set in again. The pressure was back, as sharp and intimidating as ever before. All the same negative feelings I'd had in Brighton more than two years earlier had returned. *I don't want to go, but how can I not? Why is this happening all over again?*

I didn't play badly but I managed to pick up yet another yellow card, for elbowing Bristol's young scrum-half, as we went on to lose the game 20–13. I had let the team down with my lack of discipline, again. What had Olly Kohn warned me about all those years ago? I hadn't listened. I was still being a dickhead, still selfishly fucking it up for the whole team.

We got back into the changing room after the game and I sat there with my head down. I couldn't look my teammates in the eyes. My mind was in a mess. I was thinking about going on tour, leaving the family again, and I was struggling massively with it. I didn't want to go back into the high-pressured England environment. Why was I doing it? What was the point?

I thought not having to do it all again would solve everything. *Retire from England for good this time and all my troubles would melt away,* I thought. There were other things that weren't perfect in my life, same as anyone else. But I thought escaping from international rugby was the answer to all my woes.

I made the call to Eddie, who was fantastic. Understated but understanding, he made it clear he was keeping the door open for me once again. I was grateful for that, even though I never for one second thought I'd have a change of heart.

I told the media I was retiring for 'personal reasons' and that I wanted to spend more time with my family, which was true. You have to give a hundred per cent, I said, and I wasn't in that place. There was more to it than that, of course. But I was still finding a lot of stuff out for myself.

*

It was six months since my retirement and I was clearly still not right. Shortly after the night I was accused of attempted squirrel murder, I went to see a psychiatrist called Humphrey. I had a lot to get off my chest and I needed to make sense of my moods. Most of all, I never, ever wanted to put Daisy through anything like that again. (She had since told me that she was not scared, as I feared she was. She was angry and pissed off, and stunned at what had happened. Even so, that was bad enough. I'd put her through a terrible ordeal.)

It was very good to talk. I went back to the beginning and I didn't hold back. I told Humphrey that every time I was called up to play for England I started to feel anxious. It had been the same for six years, ever since my debut. Despite earning dozens and dozens of caps and being praised for my ability and performance, I still didn't quite believe in myself. I'd ask myself, *Should I be in the team? Do I deserve to be here?* When I'd felt like that before my England debut it had seemed only natural. I was a youngster with everything to prove. But it didn't get better in time; it got worse. I was never able to shake off the 'imposter syndrome' I felt at my first ever England training camp.

I didn't fully recognise the cycle when I was in it, but I was seeing it now that I'd finally sought help. When England came calling I was more grumpy and negative, at home and at work. I'd try to compensate by pissing around a bit more than usual or trying to have a laugh, but nothing worked. I was in a rut, feeling trapped and anxious with seemingly no way of escape.

One day a coach said about my mood swings, 'Joe, you have the capacity to do good or evil.' High jinks and positivity one minute – making teammates laugh, raising the energy in the room, enjoying mentoring a youngster – then *crash!* A flick of a switch and I was as miserable as sin, sniping and griping and lashing out. But it wasn't the old red mist. It was more like black mist. Gloom. Despondency. I had no idea where it came from.

I confessed to Humphrey not only that I had smashed up the house and upset Daisy, but also that I'd had dark thoughts for months and months. Retiring from international duty had not been the magic dart I'd hoped it would be, not by a long stretch. I was still feeling the pressure just playing for Quins, trying to juggle being a rugby player with being a good dad and husband. I felt like I was being suffocated inside the rugby bubble.

So many times I'd cried all the way to work, blubbing in my truck, not understanding why. The tears would come from nowhere, engulfing me. It had been happening for a long time by now, though I'd never told a soul.

Some days I didn't just want to escape the rugby bubble, I thought it would be easier to end it all, that it would be better for everyone if I wasn't here. It terrified me to think that way. I didn't tell Daisy. I didn't tell anyone. How could I?

I was really struggling with the 'why?'. I had a beautiful wife, a lovely family, great friends, a nice house and a job plenty of other people would give their right arm for. Why was I so unhappy? I didn't think I had the right to feel the way I did.

After I smashed up the house everything felt so much worse. I'd hit rock bottom and I didn't like who I was. I was afraid of what I might do next.

Talking to Humphrey and articulating how I felt was liberating. I could feel some of the pressure releasing, straight away. I'd bottled so much up, thinking that was what I had to do. And I also found myself addressing issues that I'd never stopped to think about before.

I've been labelled 'non-conformist' and 'unconventional' many times over the years. I realise it's a response to the mohawks, my bizarre collection of bans, my gobbing off and the way I talk to the media. All the stuff that's obvious and in your face. But the thing is, I'm not as rebellious or unusual as people might think, or as the media likes to make out. I'm an ordinary bloke who does an unusually high-pressured job, and marrying the two had taken its toll on me.

I've conformed at the highest level for the vast majority of my career. Working my way up from the Quins academy to the first team, doing everything that was expected of me. Going up through the age groups in England. Responding to call-ups the only way you can, by saying yes and thank you very much for the opportunity.

You can't follow micromanaged training-and-conditioning programmes if you're not prepared to toe the line, and I've always cracked on and worked my buns off. I did it even when I didn't want to, and when anxiety crept in I tried to deny it and push it away, hoping it wouldn't reappear next time, even though I knew it would.

The stress that gripped me before an England campaign manifested itself on the pitch, clearly. The Bristol game had shown me that, and now that I was looking back with my eyes wide open I could see the pattern more clearly than before. For a long time I'd been giving away dull penalties, subconsciously looking for 'outs'. I wanted a yellow card, a red card even. I knew this. It had gone on for years, but I had never addressed it so honestly or attempted to analyse it in the way I was prepared to now. 'A ban would be an easy way out without actually pulling the trigger,' I said.

Humphrey listened without prejudice. There was no danger he would look at me and think, *What the fuck? You wear the number-one shirt for England and you're crying about pressure? Get a grip!*

I know only a minority of people in this day and age would hold that view, but it's a stigma I'd subconsciously carried throughout my career. I couldn't be honest. I didn't know how to be honest about my mental health, until now.

Humphrey identified that I had been suffering from depression, which explained my bouncing moods. Part of the reason I'd left the England squad in the first place, back in the summer of 2016, was because of a lack of recognition of how severe my depression was. That's one of the conclusions Humphrey came to. He wrote this down, and seeing it in black and white was incredibly liberating.

He put me on antidepressants, but the real ongoing treatment for me is being able to talk about my mental health. Realising it's OK to admit that I feel the pressure of playing top-flight rugby. Knowing it's 'allowed' to be a rugby player who suffers from depression. That you can still make it to the World Cup final if you have mental-health issues. It has been a massive break-through for me.

It's not always easy to talk. I'm still learning and encouraging other people – particularly men – to do the same. We all need to be able to talk openly, without fear of judgement. I wish someone had told me that years ago because my world didn't collapse when I admitted to my problems and opened up about my struggles. Life got better, for me and everyone around me. Even the squirrels of Heathfield have a happier time of it, much to Daisy's delight.

13

ON TOUR

Weird, wonderful and downright stupid stuff goes on when a squad of rugby boys are thrown together in hotel rooms and on tour buses for weeks or even months on end. Take the time Welsh scrum-half Dwayne Peel had a taste of his own medicine during the 2007 World Cup in France. Peel was a persistent prankster, and early on in the tournament he'd tested his teammates' patience by putting bikes and baked beans in their beds. The lads decided to retaliate, with one of them borrowing a sheep from a local farmer and leaving it in Peel's hotel room. The flea-ridden sheep had pooed on the carpet before Peel discovered it, and legend has it he was itching for days afterwards.

I was a young teenager when I first heard that story. I loved it because it painted a picture I really wanted to believe in: rugby tours are full of high jinks and crazy amateur-era antics, and professional players can still have a great laugh. We can and we do, but, having been on more tours than I can count on all my fingers and toes, I know that's not the whole story.

Still, I like the tales, even if you never know if they're entirely true or have been massaged in time. Ireland's Neil Best had a tale to tell after their tour of Argentina in 2007. He decided to give away his kit before heading home. Nothing unusual about that. But did he give it to a fan in the stadium after the last Test? No. On the way to the airport, after the last-night piss-up in Buenos Aires, he sprinted across a six-lane motorway, kit bag in hand, and approached a homeless man who was sleeping under blankets. 'You alright, mate?' said Best. 'Do you want some kit?' The elderly man was delighted to be handed a bag full of official IRFU gear.

It's a story that brings back memories from when I toured with the Lions. It was a blast from start to finish, which I guess sheds a lot of light on why I struggled so badly on other tours. There was no pressure on this one. I was in the midweek team, the shags, not the Test team, so I could enjoy myself without the fear of failing to perform as an England player under that intense spotlight. I still wanted to play my best rugby and show the other Lions what I could do, but the stress and pressure were minuscule in comparison to playing for England.

I made the most of every minute. One night, deep into the two-month tour, I decided to take myself out of our Wellington hotel very late at night. The harbour outside was deserted, which was perfect, as I'd been on the beers with the boys and didn't want to run into anyone – least of all any rugby-mad fans who might recognise me.

I sat myself down on the harbour wall and tucked into a packet of Quavers, enjoying just chilling on my own. I was very pissed, to be honest, and when I'd finished my crisps I decided to have a sneaky fag as I sat there looking out to sea. I thought about my best moment on the field. Drawing 31–31 with the Hurricanes had been a fantastic experience, one I'd always remember. Just wearing the Lions shirt was amazing enough, but to play as good a game as we did, in that famous Cake Tin stadium in Wellington, was phenomenal.

I was loving the peace and quiet on the harbour. All alone with my thoughts, time slipped by. I made myself more comfortable, and by that I mean I was lying down on the ground. I thought I might just shut my eyes for a minute or two …

All of a sudden I heard something in the distance. I lifted my head off the pavement and saw a couple of lads and a girl walking in my direction, chattering away. *Shit.*

I wasn't wearing anything that said I was a Lion, just some plain shorts and a hoodie, but I couldn't take any risk at all of being recognised, not like this. I was sprawled on the floor, fag end at my side, crisp crumbs down my top and smelling pungently of beer.

There was nothing for it but to hold my position. I pulled my hood up and told myself not to worry. Even if they were the biggest rugby nuts in the world they wouldn't recognise me as one of the boys on the tour, would they?

As they got closer I shut my eyes and pulled my hood down a bit further over my face, to be extra careful. I'd just stay like that until they walked past. Their footsteps got louder and I could tell they were almost in front of me.

I stayed very still, holding my breath, trying to be as invisible as possible. Then the footsteps stopped, right in front of me. *Shit!*

My heart lurched. Had they clocked me before I pulled my hood down? Did they know the Lions were staying in the hotel behind me and had put two and two together? More importantly, what would I say if they confronted me?

'Clink-clink!' It was the unmistakeable sound of coins hitting the pavement, right beside me. I didn't move a muscle as I listened to the sound of their footsteps and chatter fade away.

When the coast was clear I tentatively pushed back my hood and there it was – enough money for me to buy a cup of tea and a sandwich. *Fuck me, they thought I was a hobo!* Proof I didn't need that Prince Harry wasn't the only one who thought I looked like that.

★

'This isn't gonna be a walk in the park.' At the team meeting before our 2013 tour of Argentina we were told that England had not won a series out there since 1981 and it was a hostile environment, which was a legacy of the Falklands War. Previous players had been spat at, had oranges thrown at them – why oranges, I have no idea – and one of the stadiums had a moat around it to stop angry fans invading the pitch. I was too young to remember the Falklands War and was slightly alarmed by it all.

When you go on tour you put yourself in the hands of others. It's not like going on a trip you've chosen and booked yourself. You're told what to wear, where to meet and where you are staying. The whole itinerary is organised for you, and you have to have faith in the staff and managers who work out all the arrangements. I trusted them, of course, but when I was a youngster getting used to touring it was something I had to get my head round. It's unnatural not to have any say in your own plans for weeks on end on the other side of the world. Especially when people start talking about hostile environments and angry fans.

I don't turn a hair nowadays. I love just turning up and having it all laid on. On the majority of tours you spend a big chunk of your time in a hotel, in training, on the team bus or at a rugby stadium. There's generally not a huge amount of time for sight-seeing or day trips, so it doesn't matter that your schedule is all mapped out for you. In fact, it needs to be, so you can concentrate on your game and you don't have to think about anything else, unless you want to.

We were playing two Tests in Argentina, but first we flew over to Montevideo for an opening game against the South American XV side. The team was made up of players from Argentina, Brazil, Chile and Uruguay. 'This is it,' our coach driver said, pulling up at the address we'd been given for the rugby ground. 'We're here.'

All the boys looked at each other. We'd been expecting a stadium and a proper pitch, but this looked like a public park with a few dog walkers in it and a big shed. 'Surely this isn't right? We must be lost.'

It turned out we weren't. *Who said it wasn't gonna be a walk in the park?* I thought to myself. *That's exactly what it is!*

Seeing the opposition was another surprise. They looked like they'd come straight from their day jobs as plumbers and builders, ready to swap their paint-splattered overalls for a rugby kit.

A crowd of about 150 people watched the game. I hesitate to call them fans because they seemed to be passers-by who just happened to stumble upon the pitch and came over to have a look at what was going on.

My opposite number looked like Augustus Gloop from *Charlie and the Chocolate Factory*. *This'll be a doddle,* I thought. It wasn't. He was surprisingly good – a sneaky git in the scrum – and he really gave me a run for my money. I struggled through 60 exhausting minutes before Alex Corbisiero came off the bench to replace me.

Corbs had a stinker, struggling just like I had. Augustus Gloop forced him to give away four or five penalties before he was yellow-carded and I had to go back on. We won 21–41 but Corbs was gutted, especially when we all ribbed him relentlessly about how he'd had his pants pulled down so spectacularly.

Corbs had the last laugh, eventually. There were a couple of injuries on the Lions tour in Australia not long afterwards, and he was called up as a replacement. He played in two out of the three Tests and ripped it up, even getting a man of the match.

We were all scratching our heads. 'How the fuck did he go from having Augustus Gloop whip his arse to being the star of the Lions tour?' That's life for you. Who knows how the ball will bounce? One minute you're cock of the walk, the next you're a feather duster.

We went on to win both our games against Argentina, beating them 3–32 and 26–51, and we had some old-school fun along the way, with one member of the senior staff leading the charge. One night, after sinking a few beers together, he asked me to walk with him to the nearby petrol station.

Like all foreign visitors, we'd been warned not to leave our hotel after dark or walk the streets alone. Buenos Aries is an incredible city with stunning architecture but there's extreme poverty too. The shanty towns could be dangerous, we were told. And yet here we were, turning a corner and walking right through the middle of a shanty town.

I was on edge. 'We shouldn't really be doing this, should we?'

He shrugged. 'It'll be fine.'

'Er, what was it you were after from the petrol station?' I wondered exactly what it was that we were potentially putting our necks on the line for. Surely not a microwaved Rustlers burger?

'Oh, I thought we could have a couple of cigars, Joe.'

'Fair enough,' I squeaked. I was too young to say anything, but I loved his attitude. It felt great heading into the night for contraband with one of the grown-ups, and it did wonders for my confidence and self-esteem.

★

Roommates play an important role in the tour experience. It's tradition for boys to share a room. You can support each other through highs and lows and it's good for morale and team-building, the bosses say. Having a roommate also helps with homesickness and the feelings of isolation that can creep in when you're a long way from your home and family. I agree with all of that.

Though I didn't open up to my roommates about how much I struggled mentally – I should have, I realise now – I can see how things would have been a whole lot worse if I'd been shut away in a room on my own. At low points, when I was missing home and disappearing into a cloud of gloom, having a teammate there brought me back into the room. Even if you're bickering about the air con, at least there's another human being there to stop you wallowing – even if that human being is Coley.

In Argentina I shared with my old mate Jonny May. Having come up through the age groups together, Jonny and I stuck together in the early years of our England careers, when we were still finding our feet. He'd forgiven me for stitching him up with his 'Ice Ice Baby' performance the year before and we'd become quite close. Of all the boys he was someone I felt I could have a little whinge to if I was feeling a bit homesick or pissed off with the training drills. We were in the same boat and on the same wavelength, and we were comfortable in each other's company.

One morning Mike Catt, the attack team coach and World Cup 2003 winner, approached, shaking his head and looking at us suspiciously. 'What the fuck were you guys up to in your room last night?'

We both knew what Catty must have been talking about, but how had he found out what we did behind closed doors?

'Weird,' he said. 'You are two of the weirdest guys I've ever met. I saw it with my own eyes.'

Jonny and I looked at each other in confusion. Our room in the Buenos Aires hotel was perfectly private. How could he see us? It didn't make sense. 'How d'you mean, you saw us?'

'I was sitting in the hot tub, minding my own business, when I happened to tip my head back to relax in the bubbles,' Catty said, looking at us through narrowed eyes. 'That's when I saw you pair of weirdos, in your underpants. Jonny getting flipped back and forth.' He paused and pointed at me. 'Your arse going up and down. What the fuck were you doing?'

I realised that not telling the truth would only make it look worse. We'd have to come clean. 'Oh, that,' I said as flippantly as I could. 'We were just naked wrestling, that's all.'

Catty's jaw dropped three inches. I don't know why I didn't just say wrestling, because we did have our underpants on and weren't technically naked, but it was the first thing that came to mind. Jonny blushed and smirked.

We'd been indulging in a bit of wrestling on and off for years. We'd upped the ante on this tour, taking advantage of the fact that we were sharing a room. We took it very seriously, stripping to our pants every night so we looked as much like professional wrestlers as possible, and even strapping up our wrists and ankles. 'We don't want to do any damage, do we?' we'd laugh. 'How would we explain to the physio that we'd been naked wrestling in our bedroom?'

We really threw ourselves into it, arms and legs flying everywhere and playing on until we were sweating and panting and Jonny was tapping out. It was always Jonny who tapped out. He was incredibly fit and strong and his wrestling skills were awesome, but being the much chunkier bloke I beat him every time.

It was all good, clean fun and we had no inhibitions – why would we? It never occurred to us that anyone in the hot tub down below could look up and see us through the window. What were the chances of Catty clocking us like that?

Inevitably, the coach couldn't keep the story to himself and word quickly spread around the camp. Mike Brown, Joe Launchbury and Courtney Lawes thought it was hilarious. 'We want to see you in action,' they said. 'We've gotta see this for ourselves. It'll be perfect entertainment on the last night, before we go out on the beers.' We couldn't wriggle out of it and reluctantly agreed.

When the big night came I was glad to learn that we were allowed to wear shorts, as we were wrestling outside, where other hotel guests might see us. Jonny was as fit as a butcher's dog but I was four stone heavier than him and wobbly by comparison. Having unsuspecting members of the public stumble across me in my undies was simply not an option.

'On your knees,' Mike Brown said.

'What?'

I looked around and all the boys in the squad were nodding in agreement. They had decided that I had too great a weight advantage so we were to wrestle on our knees.

'Fair enough. Whatever you say, boys.' I wasn't arguing with a load of hyped-up and pumped rugby players looking forward to the wrestling match and our last-night piss-up. Besides, I'd trounced Jonny every time and being on my knees would make no difference to me.

Billy Twelvetrees was adjudicating and my adrenaline was spiking as he gave the signal to start the match. Cheers went up all around and I rose to the occasion, feeding off the buzz and wrestling brilliantly. Or so I initially thought.

Jonny's blood was also up, and he was wrestling out of his skin. Not only that, but the fact that we were on our knees had made a massive difference to him. Within a few minutes I was on my back, completely overpowered. Pathetic.

Jonny had bitched me. Totally outwrestled me. *How the fuck did this happen?* I thought. *And how am I ever gonna live this down?*

I couldn't get out on the beers quick enough.

★

Adam Jones had more than 70 caps for Wales when I was still at school. He'd toured five times with the Lions, played twice for the Barbarians and won countless Six Nations Championships. He was also the player who'd bent me in two in the hideous Six Nations defeat to Wales in 2013, outplaying me so comprehensively that I thought he'd ended my international career early. After that stinker of a game I never wanted to see Adam Jones's face again.

Now here I was, just three years later, watching him unpack his undies and his Afro comb in the hotel room we were sharing in San Francisco. We were there for some pre-season training, in preparation for the club's 150th season.

Bomb had joined Quins the previous season and I liked him straight away. There was absolutely no pomp or pulling rank, despite his vast experience and the history between us. He just slotted in as one of the boys, down to earth and obviously up for a laugh, which I guess shouldn't have come as a surprise. What rugby player would have a curly perm and embrace being named after a WWF wrestler from the 1990s if he didn't have a sense of humour?

I was looking forward to getting to know Bomb better on this trip, because you always get to know your roommates better. It's impossible not to when you're sharing a bathroom and listening to each other snore and call home and sing in the shower every day.

We got on great guns as roommates, just as I'd hoped. He liked drinking as much as I did and it quickly became apparent that we shared a love of food. Any food, as long as it came in big portions.

Everything was going so well until one morning, when I woke with a start very early. *What the fuck?* I looked over to Bomb's bed and saw him sitting at the end of it, in his underpants, sobbing his heart out. 'What's the matter, mate?'

He was too upset to speak at first. I sat myself up and wasn't sure what to do. Something had clearly happened and I wanted to go over and comfort him. What would he want me to do? I really wasn't sure. We weren't close friends, just good teammates who were still getting to know one another properly.

'I've just had a phonecall,' he eventually said. 'From my wife.'

My blood ran cold. I knew Bomb was a big family man and dreaded what he was going to say next. I waited for him to gather himself together enough to tell me the news.

'It's my mum …' he started. 'My mum's dead.'

I felt sick. 'Shit, shit. I'm so sorry!' I jumped out of my bed and went over to his. Bomb still had his head in his hands at the end of the bed. I hovered in front of him, telling him again how sorry I was and wondering what I should do next, what I could do to help. I wanted to give him a hug. That's what felt right. I opened my arms out wide and Bomb looked up to see me standing there with my arms outstretched, ready to cuddle him.

He stopped crying and his eyes widened as he took in the image before him. Then there was an embarrassing little pause before he cleared his throat and said in his strong Welsh accent, 'I'm alright, actually. It'll be better when you put some clothes on.'

We're great mates and laugh about that moment now, but nothing was funny at the time, far from it. Bomb's mum had died very unexpectedly and he was in terrible shock. I put some clothes on and took him out to a 24-hour Wendy's that morning, where we had the biggest breakfast either of us had ever eaten. As two large rugby players who are obliged to smash through 4–5,000 calories a day – double the recommended intake for the average person – that's saying something. We ordered every single item on the breakfast menu – and I mean *everything* – and there was a calorie count next to each of them. We'd put away just over 7,000 calories each as the sun came up.

Bomb now coaches at Quins and we've remembered that fateful morning several times since. He always says the blow-out breakfast was just what he needed, and I always question his rebuttal of me in my underpants.

'What better way to pick someone up than to offer them a naked cuddle?' I say, while Bomb shakes his head. 'No, no, no. I'd take the 7,000-calorie breakfast any day, bud.'

★

Danny Care was my England roommate for years, which was brilliant. Not just because we were good mates from Quins, but because the Talisman is always upbeat, even when it's supposedly 'down time'.

There have been times when Danny and his sunny smile have really lifted my mood. I know that if he hadn't been there I might have sunk into despair on more than one occasion, pining for home, fretting about a mistake on the pitch or questioning my future. Instead he's been there to listen and to fill the room with his positive energy and excessive amount of toiletries.

During a long campaign you're encouraged to change room-mates from time to time, to allow more players in the squad to bond. The team manager always organises who rooms with who, but you can usually put in a quiet word and sway it your way, if you feel the need.

In Japan I got to share with Mako, then Gengey, Slosh and finally Coley. All different beasts, all great blokes. Mako was a fantastic roommate. Immaculately clean and tidy, if he wasn't gaming he was sleeping the sleep of the dead. I invited boys back every night and there were always a few of us in the room. I like to think it was because they enjoyed my company, not because they always gorged on the extensive selection of chocolates and biscuits I had to offer.

'Does Mako mind us being here?' the players would ask.

'Mind? He won't even know you've been,' I'd say, holding a mirror in front of his face to check he was still breathing.

Slosh was very easy-going, as chilled as could be, even when I took the mickey out of him, which was pretty much all the time. 'What's up, mate? The bed's too small for you? Duvet not big enough to cover your arse? Careful with that toilet seat, mate. We don't want to have to pay for any accidental damage.'

Gengey played *League of Legends* deep into the night, often hooked up online with Jack Singleton, Courtney Lawes or Luke Cowan-Dickie. I haven't owned a PlayStation since I had my kids, and it was nice to relive some of my youth seeing him up all night like a teenager.

Coley was my last roommate in Japan. I think most of us gravitated towards the person we felt most comfortable with in the end. Let's just say that bathroom etiquette is always a bit awkward, whoever you share with, but Coley knows my movements and has long since stopped complaining when I get up to go to the toilet at 5am every day.

From my perspective it worked out really well with all four roommates, although maybe you'd have to ask them to see if they agreed. I heard Eddie Jones being interviewed by Ugo Monye during lockdown in 2020. 'If there was one person you couldn't be in isolation with, who would that be?' he was asked.

'Joe Marler,' Eddie replied, without skipping a beat. 'That's pretty self-evident. As much as I love him I wouldn't like to be in isolation with that guy.'

★

Fancy a peek through the keyhole of the other England players' rooms?

WHO WOULD LIVE IN A HOTEL ROOM LIKE THIS? ANSWERS AT THE END.

1. Makes a good cuppa. Likes a chat and tells it to you straight. Tends to have the best suite in the hotel and when he sings in the shower it's amazing. He has an unbelievable voice and totally loses his Wigan accent.

2. Uses a lavender diffuser to help him get off to sleep. Also enjoys doing Lego in his room, which makes up for him missing all his

big-boy toys at home, like his boat, motorcycle, paddle boards and electric bikes.

3. Loves to FaceTime his four kids, as well as using his iPad, laptop, Bluetooth speaker, headphones, iPhone and PlayStation all at the same time. The Pennyhill Park Hotel had to get an Internet boosting system installed due to his habits, and his room is often referred to as 'mission control'.

4. A young pup, he calls his folks back home every single night. Favours old-fashioned baggy underpants and often found texting me and Coley, asking if he can tag along on our day trips and coffee excursions. Also has a terrible line in jokes, which often involve nuns and cats and are always in poor taste.

5. Loves lying on the bed with his headphones in and listening to podcasts in the dark or watching the latest season of *Hard Knocks*. A massive all-round sports nut, he'll give you facts on any sport quicker than Google. Also likes to disable the hotel smoke alarm so he can burn white sage and lavender incense sticks, which gets him a rap on the knuckles from time to time.

*

Sam Underhill was in charge of the music for the team bus in Japan. It's a tough gig because you have to create playlists that appeal to everyone. Not an easy task when there are more musical tastes in the squad than positions on a rugby pitch.

Answers:
1. Owen Farrell. 2. Jack Nowell. 3. Courtney Lawes. 4. Tom Curry. 5. Kyle Sinckler.

Courtney likes his R&B. Sink's into hardcore rap that doesn't sound like music at all, not to me, anyhow. Gengey loves his grime. Faz is a big fan of Kings of Leon. Coley favours Mozart and Beethoven, or at least that's the image he likes to put out there. I like my emotional power ballads, Adele, Whitney, U2, John Denver, Etta James. The darker and gloomier the lyrics, the happier I am. I also like to sing along to the tracks. Adele's one of my go-tos, of course. Tina Turner's another.

I'd belt out a bit of Tina's version of 'Let's Stay Together', and the bottles would rain down on me taking me back to when I got my first cap. 'Shut up, Marler! Sit down!'

I'd grown in stature now, though. The bottles were being thrown backwards rather than forwards down the bus, and I had a right to reply. 'What's not to like, boys?' I'd say. 'These lyrics are team-building. You've got to listen!'

Sam would pull out his guitar. Close your eyes and you could have been listening to George Ezra, but we didn't hand it to him. He got booed and abused as I had – and the bottles rained down once again. That's the way it goes on tour.

★

It feels fitting to end the book here, having relived some fantastic memories of the World Cup. I've had my ups and downs – plenty of them – but I'm very glad I got back on my horse and clippity-clopped all the way to Japan.

It was a huge honour to be there. An unbelievable experience for a fat lad from East Sussex who never even set out to be a rugby player, let alone wear the number-one jersey for England. Proof, I hope, that, though you never know which way life is going to take you, you need to keep getting up and kicking that ball. It's going to bounce your way some of the time, and those moments are worth taking the horse to water for, mixed-metaphorically speaking.

Thank you for reading my story. Having the chance to tell it is more important to me than you might think, and I hope it encourages other rugby players to open up and talk.

*

I'm a big supporter of CALM (Campaign Against Living Miserably) Every week 125 people in the UK take their own lives. Three quarters of those are men, and suicide is the single biggest killer of men under 45.

I made the mistake of being silent for far too long, thinking I would be showing weakness if I admitted I felt anxious and depressed. I told myself I had no right to feel that way and would be letting my family and my club down if I said I was struggling to cope.

But men who play rugby, or fit any other old-fashioned 'macho' stereotype, are not immune from feeling low, and there is no shame in seeking help. You don't need to lie on a chaise longue in a psychiatrist's office in order to open up and talk, and don't forget that talking works both ways. I now check in more with the boys, asking questions, making sure they are feeling OK and I'm trying to be a better listener. So, if you're struggling give CALM a call on 0800 58 58 58. It's free and confidential. Or if you need advice on how to talk to a mate you're worried about, you can visit the CALM website at www.thecalmzone.net.